Flightdeck Performance

THE HUMAN FACTOR

Flightdeck Performance
THE HUMAN FACTOR

David O'Hare ■ Stanley Roscoe
With contributions by **Gordon Vette** *and* **Michael Young**

Iowa State University Press / Ames

David O'Hare is senior lecturer in psychology at the University of Otago, Dunedin, New Zealand.

Stanley Roscoe is president of ILLIANA Aviation Sciences Limited, professor emeritus of psychology at the University of Illinois at Urbana-Champaign and at New Mexico State University, and former manager of the Display Systems Department of Hughes Aircraft Company.

Gordon Vette is an aviation safety consultant, test pilot, and former B747 senior flight instructor with Air New Zealand.

Michael Young is a commercial pilot and manager of a large flight training organization in Auckland, New Zealand.

© 1990 Iowa State University Press, Ames, Iowa 50014
All rights reserved

No part of this book may be reproduced in any form or by any electronic or mechanical means, including information storage and retrieval systems, without written permission from the publisher, except for brief passages quoted in a review.

Authorization to photocopy items for internal or personal use, or the internal or personal use of specific clients, is granted by Iowa State University Press, provided that the base fee of $.10 per copy is paid directly to the Copyright Clearance Center, 27 Congress Street, Salem, MA 01970. For those organizations that have been granted a photocopy license by CCC, a separate system of payments has been arranged. The fee code for users of the Transactional Reporting Service is 0-8138-0173-7/90 $.10.

∞ Printed on acid-free paper in the United States of America

First edition, 1990
First paperback printing, 1992
Second paperback printing, 1994

Library of Congress Cataloging-in-Publication Data

O'Hare, David.
   Flightdeck performance : the human factor / David O'Hare, Stanley Roscoe; with contributions by Gordon Vette and Michael Young.—1st ed.
      p.   cm.
   Includes bibliographical references.
   ISBN 0-8138-0161-3   ISBN 0-8138-0173-7 (pbk)
   1. Airplanes—Design and construction—Human Factors. 2. Airplanes—Piloting—Human factors. I. Roscoe, Stanley Nelson. II. Title.
TL671.2.038   1990
   629.13′028′9—dc20   89-19904

Contents

Preface

WE PILOTS must continue to work toward improvement—through books and articles, studies, seminars, retraining, and occasional regulatory changes. The next significant gains in safety must come from improved human factors and better presentation of vital information.

ARCHIE TRAMMELL, *Cause and Circumstance*

UNFORTUNATELY, following the safest year in aviation history, 1985 was the worst year on record in terms of the number of lives lost in major airliner accidents. Although the yearly numbers of fatalities involved represent a small fraction of the numbers of lives lost to automobile accidents, suicides, or any of the major diseases, the news impact of aviation accidents is far greater because so many die at once. Adding to the public shock is the realization that the safe operation of an airliner with the most advanced technology depends ultimately on the skill and airmanship of a small flight crew and the vigilance and judgment of one or two often overworked air traffic controllers.

The development of flying from its relatively recent origins at the beginning of the twentieth century was given enormous boosts by the two world wars. The image of the glamorous but slightly reckless fighter pilot, magnified through the lenses of the film industry, probably still colors the popular perception of the pilot today. This may be one reason why any hint of recklessness or error on behalf of the pilot is so readily seized on in the aftermath of any accident. There may seem to be justification for this attitude in view of the fact that typically 65 percent and as high as 80 percent of the accidents investigated have been attributed to pilot error.

Because accident investigators have traditionally been drawn exclusively from the engineering and aviation communities, there is reason to believe that the real causes of accidents attributed to "pilot error" are seldom explained. Understanding of the capabilities and limitations of the human operator has been developing for a period not much greater than aviation itself. Specific expertise in aviation psychology is to be found in a relatively small number of departments of psychology scattered around the world. These departments include psychologists who aim to achieve a broad understanding of pilot behavior through the study of specific human abilities and limitations critical to flight operations.

Learning, memory, attention, perception, thinking and problem solving, verbalization, and social facility are traditional subject divisions within psychology. A complex activity like flying involves all of these capacities. In addition to developing basic knowledge, psychologists have been strongly connected to the provision of applied services, and a vigorous branch of psychology is oriented toward understanding the roles of people in the context of technology. The fields of "human factors" and "behavioral engineering" also draw on other academic disciplines to provide answers to increasingly complex questions regarding our roles in modern technological systems.

A result of these developments has been a widespread recognition of the need to understand the abilities and limitations of the human in performing the complex activity of flying an aircraft. An important aspect of this is that more detailed attention is now given to the causes of error and the necessity to consider the human and technological aspects of flying as mutually interdependent rather than entirely separate factors. Pilot error is being tied ever closer to the design of equipment and air traffic procedures, to inadequate and sometimes inappropriate training, and to questionable operational doctrine by management.

The evidence for this change can be found in several places. Journals in the human factors and ergonomics areas frequently report studies of pilot performance, and the international Human Factors Society and Ergonomics Society are currently enjoying a period of accelerating growth. Several associations of aviation psychologists now exist whose members meet and correspond regularly. Most signficantly, there has been a filtering down of this information through the professional and amateur pilot magazines and safety literature and the mass news media.

In addition, an increasing number of national and international aviation agencies and accident investigation departments now include representatives from the psychology and human factors areas. In the past, accident investigators have identified the human factors aspect of an investigation almost exclusively with the medical evidence provided by an aviation pathologist. No doubt this can be of great significance in some accidents, but it is unfortunately true that a lack of understanding of human behavior has limited many accident investigators to the simple recognition that the accident must have been caused by some human defection. They close their reports with the cause simply stated as "pilot error."

In so doing they deny themselves the opportunity to discover the true reasons for the accident. More importantly, another opportunity has been missed to analyze the recorded events and system design characteristics that could have induced the human behavior leading to the accident. Such analyses together with simulated recreations of circumstances preceding an accident can contribute greatly to the prevention of another of similar type. The uncritical acceptance of pilot error as a cause of aircraft accidents, by the general public as well as the aviation community, has always been easy because "to err is human."

What is not so readily appreciated is that to err is also much more probable given certain circumstances and can be predicted by students of human behavior well informed in the type of operation in which the crew was engaged. Some of the most horrendous accidents of the past have failed to make their due contribution to our understanding of the human factors involved, and quite inevitably similar accidents occur repeatedly. Certain types of accidents, such as controlled flight into terrain in light general aviation airplanes and in military airplanes with head-up displays, occur many times every year without having their respective causes recognized.

The research surveyed in this book sometimes relates to technological innovations that have yet to appear or are only just appearing on the latest generations of airliners or combat aircraft. The main body of information considered is concerned with the more fundamental limitations of our sensory systems and our strategies for dealing with information. These set the limits on what is possible for the pilot and contribute to our understanding of errors in performance. This book also presents much of what is known about human behavior that is relevant to the primary task of designing aircraft to make them safer to fly and selecting and training pilots to achieve the same goal.

For the psychologist or psychology student, the book gives an insight into the ways in which the knowledge and methods of psychology have been applied with much success to a huge class of practical problems. The span of problems covered, ranging from vision (Chapter 1) to social psychology (Chapter 8), illustrates the close relationship between theoretical and applied research and the authors' conviction that research is truly basic to the degree that its findings are generalizable to a wide range of real-world applications.

Finally, a glossary of aviation terminology is included that should provide sufficient background to illuminate some of the abbreviations that seem impossible to avoid in any discussion of aviation matters.

Acknowledgments

MANY PEOPLE have contributed to the preparation of this book. The manuscript was produced at the University of Otago, Dunedin, New Zealand. The University of Otago provided computer facilities and assistance that are gratefully acknowledged. The support and encouragement of the late Professor Graham Goddard were much appreciated. The Office of Air Accidents Investigation, Wellington, New Zealand, kindly provided access to its library of accident reports. We gratefully acknowledge the support of the Captain A. G. Vette Flight Safety Trust Fund of Auckland, New Zealand.

Isabel Campbell typed and retyped the manuscript with remarkable cheerfulness and outstanding efficiency. Her appetite for work helped to propel the manuscript through its revisions and additions. Dianne Morrison contributed long hours at the word processor. Louis Corl of ILLIANA Aviation Sciences critically reviewed the entire manuscript and made suggestions for improvement. Our main debt, of course, is to the many people throughout the world who have dedicated their enthusiasm and expertise to understanding the causes of human performance failures in aviation. As a result it is now possible to draw on a body of knowledge of human performance in the pursuit of improvement in aviation safety and effectiveness.

The Senses

[1] Vision and Visibility: The Pilot's Eye View

WE HAD no means of angular orientation, were already deafened, and were bit by bit growing blind. Overhead the sky was filling with clouds and we flew thenceforth between cloud and fog in a world voided of substance and all light. Already our tired eyes were seeing things—errant signs, delusive flashes, phantoms.

ANTOINE DE SAINT-EXUPÉRY, *Wind, Sand and Stars*

INTRODUCTION

Whether the first powered flight was undertaken by the Wright brothers, as most people believe, or by a pioneering New Zealander by the name of Richard Pearse is now a matter of some debate. Born into a New Zealand farming family in December 1877, Pearse pursued his interest in the problems of heavier-than-air powered flight from his farm workshop. He constructed an aircraft equipped with three wheels in a tricycle configuration with a wood and metal-tube framework that supported the engine and wing mounted above the pilot's head. The two-cylinder, double-action, horizontally opposed engine was also constructed by Pearse in the same workshop.

There is no doubt that Pearse assembled and tested this aircraft. The exact date of his first flight can only be estimated from contemporary eyewitness accounts. One of these puts the date as early as March 1902, although other witnesses put the date as April 1903. The first reasonably sucessful flight, now known as the "terrace flight,"

3

started with a downhill takeoff from a 35-foot-high terrace above the Opihi River. The plane traveled approximately one quarter of a mile up the river before landing on the riverbed. Pearse himself did not consider this flight or the Wright brothers' flight at Kittyhawk in December 1903 to be properly sustained and controlled flights.

If the origins of powered flight are cloaked in uncertainty and controversy, there is no doubt that in a period spanning less than a century an astonishingly rapid development of the airplane has taken place. This single term encompasses a remarkable diversity from the low-powered, easy-to-fly, single-engine trainer or touring aircraft to rocket-powered hypersonics designed to fly in the outer limits of the atmosphere. With rare exceptions, all these machines are controlled and flown by a human operator—the pilot.

In contrast to the rapid evolution of the airplane, the sensory, motor, and cognitive capacities with which humans are equipped are the outcome of millions of years of gradual evolution and adaptation to environments quite different from those encountered while flying. Some animals have highly developed senses that far exceed human capacities—the unique ultrasonic system of the bat, the highly developed chemical sense of certain insects, and the supremely sensitive sense of smell of the shark are a few examples.

All these capacities represent superb examples of adaptation to the demands posed by a particular environment—tracking small insects at night, finding a mate across thousands of square kilometers of countryside, or locating a food source in as many cubic kilometers of ocean. Human sensory equipment can be seen as the result of evolutionary adaptation for survival on the earth's surface—forward facing eyes, for example, being ideally suited for the fine depth discrimination and manipulative precision at relatively short distances exhibited by all the primates. In contrast, the eyes of hawks are better suited for detecting small prey from the air.

Our evolutionary background has favored the development of a highly flexible visual system, and vision is generally considered to be our primary sensory modality. Its importance in flying is recognized in the medical requirements for the issue of any form of pilot license from the private certificate onward. The visual system has evolved to perform the functions of gathering information and guiding action, and there are intimate links between the two. For example, it is possible to demonstrate this by imposing unnatural demands, such as wearing inverting goggles.

At first, the wearer sees the world upside down, but over a period of two or three days vision and action become more coordinated, and after about a week the wearer is able to undertake complex activities, such as riding a bicycle. When the goggles are removed, everything reverts to being upside down, and actions are again uncoordinated for a relatively brief period before things return to normal. For the visual system to adapt to such changes, it is necessary for the brain to receive the additional information provided by movement to close the control loop effectively.

The task of piloting an aircraft off a small area of ground, flying safely in all kinds of weather, avoiding collision with the ground or other aircraft, and then smoothly reuniting the craft with another small area of ground places remarkably challenging demands on our sensory processes. To accomplish this task, the visual system operates both directly and indirectly on the objectively available optical information that is present in the light reaching the eye. This consists of light emitted or reflected from surfaces that is modified by the observer's movement through the environment.[1] This is a further example of the close links between perception and action.

There is evidence from both animal and human studies that some actions are geared directly to the available optical information.[2] From this follow the requirement that the pilot possess a fully functioning visual system and the emphasis on visual testing in pilot medical examinations. In contrast to "direct" perception, what we see is influenced indirectly by the perceiver's expectations or hypotheses to guide the processing of incoming information. In this case, it could be said that "believing is seeing" rather than "seeing is believing"!

If a particular ability is nonexistent (for example, seeing through clouds or detecting energy in the radio or microwave spectra), another highly evolved human capacity comes into play—the ability to create artificial sensory systems to supplement our own senses. In other cases, in which we have quite limited abilities (for example, judging height and speed), we develop artificial systems to augment those abilities (the altimeter and airspeed indicator). It can readily be seen that manned flight has placed demands on human sensory systems that exceed their normal limits.

Furthermore, it is a nearly universal part of pilot training for the trainee to be made aware of the necessity to disregard the sensations from certain senses, particularly the acceleration receptors in the inner ear. The reasons for this will be outlined in Chapter 2. Despite this, experienced professional airline crews can still be trapped by highly misleading perceptual cues with disastrous results. An example, to be discussed later, was the Antarctic tragedy in which an Air New Zealand DC-10 flew under visual "sector whiteout" conditions into the side of the Mount Erebus volcano.

It is not surprising that in our rapid evolution of flight, we have also created situations in which our sensory systems malfunction or are liable to produce erroneous interpretations. In the interest of safety, these situations attract the prime attention of aviation psychologists. We shall also deal with situations in which the visual system operates relatively well, but the sensory sensitivity or perceptual precision required exceeds normal human abilities.

OUTLINE OF THE VISUAL SYSTEM

We shall not deal in great detail with the anatomy or physiology of the visual system as there are excellent sources of material already available for this purpose. (See Further Reading at the end of this chapter.) Our emphasis will be on what the visual system does (and does not!) and how the structures of the eye and the brain accomplish the task of guiding action. Figure 1.1 shows a schematic outline of the principal structures of the nervous system involved in vision.

The eyes are only the first stage in a system that enables the transmission of nerve impulses from the retina to the visual cortex. Each structure plays an essential part in vision, with complex processing activities being performed in the retina and even more complex activities in the cortex. For example, a person whose optic tract has been cut or damaged on one side will suffer blindness in one-half of the visual field. However, damage to the visual cortex itself may produce a much more complex disorder, such as a complete inability to recognize faces or words.

Such conditions, known as "agnosias," have excited much interest among psychologists for the insight they provide in the operation of the visual system as a whole. The existence of complex pathways and links to the hindmost quarter of the brain, the visual cortex, can be taken as an indication that vision, or seeing, involves much more than simply registering information on the retina. The popular notion of vision as a kind of internal cinema screen must be quite wrong for at least two reasons.

First, it is illogical. Presumably some kind of inner eye would have to be responsible for scanning the picture on the retina. But this is no kind of explanation at all as it leaves the working of the inner eye completely unexplained. Second, advances in neurophysiology and computer picture recognition have shown ways in which the various pathways and cortical structures might process the nerve impulses caused by light striking the retina to allow us to "see" the world and react adaptively.

Naturally, this has become a highly technical undertaking, but there is no doubt that major advances have been made in understanding the complexities of the visual system. The practical relevance of this point to flying is that determining what is there to be seen is by no means a simple matter. The amount of work the visual system has to engage in means that there is considerable opportunity for error whenever unusual demands are placed on the system. As we have

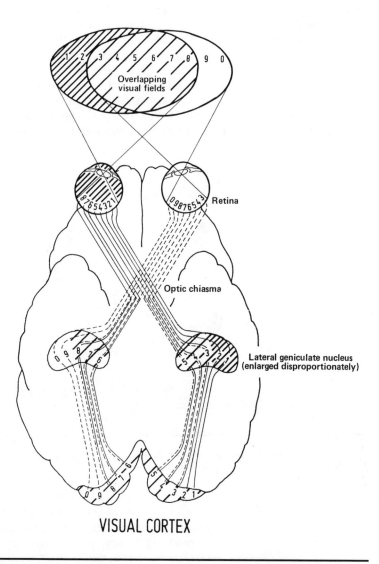

Overlapping
visual fields

Retina

Optic chiasma

Lateral geniculate nucleus
(enlarged disproportionately)

VISUAL CORTEX

Fig. 1.1 A schematic outline of the structure of the visual system. Information located in the left field of view (represented by the numbers 1 to 5) is received by part of the visual cortex in the right hemisphere, and information in the right field is processed in the left hemisphere. The eyes are actually an extension of the brain devoted to processing visual information. From *Human Information Processing* by P. H. Lindsay and D. A. Norman. Copyright 1972 by Academic Press. Reproduced by permission of Harcourt Brace Jovanovich.

already said, flying is by nature an activity that can cause us to err unexpectedly—but not necessarily without warning.

The basic structure of the eye can be represented as shown in Figure 1.2. Two types of photoreceptors are found in the human eye—rods and cones. Most of the receptors are rods, and these are found only in the periphery of the retina, whereas the cones fill the central fovea and spread to the near periphery. Rods have a much higher sensitivity to light than the cones but cannot distinguish colors. Although there are approximately 17 rods for every cone, the cones, concentrated centrally, allow us to resolve fine detail and distinguish colors.

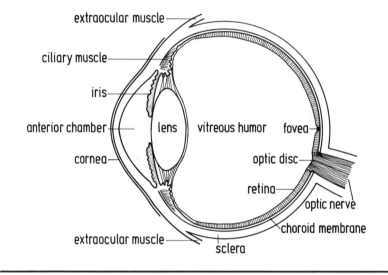

Fig. 1.2 Schematic outline of the eye. Cones are most densely packed in the fovea while rods are more widely distributed around the retina.

Unlike the rods, the cones operate only at relatively high levels of illumination—that is, they are much less sensitive to light—and color discrimination requires even more light than shape discrimination. This can be easily confirmed by noting that at dusk the different colors of the flowers in a garden become virtually indistinguishable. The density of the cones at the fovea gives this area of the retina its extremely high acuity, the ability to resolve fine detail.

Unlike those animals whose eyes are predominantly endowed with rods for sensitive night vision (e.g., rats and mice) or with cones for powerfully acute vision (e.g., hawks), the human eye manages to combine some of the advantages of both systems. In terms of sensitivity, the human eye is able to detect very small quantities of light—the equivalent of a match being struck 16 kilometers away on a dark night. Such targets can only be detected by allowing light to fall on the rods in peripheral vision. Once a target is detected in twilight or at night, one should avoid looking directly at it but rather look to one side to allow peripheral target recognition.

With better illumination, our eyes are remarkably acute with an ability to detect a telephone wire at a distance of 2 kilometers. However, this can only be achieved by looking directly at the wire and focusing the eyes at or near its distance. Moving targets, on the other hand, can be detected without looking at them or focusing on them. Unfortunately another airplane on a precise collision course with you doesn't move, it only grows, and unless the intruder flashes or glints or leaves a contrail (a condensed vapor trail), it will be virtually impossible to avert a midair collision.

ACUITY

Visual acuity is the capacity of the visual system to resolve detail. The commonly agreed measure of acuity is the angular size of the object, which can be measured using elementary trigonometry. Expressed this way, the visual system is normally capable of resolving detail as small as one minute of arc ($\frac{1}{60}$ of a degree). A number of methods can be used to measure acuity as shown in Figure 1.3.

The most common test used in aviation medical examinations is the Snellen chart, which presents capital letters of decreasing size on successive lines. The smallest letters read correctly determine visual acuity. Different methods yield different values, and the Snellen test can be compromised by a testee who remembers letters read with the stronger eye when using the weaker eye or one who memorizes all such charts in advance! Nevertheless, these assessment procedures are usually adequate for screening candidates with gross deficits.

Snellen acuity is typically measured at a viewing distance of 6 meters or 20 feet. However, pilots must read flight instruments at shorter distances and detect and identify airborne and surface objects at longer distances. Near and far vision depend on the eye's ability to accommodate—to shift its plane of best focus inward and outward from its neutral resting state, or "dark focus" distance. Near and far focus are mediated by a ring of intermingled tangential and radial muscle fibers forming the ciliary body that supports and controls the shape of the lens.

Constriction of the tangential fibers squeezes the lens, fattening it to focus near objects; contraction of the radial fibers stretches the lens, flattening it to focus far objects. The iris, or pupil, of the eye works in

TECHNIQUE	EXAMPLES	MINIMUM (ANGULAR) VALUE
1. *Minimum visible* (detecting single line or dot)	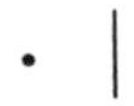 • |	0.5 sec of arc
2. *Minimum separable* (resolution of interspaces between contours)	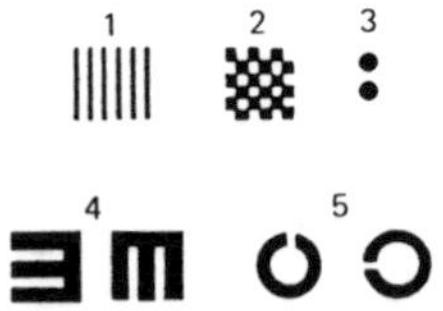 1 2 3 ‖‖‖ ▓ : 4 5 ∃Ⅲ O O	30 sec–1 min of arc (20/10 to 20/20)
3. *Recognition* (naming target)	 L O B T C L	30 sec–1 min of arc
4. *Vernier acuity* (detecting discontinuity)	 | |	2 sec of arc
5. *Stereoscopic acuity* (detecting depth displacement)	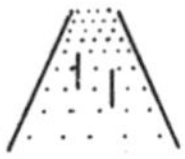 /\·|·\	1.5 sec of arc
6. *Dynamic acuity* (detecting and locating interspace in moving target)	 O ←	1–2 min of arc up to 60°/sec

Varieties of minimum separable acuity include: (1) Ives grating, (2) checkerboard pattern, (3) dot pairs, (4) Illiterate Snellen, (5) Landolt circles. Note that in several of these, the viewer must not only detect interspaces, but must localize them (Illiterate Snellen and Landolt circle).

Fig. 1.3   A variety of techniques for measuring visual acuity. From *Perception: An Applied Approach* by W. Schiff. Copyright 1980 by Houghton Mifflin. Reproduced by permission of the author.

conjunction with the lens, constricting to increase the depth of field to compensate for its reduction by the *fattened* lens and dilating to gather more light from distant scenes, taking advantage of the increased depth of field of the *flattened* lens. (This explanation of the functions of the internal eye muscles is a gross simplification of a complex autonomic process.)

Tests for near vision are a routine part of all classes of pilot medicals and can be accomplished by drawing a line of print toward the eye until the print becomes blurred. Near vision is assessed for each eye separately. This capacity is particularly affected by aging as the lens gradually loses elasticity from approximately age 30 onward. The main effect is to push outward the nearest distance at which the eye can accommodate. However, the far point and dark focus also slowly migrate outward throughout one's life, as illustrated in Figure 1.4. It is generally acceptable to correct focusing deficiencies with spectacles, and such correction does not preclude the issue of any class of pilot certification.

The conventional term of measurement of eye accommodation is the diopter (D): the reciprocal of the focal length of a lens in meters. Thus 1 D refers to a lens of focal length 1 meter. A child who can focus on an object 10 centimeters from the eye therefore has a power of accommodation of 10 D. Power of positive accommodation diminishes gradually with age. A typical value at 45 years might be 3.5 D (29 centimeters or about 11 inches). These values are shown by the line marked "near point" in Figure 1.4. The normal state of the eye in

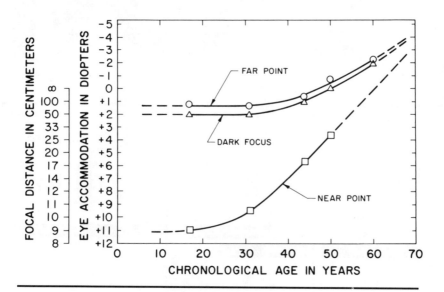

Fig. 1.4 Changes in near point (nearest distances to which the eyes can be focused), far point, and dark focus with increasing age, expressed both in diopters and in the corresponding focal distances out to optical infinity. Beyond optical infinity accomodation is expressed only in negative dioptric values. The outward migration of near focus typically becomes of functional significance after the age of 40, by which time the near point has moved out from approximately 9 to 14 centimeters and corrective lenses are needed for close work. (For an occasional fortunate myope, the outward migration of the far point makes it possible to dispense with glasses.) Based on data presented by N. A. Simonelli (1983) and adapted by S. N. Roscoe (1985) in *Human Factors*, 27, 630.

which there are no refractive errors is referred to as emmetropia. The most common refractive error is myopia in which light tends to be focused in front of the retina, causing the individual to be nearsighted.

COLOR VISION

Color vision is mediated by three types of cones maximally sensitive to red, green, and blue light, respectively. Cones are mostly packed together in the central or foveal area of the retina and in the

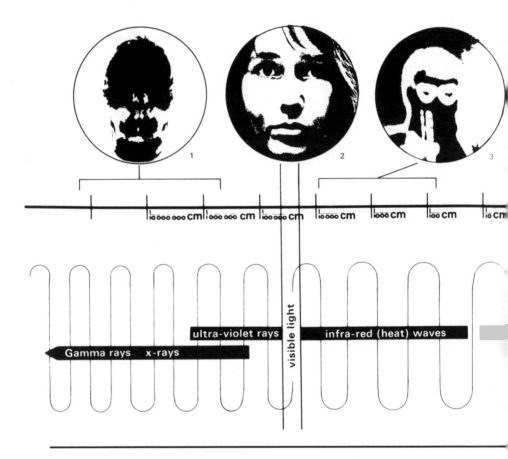

Fig. 1.5 The electromagnetic spectrum. The wavelengths that we detect as visible light cover a very narrow band in the spectrum. Pictures 1 to 4 show how the human face would appear to us if we were sensitive to energy in (1) the X-ray, (2) visible, (3) infrared, or (4) long-wave parts of the spectrum. From *Illusions* by E. Lanners. Copyright 1977 by Bucher-Verlag. Adapted by permission.

surrounding near periphery, thereby maximizing acuity as well as color discrimination in that region. It must be remembered that the eye is essentially a specially tuned receptor for energy in one portion of the electromagnetic spectrum (see Figure 1.5). Energy in most of the wavelengths will not excite the receptors in the retina. Energy in wavelengths outside the visible spectrum can, of course, be used through the design of artificial receptors, such as UHF and VHF radio, microwave landing systems, television, and radar and infrared scanning systems.

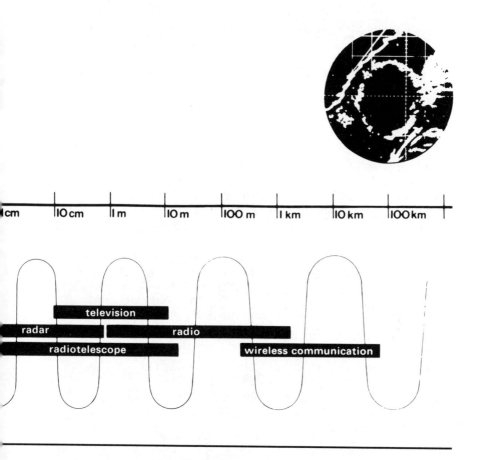

Visible light is composed of a range of different wavelengths. When light is refracted through a prism or through raindrops, the familiar rainbow of pure colors from red (the longest visible wavelength) through orange, yellow, green, blue, indigo, and violet (the shortest visible wavelength) can be seen. Since wavelength varies continuously, the division of the spectrum into discrete color names is arbitrary. The degree to which one wavelength can be discriminated from another by the human eye can be measured experimentally.

The eye is not equally sensitive to small changes across the spectrum but is slightly better at discriminating colors in the central region at about 550 nanometers, corresponding to a yellowish green light. Although individuals differ from one another, there are on the order of 130 discriminable steps across the visible spectrum. The extent to which individuals are aware of such color differences is likely to depend on genetic factors as well as cultural differences in the availability of suitable names.

Although the rods do not yield color discrimination, their sensitivity to light of different colors varies slightly. The rods are least sensitive to light at the red end of the visible spectrum. This fact, unfortunately, was the basis for restricting cockpit lighting to the color red for many years in the mistaken belief that the rods would thereby maintain a high level of dark adaptation. Because of the vast differences in the brightness of the light emitted from different instruments and from different areas of control panels (typically on the order of 100 to 1), the resulting hot spots of red light undid any advantage the restriction might have had.

The mechanisms that are involved between the reception of light at the rods and cones and the processing of signals from these receptors in the visual cortex are much more complicated than we have described. There are additional cells other than rods and cones that respond only when the level of illumination presented to the retina changes. It is now known that these cells actually cause changes in visual sensitivity in the absence of changes in dark adaptation. This is rather like having low-speed and high-speed film simultaneously available in your camera.[3] This shift in sensitivity applies primarily to the cones, because the rods become quickly saturated with increasing background illumination.

The retina adapts to the level of ambient illumination by synthesizing a substance called rhodopsin, or visual purple. The time taken for the rods to become fully dark adapted is approximately 30 minutes. Several experimental studies have compared the effects of different cockpit lighting systems. Low-level red lighting does result in a lower threshold for discriminating gross shapes than green or white lighting, but this difference is extremely small, even with carefully balanced lighting systems, and any advantage is offset by the advantages of white light in allowing color coding of instruments and controls and easier accommodation to instrument detail.[4]

Measurement of color vision is routinely included in all classes of pilot medical examination. Although the complete absence of color vision is extremely rare, approximately 9 percent of males show some form of deficiency when tested. The rate is much lower for females (0.5 percent), as most types of color deficiency are caused genetically in a form carried by females but affecting males only. Testing is most commonly carried out by means of the Ishihara plates. These consist of patterns of dots of different sizes and hues. If color vision is normal, the testee will be able to see patterns within other patterns—often consisting of hidden numbers.

The different forms of color vision defects will show up as the candidate fails to discriminate the correct patterns. The most common of these involves a slight weakness in differentiating between reds and greens. Much less common is a similar weakness in regard to yellows and blues. As with the tests of visual acuity, the tests of color sensitivity are suitable as an initial screening device. Any defects detected at this stage will be explored further by a more detailed opthalmological examination. With the changes in aviation from signal lantern systems to radio communication, the importance of color vision to flying has probably decreased slightly.

Nevertheless, night flying in particular presents problems of picking out taxiways (usually marked by blue and/or green lights) and distinguishing aircraft navigation lights (red for port and green for starboard). Night landing guidance systems in common use such as VASIs and T-VASIs typically involve red light but usually can be read correctly without full color vision. Many people with defective color vision cope successfully with tasks such as driving because there are normally other clues to guide action—the position of lights on traffic signals and different brightnesses normally associated with different hues.

Now that we have covered some of the basic aspects of vision relevant to flying, we will look in more detail at the kinds of tasks the visual system is asked to perform in flight. The most crucial, as far as flight safety is concerned, is the avoidance of other aircraft. The development of complex and expensive air traffic control systems to regulate traffic in busy airways and at airports has meant that the midair collision is a statistically insignificant event, particularly for scheduled air carriers, although examples still occur with tragic results. Light aircraft on local flights are the most exposed to this hazard. A look at how the visual system operates to detect collisions can be used to generate some practical advice for collision avoidance.

COLLISION AVOIDANCE AND THE MIDAIR

HELICOPTOR IN NEAR MISS WITH LARGE PINK PIG

> *The Gazelle was en route from Northolt, England, at 130 knots, at 1,250 feet. The helicopter was turning right when its pilot saw a large pink pig at one o'clock, half a mile away. The turn was stopped, and the Gazelle overtook the pig, passing 500 to 1,000 feet from its port flank. The pig had its back to the Gazelle and was therefore unable to take evasive action. (The "pig" was a publicity balloon that had broken away from its moorings.)*[5]

As we said earlier, the human visual system has evolved to guide action. A critical action for any animal to take is to avoid imminent danger. The approach of any threatening object is therefore an event of great significance, and the human visual system has a variety of ways of detecting and reacting to impending intrusion. The first of these involves the activation of the combined eye muscle and head rotation mechanisms. The rods in the eye's periphery are especially suitable for the detection of small differences in energy from low-contrast light sources. However, for a target to be detected by the rods in the eye's periphery, it must be moving, flashing, glinting, or very large, such as a trail of condensed water vapor behind a high-flying airplane.

Unfortunately, another airplane on a collision course may possess none of these critical characteristics until the moment before impact when it suddenly fills the whole windscreen. If a target is detected in peripheral vision, which in humans covers nearly 180 degrees of horizontal visual angle, head and eye movements can then be used to bring the object onto foveal vision where the greatest acuity is to be found. Unfortunately another airplane, whether moving rapidly in the visual field or maintaining a stationary bearing (on a collision course), is easily lost again after being detected.

Most animals, including humans, have an innate or automatic avoidance response to a suddenly appearing or looming target. Human babies as young as six days old have been shown to have an innate response to such stimulation—they move the head back, thrust the hands up, and stare straight ahead. Relatively little visual processing seems to be required as the action follows immediately from the optical stimulation provided by a rapidly expanding target. A far-off object moving toward us at a constant velocity will occupy an increasing angular size at the eye (see Figure 1.6), but the angular increase is barely detectable and seldom noticed until the final second before the two airplanes near-miss or collide.

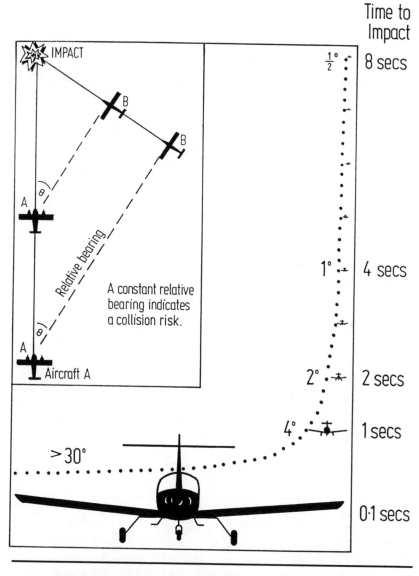

Fig. 1.6 The angular size of an oncoming aircraft expands slowly until moments before impact, when it expands rapidly to fill the field of view. The angular sizes are not drawn exactly to scale. Adapted from a drawing by R. Green with his permission.

This is because the increase in visual angle is not linear but positively accelerated; it expands slowly at first, then explodes as the target comes closer to the eye. When a target has suddenly loomed into view by occupying about 30 degrees of visual angle, a collision is imminent. At this point, two light planes would be only one-tenth second away from impact! This would already be about ten seconds too late for the pilot to recognize that the other plane was maintaining a constant bearing both horizontally and vertically; decide which way to turn, climb, or dive; make the control inputs; and wait for the plane to complete the evasive maneuver. Fortunately 60 to 65 percent of those involved in midair collisions survive.

The "looming" phenomenon of the midair closure is similar to the groundrush experienced by parachutists during the last few meters of descent as the ground appears to rise to meet the jumper. This may also account for some of the difficulties experienced in learning to land an aircraft. For most of the approach the optical picture expands slowly as in the upper portions of Figure 1.6. Once over the boundary fence, however, there is a sudden optical expansion similar to that of the impending collision. Learning to land an aircraft involves the precise coordination of this high-velocity perceptual information with smooth, small adjustments of the aircraft's controls. Overcontrol, often resulting in "ballooning," is a common problem at this stage.

Several strategies are recommended to minimize the likelihood of a midair collision.

• Be aware of the high-risk areas—pleasure flights below five thousand feet in the vicinity of an airport are most likely to be involved in such accidents.

• Be aware that not all collisions are head-on or from some other stationary collision angle. A greater danger exists when one or both planes are turning in the landing pattern. The risk will come from the side and slightly behind—an area of poor visibility on most aircraft.

• Be careful not to relax when under radar contact. It is still the pilot's responsibility to see and avoid other aircraft. The tendency to diffuse responsibility (see Chapter 8) can lead to a dangerous sense of complacency.

• Keep up a systematic scan at all times. Do not fixate on any one spot but keep moving the head and eyes, thus maximizing the chance of detecting a target with peripheral vision.

• Remember that the most difficult target to detect will be one that is on a constant bearing from you—one that will remain in the same spot on the windscreen. An intruder that changes angular position, either horizontally or vertically, is not a collision threat unless one or the other turns. The one that you will be able to reach over and shake hands with is the target that remains in a constant angular position relative to your aircraft.

NIGHT FLYING

For the private pilot, flying at night is an opportunity to develop basic instrument skills as well as to extend visual flying abilities. For the professional pilot it is a routine operation. For both it is a situation that places unusual demands on the visual system. This is reflected in the rate and type of aircraft accidents that occur at night. The most common of these involves a tendency to fly a long, low approach, particularly in so-called black hole conditions. These exist when, for example, an aircraft descends through clouds on a completely dark night. On breaking out, the pilot can see the airfield lights in the distance, but there is no other illumination.

Often these conditions involve an approach over the sea where there is no light source or reflected light under or around the aircraft. The black hole conditions are particularly conducive to the pilot's illusion that the aircraft is too high. As a result, the pilot reduces power and allows the aircraft to descend short of the runway, in some cases into the sea. Classic accidents of this type have occurred at Los Angeles, Salt Lake City, and Tokyo, to name a few. Several factors seem to be involved here, most notably where the pilot's eyes focus in the dark.

Eye accommodation and apparent size. As introduced earlier, the distance at which the eye spontaneously focuses in darkness is known as the dark focus or resting state. For young adults with normal eyes, this tends to be at about arm's length, but for some it may be at optical infinity or well *beyond* optical infinity. Although this has been shown to be a determinant of various kinds of visual performance, there is at present no test made of it in the medical examinations for any class of pilot license. The importance of the dark focus is that the apparent size of an object alters with changes in the distance to which the eyes accommodate.

This can be demonstrated by looking with one eye at a small distant object, such as the moon, through a small opening, or peekhole, made by the fist, and alternately closing and opening the other eye. This causes the focus of the eyes to jump inward and outward making the object appear smaller and larger, respectively. This fact seems to account for the puzzling "moon illusion" in which the moon appears larger when viewed low against the horizon than when it is overhead.

Many ingenious explanations for this have been proposed, but it has now been shown experimentally to depend on the distance to which the eyes are focused.[6]

Experimental work involving professional pilots flying simulated night approaches on autopilot has demonstrated that there is a relationship between the individual's focal response to the simulator's visual display and judgments of whether the aircraft will overshoot or undershoot the landing aimpoint. In the black hole conditions, the first visual contact with the runway lights far in the distance moves the focus forward from its resting position, causing an apparent expansion of the visual scene with a consequent lowering of the runway threshold relative to the more distant band of lights defining the horizon.

For pilots with a distant far point of accommodation, a serious height illusion can result. At this stage such pilots are likely to regard themselves as overshooting—as would be natural if the image of the runway seemed larger and the threshold lower than they should. When closer in, with the pattern of runway lights and the other airport and city lights more easily resolved, the eye's focus can lapse back toward the dark focus, causing the runway to decrease in apparent size and increase in apparent distance. The pilots will see that they are undershooting, but it may be too late to add power and avert a premature touchdown.

Partially offsetting the effect just described is the tendency of eye accommodation to shift outward during the performance of a stressful task. On average for the 20 pilots in the simulator experiment, there was a net outward shift in focus between 20 and 10 seconds before touchdown as the adrenalin flow increased, but the perceptual effects were as described. The clear conclusion of this research was that the focus of the eye could be misled by several phenomena that can occur in flight, and when so disturbed, both size and distance perception are distorted, and the pilot's controlling responses can be correspondingly biased.[7]

Although these phenomena are not as yet fully understood, it is known that the dark focus changes with age, moving slowly outward. As was shown in Figure 1.4, the rate of change for both the dark focus and the far point as well as the near point increases after age 40–45 years. There is considerable individual variation in dark focus, and there is reason to suggest that older individuals with a distant dark focus may be particularly susceptible to the illusions generated by the black hole approach.

There is some evidence, however, that individuals can learn to control the dark focus distance, and its effects can be partially compensated for by wearing appropriate lenses.[8] As we noted earlier, it is possible to compensate for even extremely distorted visual input by taking the appropriate actions, and undoubtedly pilots do learn to compensate for such biased judgments. Nevertheless it remains somewhat surprising that dark focus is not taken into account in medical examinations or pilot selection. The potential effects are nicely summarized in the title of Roscoe's 1979 article, "When day is done and shadows fall, we miss the airport most of all."

The runway size-width illusion. Another factor that may contribute to the relatively high accident rate for night visual landing approaches is the size-width illusion. This has been described as follows: "Some researchers have suggested that if the width and/or length of an unfamiliar runway differs radically from that to which the pilot is accustomed, then the resulting illusion may cause systematic deviations above or below the desired glidepath."[9] Figure 1.7 shows how the image of an 8,000-foot runway of widths ranging from 75 to 300 feet would appear to a pilot 5,000 feet out flying a typical 3-degree approach angle.

Pilots used to flying at airport A will have learned that this is how the image should look if they were flying the correct glidepath. If the image were to appear as in E, then this would provide a correct cue to infer that the aircraft is overshooting and take the appropriate actions. Unfortunately the image projected by runway A, indicating such an overshoot, would be virtually identical to the image projected by runway E, indicating the correct glidepath. Pilots used to airport A are likely to fly a low approach to runway E. If this tendency is combined with other factors referred to in the black hole situation, the chances of a dangerously low approach are greatly increased.

In a series of experiments, professional pilots with an average of 3,800 hours of flight experience flew simulated night visual approaches to a series of runways varying in widths as shown in Figure

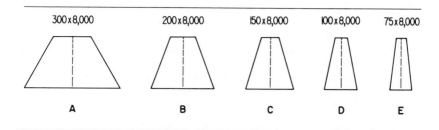

300×8,000	200×8,000	150×8,000	100×8,000	75×8,000
A	B	C	D	E

Fig. 1.7 Schematic outlines of the projected images of five different runways of the same length but different widths, seen from the same approach point. In the experiments, the images were computer generated and displayed on a 17-inch multicolor CRT. Adapted from H. W. Mertens and M. F. Lewis (1982). *Aviation, Space, and Environmental Medicine, 53,* 464.

1.7. Over the last mile of approach, the variation produced with decreasing runway widths was as much as 1 degree, with average approach angles dropping from 2.77 degrees to 1.96 degrees. This illusion affects highly experienced pilots even when they have been warned to expect it. These findings highlight the danger in night visual approaches at airports with no visual approach angle indicators (such as VASIs) by pilots accustomed to runways of smaller length-to-width ratios.

These last two sections have illustrated one kind of visual perception in which sufficient information about impending collisions and approach angles is directly available from the optical environment. A more insidious situation is one in which the optical cues bear little relation to the true situation, and this is best illustrated by the circumstances surrounding the Air New Zealand DC-10 tragedy on the slopes of Mount Erebus in Antarctica.

TEXTURE, SIZE, AND DISTANCE

IMPACT EREBUS

On 28 November 1979, an Air New Zealand DC-10 on a sightseeing flight over the Antarctic flew into the side of a 12,000-foot volcano near Scott Base. The aircraft had descended below a 6,000-foot overcast to give the passengers a view of the ice-shelf below. The initial report of the New Zealand accident investigators criticized the crew for flying at low level in conditions of poor visibility. This finding was overturned by the Royal Commission of Inquiry, which put the blame on the airline's navigation section for providing the crew with a different set of navigational coordinates from those presented at the preflight briefing. The revised coordinates, entered by the crew immediately before departure, put the DC-10 25 miles to the side of the correct track up McMurdo Sound and directly in line with Mount Erebus. The mystery of why the crew, even then, failed to see the slopes of Erebus in conditions of 70-kilometer visibility could only be solved by a close examination of the effects of visible (and invisible) texture on visual perception and the illusion caused by sector whiteout.[10]

For a small country like New Zealand, the DC-10 crash was traumatic. Reverberations are still being felt from the controversy aroused by the conflicting attributions of responsibility for the tragedy. In his official accident report, the New Zealand chief accident investigator found the cause to be solely pilot error by the captain in command. The report of the Royal Commission for the government arrived at a quite different conclusion. A more thorough investigation of the accident suggested that the crew members were subject to a variety of misleading visual cues, including an insidious illusion known to experienced polar fliers as "sector whiteout."

The phenomenon of sector whiteout is of general interest, not only for its role in the tragic outcome of Flight 901, but as an example of the importance of visible texture in eye accommodation and the pilot's perception of size and distance. The crash of Flight 901 also highlights the part played by mental set or expectation in visual perception. This will be discussed in detail at the end of the chapter.

Visual cues and clues.   In normal circumstances there are numerous clues to the size and distance of objects. We learn to expect familiar objects at a certain distance to subtend a certain visual angle, and if the visual angle subtended by such an object is very much smaller than expected, we will see the object as being farther away. This is usually referred to as "size constancy." When the eyes are properly focused, objects do not appear to shrink or expand according to the visual angles they create but remain constant in apparent size with their apparent distance changing.

The world would be an unpredictable and confusing place if some such mechanism did not operate! Size constancy played its part in the Air New Zealand DC-10 crash. The final route of Flight 901 is shown in Figure 1.8. The transcript from the cockpit voice recorder and photographs taken by passengers and recovered from the wreckage provide detailed evidence that the crew members were misled by a remarkable correspondence between the appearance of the features they were observing as they flew into Lewis Bay and the appearance of the features they would have seen had the aircraft been following its planned course up the middle of McMurdo Sound.

Some four hours after leaving the New Zealand coastline, the DC-10 descended from its cruising altitude to give the passengers the promised view of the Antarctic continent. The inertial navigation systems showed the aircraft's track to be on course, supposedly in the middle of McMurdo Sound. Several descending orbits were flown beneath the 6,000-foot overcast. The crew and the Antarctic expert, who was providing a commentary from the flight deck, were able to pick out features from the landscape on either side.

At the position where the crew expected to see the cliffs of McMurdo's Cape Rhoyds, they saw instead the cliff faces of Lewis Bay's Cape

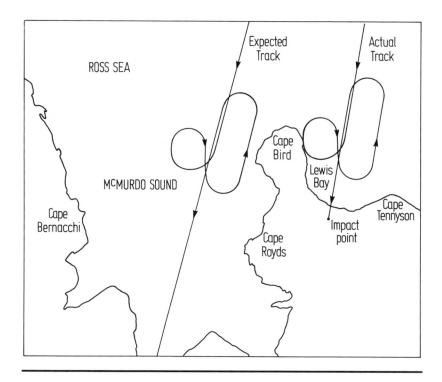

Fig. 1.8 A simplified map of the McMurdo Sound area, showing the course that the crew of Flight 901 expected to be on and the actual track that the aircraft flew because of the change in coordinates entered into the INS.

Tennyson. The cliffs were of similar size and appeared at the expected distance from the aircraft. In addition, the cliff faces of Lewis Bay's Cape Bird matched the expected appearance of the cliffs of McMurdo's Cape Bernacchi. Whereas the cliffs of Tennyson matched Rhoyds in both size and distance, the cliffs of Bird were only approximately one-third as high as those of Bernacchi but subtended the same visual angle because they were about one-third as far away.

This apparent correspondence between the observed terrain features and the features marked on their charts of McMurdo Sound, together with the agreement of all three navigational systems, provided further confirmation of their expectations. Their mental set assured them that they were proceeding up the 40-mile-wide expanse of sea ice in McMurdo Sound. This error would not in itself have led to the accident were it not for the sector whiteout. This will be discussed in detail in the next section, following a consideration of other cues to the perception of depth and distance.

A second common source of information about distance is provided by the relative displacement of objects when one moves, known as "motion parallax." Whereas objects close to the observer will be displaced considerably, objects in the far distance will hardly be displaced at all. Figure 1.9 shows how this works in practice. An example of this is provided in a moving train. Telegraph poles close to the railway line move rapidly across the field of vision, whereas the far view remains relatively unchanged. Of course we are also using our prior knowledge of the size and likely locations of telegraph poles as well as the information provided by the motion parallax.

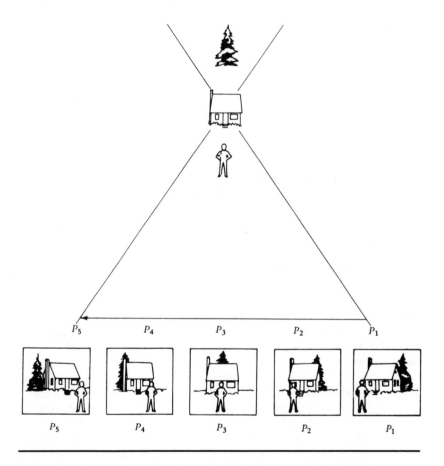

Fig. 1.9 Some of the changes known as motion parallax can be seen here. These include the greater movement across the retina of the projections of near objects (the figure) than far objects (the tree) and changes in the way the objects overlap or occlude one another as the scene shifts. The changes depicted would be seen regardless of where the observer focused. From *The Psychology of Visual Perception*, 2nd ed., by R. N. Haber and M. Hershenson. Copyright 1980 by Holt, Rinehart and Winston. Reprinted by permission.

A third source of information is provided by the fact that objects at a great distance project a less detailed image on the retina and also appear less saturated in color than they do when nearer. Thus distant hills take on an unclear and somewhat bluish appearance. Atmospheric conditions such as haze may contribute to an illusion that objects are farther away than they really are. This is because haze makes the outline of objects appear diffused and of subdued color—just as would be expected if the objects were actually more distant.

The effects can be all the more insidious when visibility over the haze is very good or in other special circumstances, such as in polar conditions. On such a day, when dry particles become trapped by an inversion creating hazy conditions beneath the inversion level, it is visibility downward and particularly on a slant that is most affected, and although horizontal visibility above the inversion remains unimpaired, distant vision suffers. Why this is so is readily understood when one considers the effects of visible texture on visual accommodation and our perception of size, distance, and angular location.

Texture, focus, and perception.   Where the eyes focus in flight is a compromise between the pull of visible texture in the distance (or the sharply defined markings in the cockpit) and the antagonistic pull of the dark focus toward its resting position. In the absence of clearly defined or distant objects to focus on, the point at which the eyes accommodate tends to move back toward the viewer. In hazy conditions, the eyes will focus only a short distance ahead even though distant terrain may be vaguely visible and horizontal visibility excellent. This condition is generally referred to as "empty sky myopia."

Under such conditions, misaccommodation has several effects. The perceived field of view appears shrunken so that objects, when seen, appear smaller, farther away, and closer to the horizon than they are. Although the outside world does not appear blurred, it is actually badly out of focus, causing a further reduction in effective contrast and the probability of detecting intruders. In addition to keeping up a regular scan for other traffic, pilots are advised in these conditions to focus periodically on their wingtips to change the distance to which their eyes are accommodated.

As they are in everyday life, the size, distance, and angular position of objects are of considerable importance when one is flying at high altitudes as well as at relatively low altitudes over the countryside. At high altitudes, and particularly over featureless terrain, available visual cues cannot be expected to provide adequate distance information. At lower altitudes, an adequate source of information about depth and distance is normally provided by the environment itself—or more specifically the light reflected from surface objects.

The information contained in this reflected light gives vital clues to distance and layout. At the simplest level, there are gross differences in the amount of light reflected by different surfaces. Snow is highly reflective; forests and rocks reflect a much smaller proportion of the available light. Differences between the amount of reflected light show up as edges, revealing for example the difference between a lake and the surrounding snow-covered ground. Edges can be seen, however, even where there are no differences in the amount of light reflected by adjacent surfaces.

Figure 1.10 shows how a definite perception of an edge can be produced by varying the optical texture gradients of two surfaces. All surfaces have some texture; they may be rough or smooth. The texture of a plowed field, for example, provides ample information for the perception of distance. The portion of the field close to the observer has a large-grained, rough texture, whereas that in the distance has a small-grained, smooth texture. Such information can also provide clues as to the slope of a surface.

Figure 1.11 shows five textured shapes on a textured background. Shape E has exactly the same texture gradient as the background and is therefore seen as parallel to it. This would be the sort of information available to a pilot looking for a suitable flat surface on which to make a landing. Having located a suitable general area (a valley floor as opposed to the adjacent hillsides), a particular field will be selected whose texture gradient appears to match the surrounding background as closely as possible.

Conditions that obscure or eliminate this texture gradient are precisely those often present when accidents occur—for example, shortly after dusk or perhaps in the presence of a low sun directly facing the aircraft. Dirt or rain on the windshield can trap a pilot's focus and impair judgment of depth and distance through misaccommodation and the loss of outside texture information. Rain may also cause misleading depth perception through refraction. This is particularly likely to take place at night when airfield lights are diffused through moisture on the windshield and can therefore appear dimmer and farther away than they really are.

Returning to Figure 1.11 we can see how the relative texture gradients of the various shapes provide sufficient information for us to judge their slopes. For the pilot this is of course vital information either in the case of making a landing in an unknown area or in judging whether the aircaft can outclimb the rising ground ahead. The number of accidents in the latter case suggests that pilots of light aircraft are prone to underestimate slope or overestimate their aircraft's performance—or both!

The effect of runway slope on the perception of approach angle can be quite dramatic.[11] Figure 1.12 shows the projected image of the same

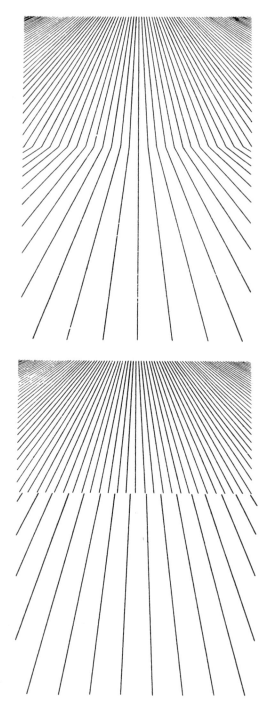

Fig. 1.10. These two figures show how the perception of a corner or an edge can be produced by differences in the texture gradient of two surfaces. From *The Psychology of Visual Perception* by R. N. Haber and M. Hershenson. Copyright 1973 by Holt, Rinehart and Winston. Reprinted by permission.

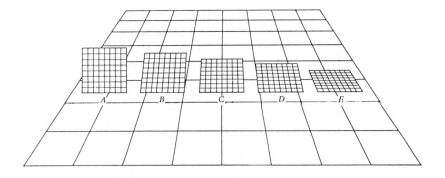

Fig. 1.11 Five textured shapes set against a textured background. The relationship between the texture gradient of the shape and the gradient of the background provides the visual system with cues to the orientation of the shapes. From *The Psychology of Visual Perception* by R. N. Haber and M. Hershenson. Copyright 1973 by Holt, Rinehart and Winston. Reprinted by permission.

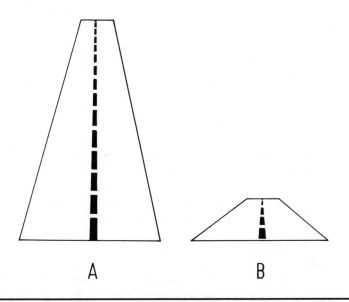

Fig. 1.12 Differences in the projected images of two runways of the same length and width, but with a two-degree upslope (A) and a two-degree downslope (B). Compared to a level runway of the same dimensions, the approach to A appears too high, and the approach to B appears too low. Both are shown from the correct three-degree approach angle.

1,220 × 30-meter runway viewed from 490 meters out at a height of 32 meters. The only difference is that runway A has a 2-degree upslope, whereas runway B has a 2-degree downslope. In the first case, the image is equivalent to being too high for a level runway of the same dimensions. Unless the pilot has learned to compensate for this through previous experience at this particular runway, there will be a strong tendency to reduce power or otherwise lower the descent angle early and consequently land short. The reverse situation could occur with the downsloping runway.

Given this information about the cues that provide us with knowledge of size, distance, and angular location of visible objects and the slope of visible surfaces, we are in a position to discuss the circumstances that may be expected to affect other perceptual judgments. There is now convincing evidence to support the view that the Air New Zealand DC-10 crew was unwittingly flying in precisely the sort of conditions that would conspire to make such judgments highly misleading.

Removal of texture and whiteout.   When pilots knowingly encounter conditions of whiteout and lack of texture, as in clouds, they must possess the skill to fly solely by instruments and are obliged to follow a different set of rules (Instrument Flight Rules) from those that apply when flying by visual reference to the ground (Visual Flight Rules). Provided the pilot has received adequate training in the necessary skills, instrument flight is unproblematic. Statistically IFR operations are far safer than VFR operations.

There are, however, circumstances that effectively remove visible surface texture but leave the pilot with the illusion of flying in normal visual circumstances. One such situation, which is known to occur frequently in the polar regions, is illustrated in Figure 1.13. The prerequisites are the sun at a low angle (38 degrees or less), snow-covered ground that reflects most of the light falling on it, and a low to medium overcast (up to 20,000 feet) that will also reflect the majority of the light falling on it. This is sometimes referred to as the albedo, or "milk bottle," effect.

In the conditions depicted in Figure 1.13, in which the aircraft is flying toward rising ground with the sun behind it, light will be reflected back and forth between the surface and the overcast with no discernible textural difference separating the two. However, a mental set can provide "in fill" or "line joining," implanting an artificial horizon line across the whiteout sector between the clearly visible cliffs to the left and right. Thus sector whiteout can be more dangerous than full whiteout, and this provided the final trap for the crew of Flight

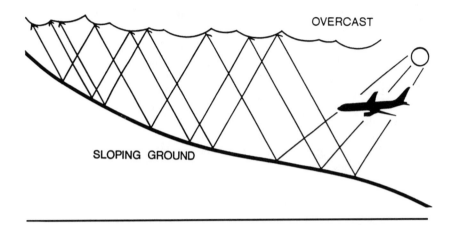

Fig. 1.13 An illustration of the sector whiteout effect. Although the aircraft is in clear air, the light from the sun behind the aircraft is reflected between the snow-covered ground and the overcast above. Differences in texture gradients that give rise to the perception of slopes, edges, and contours are not available in the light reaching the pilot.

901. Visibility was obviously excellent, and there was no visible obstruction ahead.

Antarctic flyers have become familiar with the phenomenon of sector whiteout. It must be distinguished from the popular conception of whiteout as involving a complete loss of visibility in a blizzard or snowstorm. The conditions described above are particularly deceptive because the perception of clear air is maintained, even though that clear air may be interrupted by an invisible snow-covered mountainside. Although the majority of pilots will not find themselves faced with conditions of the same severity, an important principle remains.

The crew of Flight 901 were operating visually below an overcast sky in polar conditions as they had been authorized and cleared to do by the company and by the U.S. Navy's air traffic control station at McMurdo. Unaware of the effects of sector whiteout, the crew relied on the main premise of visual flight rules—that visibility and the distance at which a pilot will be able to see and recognize an obstacle are synonymous, and thus a pilot will have time to take avoidance action if confronted by an unexpected obstacle.

If visibility and the distance at which a pilot can see and recognize the obstacle are no longer synonymous (as in the case of sector whiteout), the entire scale of VFR visibility criteria laid down by civil aviation authorities is inappropriate. Air New Zealand had permitted its pilots to descend below 6,000 feet over the ice shelf provided they were flying with visibility of at least 20 kilometers. In this case, the extended company Antarctic requirements for visibility of 20 kilometers from the regulatory 8 kilometers would have done nothing except lull the crew into a false sense of additional security.

The general rule is that conditions that lead to a degradation of surface texture will result in greatly impaired judgments of size, distance, angular location, slope, and even object recognition. Light aircraft are often involved in landing accidents at or shortly after dusk in which dim light, glare, or even interference from a dirty windshield can affect the perception of texture. Generally such accidents will have been compounded by other factors related to weather and time, but the central point remains.

Design induced misperceptions.

Design induced misperceptions.   From time to time in aviation, a new technology emerges that enables previously impossible operations. Ground and airborne radar revolutionized air traffic control and air-to-air weapon delivery; night vision goggles and forward-looking infrared (FLIR) scanners made "nap-of-the-earth" helicopter operations possible at night; and so it goes. Unfortunately, because new technologies make such operations possible, pilots (and administrators) readily accept the new hazards to safety they inevitably also introduce if they are not optimally designed. Aviation's love affair with head-up displays (HUDs) is a classic example of our acceptance of such a risk unnecessarily.

The intention of HUD designers is to provide a means for pilots to see outside the cockpit and simultaneously see flight and steering guidance symbology for ground-referenced operations. To make this possible, optically collimated virtual images of CRT symbols are reflected off a transparent combining glass mounted above the aircraft's instrument panel. The assumption has been that the eyes focus at optical infinity when viewing collimated symbology that appears to emanate from optical infinity and hence requires zero vergence to avoid double images. Not until the late 1970s was it conclusively shown that collimated images do not necessarily cause the eyes to focus at optical infinity, but many still refuse to accept this conclusion.

Meanwhile, the U.S. and U.K. flying forces have been losing on the order of five HUD-equipped planes a month since they came into wide use during the 1980s. In 1988 TV newscasters reported that between May and August of that year 19 NATO aircraft crashed into the countryside of West Germany alone. Most of these flying mishaps involve controlled-flight-into-terrain in clear daylight, and the rest follow spatial disorientation at night or in marginal weather. Both are invariably fatal, and the combined annual losses by all North Atlantic Treaty Organization members are approaching one billion American dollars. Of the 73 HUD-equipped planes lost by the United States Air Force between 1980 and 1985, 54 mishaps involved misjudgments of range and angle to terrain and 19 resulted from spatial disorientation.[12]

One of the heaviest burdens of science is to correct the misconceptions of common sense. For most of human history, common sense told us the earth was the center of the universe and that its surface, with minor perturbations, was flat. Common sense also tells us that the eyes should respond to collimated virtual images in the same way they respond to distant objects in the real, three-dimensional world; science tells us that they do not. The misaccommodation induced (or permitted?) by infinity optics has been demonstrated in at least four crucial experiments.[13]

Not only does accommodation remain near the dark focus when HUD symbology is viewed in darkness or in a cloud; in clear daylight it is drawn inward toward the dark focus by the collimated virtual imagery, as shown in Figure 1.14. In this experiment, a HUD was set up on one rooftop and a scoreboard assembly with selectively lighted numerals of various sizes was mounted on top of another building 182 meters away and of about the same height. Observers were asked to read the scoreboard numbers as they appeared and also numbers presented by the HUD on half the trials.

Figure 1.14 shows the average focal responses of each observer to the scoreboard numerals and the background terrain beyond the scoreboard alternately with the HUD turned off and with it turned on. In either case the observers' focal responses were highly dependent on their individual dark focus distances; in fact, knowing each individual's dark focus accounted for 88 percent of the variance in focal responses under all conditions of the experiment. Excluding Observer 9, whose dark focus was almost 3 diopters (D) beyond infinity, the average for the remaining nine emmetropes was 1.06 D, or just short of 1 meter.

But the striking result shown in Figure 1.14 is the fact that when the HUD was turned on, for all ten observers focus shifted inward from an average of 0.02 D, or 50 meters, to an average of 0.20 D, or 5 meters. Once again excluding Observer 9, the average inward shift was from 0.27 D, about 4 meters, to 0.47 D, about 2 meters. Although such shifts have little effect on the apparent clarity of the visual scene, they have tremendous effects on the apparent size, distance, and angular direction of terrain features, as previously described.

The apparent angular compression of the visual world with near focus causes ground targets and other objects to seem farther away and closer to the horizon than they are, and hence, to a pilot, an airplane's descent angle appears shallower and surface objects higher than they are. In a 3-degree landing approach this combination tends to result in a high roundout, a long float, and eventually a hard land-

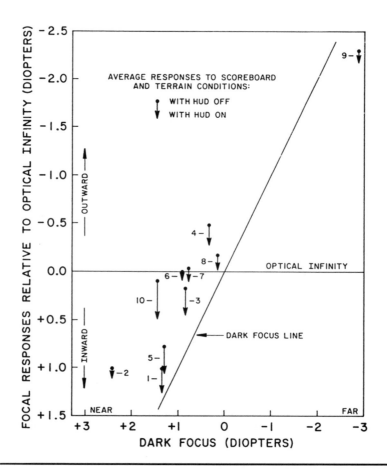

Fig. 1.14 Effects, for each of ten observers, of a head-up virtual image display on the average focal responses to the scoreboard and the terrain conditions with the HUD on and off, plotted against each individual's dark focus. From J. H. Iavecchia, H. P. Iavecchia, and S. N. Roscoe. (1988). *Human Factors, 30,* 700.

ing; in a 30-degree bombing attack, the seemingly distant target and relatively shallow apparent dive angle can result in a delayed pullup. The pilot suddenly sees the target rushing toward the aircraft, but it is too late to avert the crash.

Of course, HUDs are not all bad; indeed, any display that enables pilots to fly inherently dangerous, complex missions is better than one that does not. Furthermore, some risk is inherent and acceptable in military operations, but unnecessary risk is not acceptable. The trouble with HUDs is that they cause biased spatial judgments at best and disorientation at worst, and these create unacceptable risks if they can be largely compensated for or eliminated by design changes. In the case of HUDs there is much room for improvement and a high probability of some success.

To induce pilots to focus at optical infinity when viewing virtual images, investigators in Israel[14] introduced a negative focal demand of −0.5 D with the desired result, although there were wide individual differences in responses as a function of individual dark focus distances. Thus the first experimental fix should be the addition of variable optical refraction to offset each individual pilot's inward focal lapse induced by the HUD's virtual images.

Almost as important is the complete redesign of HUD symbology. Just how complicated and confusing it is can be appreciated from the estimate of an army instructor pilot that an average student helicopter pilot requires 300 hours of simulator and flight training to master the gaggle of symbols. Furthermore, the attitude presentation is conducive to horizon and pitch-ladder control reversals that result in disorientation and "graveyard spirals" at night and in marginal weather.

MOTION PARALLAX AND OCCLUSION

The cues discussed previously were all based on a view of the world in which various objects, such as people, houses, trees, and distant hills, can be seen to move in relation to one another (motion parallax) or to overlap one another (occlusion). These cues are normally available in abundance to the ground-based observer, and to an extent to the pilot of a relatively low-flying aircraft. In the case of flying in clouds, at night, or over featureless terrain such as desert or snow-covered regions, lack of these cues results in impaired perception of distance, angular location, and slope.

SPEED ILLUSION

> *A British Army Beaver crashed during a low-level display at the Royal Naval Air Station Culdrose airshow. At the time of the crash the wind was gusting up to 27 knots at right angles to the display axis. As the pilot was approaching his second turn, he was flying downwind and climbing slightly, which may not have been apparent to him. The combination of wind and slope could possibly have given him an impression of considerable speed over the ground as he approached the crowd line. He may have then reduced his airspeed to the point at which his safety margin above the stalling speed was insufficient.[15]*

The relative motion of objects on the ground can provide cues that mislead the pilot making a landing approach. With an unexpectedly strong headwind and a slow-moving light aircraft, the appearance of trees and buildings moving beneath unusually slowly may provide the illusion of being too high, thus leading to a dangerously low, power-on final approach. With a strong tailwind on the downwind leg of a circuit, the relative motion of objects on the ground can provide a strong sensation that the aircraft is traveling too fast and lead the pilot to reduce airspeed sharply, so that the relative motion of outside objects once again appears normal.

If attention is distracted from the airspeed indicator—for example, by turbulence—then the pilot is set up for a dangerous situation indeed, with an overruddered turn to the base leg combining with low airspeed to provide a classic stall-spin situation. This is one of the most common accident categories for light aircraft, and illusions caused by the relative motion of visible known objects have been shown to be a contributing factor in many cases. The slower the normal approach speed of an aircraft, the greater will be the potential for an illusory effect.

Movement and optic flow.   We noted at the outset that vision and movement are closely related. Apart from cases such as flying at night, at high altitude, or in clouds, movement is accompanied by what is known as optical flow. When moving toward a point, this refers to the outward expansion of objects in the field of view. Objects at the periphery of view appear to expand and move rapidly. The optic flow will appear to radiate from the point at which the pilot is aiming (see Figure 1.15).

There is evidence from both human and animal investigations that the rate of this optic flow is used by the perceptual system to guide activities, such as long jumping, controlling the braking of a car, or landing an aircraft.[16] In fact, one method of controlling drivers' perception of the speed at which they are traveling on the approach to a traffic intersection, for example, is to paint lines across the roadway at increasingly close intervals. These give rise to an apparent increase in optic flow as would normally occur at much higher speeds, causing the driver to slow down.

There is some evidence that visual sensitivity to flow patterns is correlated with some aspects of pilot performance.[17] In one experiment, groups of fighter pilots, instructor pilots, and student pilots were given a set of tasks to perform in an A-10 simulator with a visual display system. The tasks included flying in formation with another aircraft, flying a low-level bombing attack, and making a restricted visibility landing. Performance on the low-level task was highly corre-

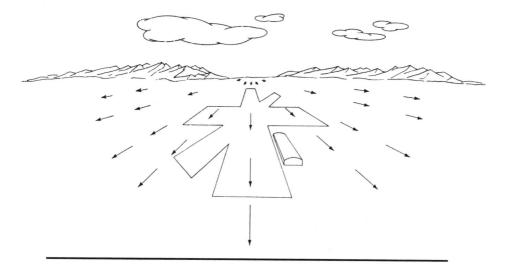

Fig. 1.15 This illustrates the optic flow seen by a pilot moving forward toward the midpoint of the horizon. From *The Perception of the Visual World* by J. J. Gibson (1950). Reproduced by permission of Eleanor J. Gibson.

lated with ability to discriminate different rates of expansion of a flow pattern as measured on a previous test. Experiments with drivers have shown that the optic flow is used directly in the estimation of time-to-collision with an obstacle.[18]

MENTAL SET

We tried to emphasize at the start of this chapter that visual perception involves a complex array of processes designed to pick up and to interpret the available optical information provided by light from the environment. This processing occurs through a sequence of stages as light enters the eye and causes cells in the retina to transmit nerve impulses through the visual pathways to the visual cortex. The processes of visual perception can be affected by damage to the eye muscles, the retina, the optic nerve, and the pathways to the visual cortex.

Although certain kinds of optical information are interpreted directly (for example, the optical expansion specifying time-to-collision), there is a large amount of evidence to show that previous expectation, or "set," plays an important role in the interpretation of other visual evidence. Nowhere is this more apparent than in the perception of written material. Figure 1.16 is easily read as "Paris in the spring." However, that is not what is there to be perceived—look closely!

Fig. 1.16 A simple example of misperceiving a stimulus because of "set" or expectation.

Although expectation can fool us, its main function is to allow us to process information more efficiently. Consider the laborious efforts of a child learning to read or an adult reading an unfamiliar foreign language. Both proceed word by word and then fit the words together to make a coherent whole. In contrast, the adult reader in the native language will read more rapidly by forming an initial expectation of the meaning of the text. Expectation reduces the words that are likely to appear and speeds perception. This may seem to put the process in the wrong order—surely the words must be understood first. In fact, Figure 1.16 shows that expectations do take a larger role.

Another way of demonstrating this is to try to recall word for word the last conversation you had with someone. Although it will be relatively easy to remember the overall sense of things—whether the encounter was friendly or tense and the general meaning of what was said—often the precise words used will be forgotten. More dangerously, when there is a clear expectation as to exactly what should have been said, the listener will often remember this as what was heard, even when something else was actually said. This has serious implications for the transfer of information between pilots and controllers (see Chapter 5).

It is precisely because it is easy to remember the general sense of something, while forgetting the particulars, that it has become standard procedure to adopt a checklist for the steps to be carried out before and after takeoffs and landings and other transitions. On simple light aircraft, the hard-copy checklist is often replaced by a mnemonic committed to memory, but on complex types, a written list is normally used. Expectations are crucially important not only in the perception of written material but also in the perception of other visual material.

This can easily be demonstrated by looking at an ambiguous visual stimulus, such as the one in Figure 1.17. Without supplementary information, such a stimulus is generally perceived as a meaningless set of black and white patches. If the subject is supplied with a prior set by being informed that the scene shows a black and white dog, the stimulus will be perceived differently, and it becomes possible to identify the various doglike features and confirm that it is indeed a Dalmatian.

This kind of confirmatory check to substantiate a prior expectation can arise frequently in flying. Instruments may be misread because the pilot expects to be at 13,000 feet, not 3,000 feet. Cockpit displays should minimize the possibility of this kind of error, as detailed in Chapter 4. Similar errors can arise when navigating in rela-

Fig. 1.17 An example of how expectation can influence the perception of ambiguous visual information. At first glance the pattern appears to consist of meaningless black and white patches. The knowledge that this is a picture of a dog allows this ambiguous pattern to be perceived in a meaningful way. Knowledge and expectations play an important role in visual perception.

tion to features visible on the ground and then looking for those features on the map. It is possible to misinterpret observed features in line with the pilot's expectancy of what should be visible. The Air New Zealand DC-10 accident provides a tragic example of this.

Unknown to the crew, the aircraft's programmed course had been shifted 25 miles to the east, in line with Mount Erebus. From the cockpit recordings recovered after the crash, it is apparent that all the flightdeck crew members were attempting to monitor position visually by looking for features that would be visible if they were on course. Unfortunately, as stated previously, the features actually visible were similar to those they expected to see and were easily misidentified, leading the pilots and the commentator to believe that they were well clear of the volcano.

The circumstances of this particular accident have been presented with great thoroughness elsewhere (see Further Reading). The tragic outcome of Air New Zealand Flight 901 serves to underline the importance of an understanding of visual perception by the pilot. The apparent obviousness of what we perceive and our lack of conscious awareness of the complex cues involved in visual tasks combine to represent a hazard to the unwary or unprepared pilot.

FURTHER READING

There are many texts on visual perception ranging from the more physiologically oriented such as F. Geldard's *The Human Senses,* 2nd ed. (New York: Wiley, 1972) to the more psychological such as J. Frisby's *Seeing* (Oxford: Oxford University Press, 1979). A useful general source is W. Schiff's *Perception: An Applied Approach* (Boston: Houghton Mifflin, 1980). The circumstances of the accident involving Air New Zealand Flight 901 are presented in greater detail by G. Vette in *Impact Erebus* (Auckland, New Zealand: Hodder & Stoughton, 1983) and by P. Mahon in *Verdict on Erebus* (Auckland, New Zealand: William Collins, 1984). A new book, edited by M. Hershenson, is devoted entirely to *The Moon Illusion* (Hillsdale, NJ: Lawrence Erlbaum Associates, 1989).

[2] Orientation:
The Spatial Senses

THE WIND is from the east, and one is blind. The sun is tossed about in these yellow spirals. Its pale dusty face emerges, sears, then disappears. Occasionally there's a glimpse of earth beneath, if one looks straight down. But not always. Am I climbing, diving, banking? How am I to know?

ANTOINE DE SAINT-EXUPÉRY, *Wind, Sand and Stars*

INTRODUCTION

The problem of orientation—knowing which way is up and whether you are leaning sideways, backward, or forward—is quite unproblematic in everyday life. Just as the visual system has evolved to supply us with detailed information about the world outside, our eyes and other sense organs keep us supplied with information about our positions in space. The most problematical of the other senses in flying is the vestibular system located in the inner ear. The flow of information from the vestibular organs may be profoundly disturbed by the changing conditions of flight.

In addition to organs that react to patterns of vibration or pressure change in the surrounding air and convert these changes to electrical signals in the auditory nerve, the inner ear contains other organs specifically adapted to the task of providing spatial information. Figure 2.1 shows the main structures of the ear. The eardrum, the bones known as the hammer, anvil, and stirrup, and the fluid-filled cochlea, all form a biological transducer that takes in energy in the form of

41

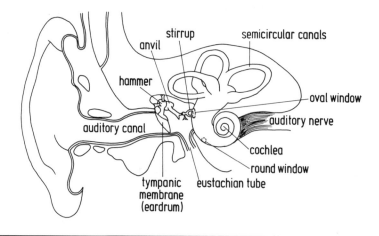

Fig. 2.1   The main structures of the auditory system. Pressure differences in the air-filled auditory canal are transformed into movement of fluid inside the cochlea via the small bones of the middle ear. The movement of hair cells inside the cochlea results in the transmission of signals along the auditory nerve to the auditory areas of the cortex. From *Aviation Medicine: Physiology and Human Factors*, edited by G. Dhenin. Copyright 1978 by Tri-Med Books. Adapted by permission.

vibration and converts this into electrical energy that is then transmitted through a complex neural network to the auditory cortex.

Just as the eye is sensitive to frequencies of light in a relatively limited range, so the ear is sensitive over a particular range of sound frequencies. This is roughly from 20 Hz (cycles per second) to 20,000 Hz with greatest sensitivity in the region of 1,000 to 3,000 Hz. The ear is sensitive to variations in sound intensity (or power) over a remarkably wide range. Table 2.1 gives a sampling of sound levels measured on several scales.

The first column lists typical sources and the second gives sound intensities in watts per square centimeter and shows that loud sounds can be at levels ten to the twelfth power or one trillion (American) or one million million (one billion English) times the power of a barely audible tone. The third column gives the pressure levels in dynes per square centimeter corresponding to the power levels of the second column. The range is not as great because the pressure is proportional to the square root of power, so there is only a range of one million in sound pressure from barely audible to quite loud.

Sound intensity is commonly measured on the decibel scale as a logarithmic ratio between the sound pressure and a standard reference level. The reference value normally used is 0.0002 dyne per square centimeter, which is approximately the threshold of hearing under

Table 2.1.   Sample Sound Levels in Different Units

Typical source	Intensity or power level in watts/cm²	Pressure level in dynes/cm²	Decibel scale
Hearing threshold	10^{-16}	0.0002	0
Rustle of leaves	10^{-15}	0.0006	10
Bedroom at night	10^{-13}	0.0063	30
Library	10^{-12}	0.02	40
Quiet office	10^{-11}	0.063	50
Average radio	10^{-9}	0.63	70
Typical factory	10^{-8}	2.0	80
Subway train	10^{-7}	6.3	90
Symphony orchestra	10^{-6}	20.0	100
Rock band	10^{-5}	63.0	110
Aircraft taking off	10^{-4}	200.0	120

ideal conditions. The decibel scale provides a more manageable measure of the wide range of sound powers and sound pressures of interest.

In many older aircraft, cockpit noise levels reach 100 decibels or more. In three separate accidents involving the Beechcraft 99,[1] the U.S. National Transportation Safety Board (NTSB) commented on the adverse effects of high levels of cockpit noise on the ability of flight crews to carry out their tasks. In these cases the measured sound level was 97 decibels, "the range where face-to-face communications are difficult, and a voice range between shouting and maximum vocal effort are required."[2]

Quite large changes in auditory sensitivity occur with age, with the largest loss for older people (over 60) occurring at the higher frequencies (4,000–8,000 Hz). This is unlikely to impair ability to conduct radio communication significantly because aircraft headsets generally have limited response beyond 3,000 Hz. However, the region most susceptible to damage from the noisy cockpits of older airplanes flown by younger pilots is from 4,000 Hz downward, and a serious hearing loss in this region does adversely affect radio intelligibility.

Such information about the auditory system is of vital importance to the designers of aircraft warning systems. For example, some commercial passenger aircraft employ 30 to 40 different auditory warning signals to provide information to the pilots on such states as autopilot disengaged, ground proximity, engine fire, excessive sink rate, and so on. A list of the auditory signals currently provided in the Boeing 747 is shown in Table 2.2. The questions of the design and suitability of such devices will be taken up in Chapter 4.

Associated with the principal structures of the ear are other nonauditory structures that collect information about the body's position and movement in space. These are generally thought of as the organs of balance but in fact consist two quite separate structures known as

Table 2.2. Sample of Auditory Alerts Used on Boeing 747 Aircraft

Alert condition	Type of alert	Frequency (Hz)	Loudness (dB)
Altitude alert	Chord	461–563, 567–704, and 691–845	95 ± 5
APU fire	Bell	600–10,000	93 ± 5
Autopilot dis-engage	Wailer	130 + 20 to 200 + 30	93 ± 5
Ground proximity	Warbler and voice	400 to 800	85–96
Decision height	Chord	As for altitude alert	
Emergency evacu-ation	Chime/tone	727–947 and 477–497	95 ± 5
Engine fire	Bell	600–10,000	93 ± 5
Excessive airspeed	Clacker	1,000–2,400	86
Excessive sink rate	Warbler and voice	400–800	85–96
Excessive terrain-closure rate	Warbler and voice	400–800	85–96
Low cabin pres-sure	Horn	220–280	93 ± 5
Negative climb after takeoff	Warbler and voice	400–800	85–96
SELCAL	Chime	588 and 488	95 ± 5
Stabilizer in mo-tion	Clacker		
Unsafe landing condition	Horn	220–280	93 ± 5
Unsafe takeoff condition	Horn	As for landing but interrupted at 3 Hz	

Source: Adapted from Kantowitz and Sorkin (1983).

the semicircular canals and the vestibular sacs. These are shown in Figure 2.2. The three semicircular canals form an interconnected tubelike structure with each canal approximately at right angles to the others. The canals are filled with liquid that shifts or circulates within the canals in response to rotational acceleration of the whole body.

The construction of the semicircular canals is such that they are maximally sensitive to rotational accelerations around three orthogonal (right-angled) axes. It is important to note that the fluid in the semicircular canals can only respond to rotational acceleration. Steady rotation results in the fluid rotating the same as the canal. This cannot be distinguished from the nonrotating case. The interpretation of such signals can prove confusing to the pilot deprived of information normally provided by the visual system.

If the semicircular canals may be thought of as rotational acceleration detectors, then the vestibular sacs can be considered to act somewhat like accelerometers. These two inner ear chambers are filled with a gelatinous substance surrounding hairlike cells. As the head tilts backward or forward, angular acceleration forces act on the hair cells. Thus the vestibular sacs primarily provide information about the body's departure from the vertical when in uniform motion.

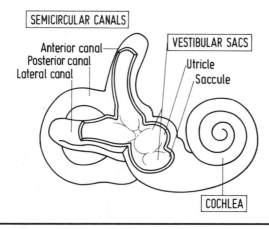

Fig. 2.2 The semicircular canals and the vestibular sacs. The fluid filled semicircular canals are arranged approximately at right angles to one another and are stimulated by angular accelerations. The vestibular sacs are filled with a denser fluid and respond to gravitational or transitional accelerations.

The vestibular sacs can only respond to accelerations, not to constant velocity motion. This is why one feels no sensation of movement in an airplane cruising smoothly at a constant 500 miles per hour.

In fact, the division between these two nonauditory organs of the ear is not so clear-cut as the above might suggest. Regardless of the anatomical complexities, the two functions of detecting the vertical and responding to acceleration and deceleration are of considerable importance and will be considered in the following sections.

ACCELERATION: TOLERANCE TO *g* FORCES

Our ability to tolerate and even adapt to high levels of gravitational (*g*) force is chiefly of interest to the military pilot. The imposition of *g* forces greater than one's normal weight at sea level (1 *g*) can be generated by powerful linear acceleration, as would be produced by takeoff power, or by radial acceleration, as produced by a pullup from a steep dive or by a steep turn. We refer to forward or upward accelerations as positive (+*g*) and backward or downward accelerations as negative (−*g*). In practice, with the exception of carrier-catapult launching or the action of afterburners on military aircraft, the linear accelerations are not of great magnitude.

It is possible, however, to generate fairly high *g*-forces through radial acceleration even in light aircraft. This, of course, is the main danger in performing aerobatics at low altitudes where the aircraft may be put in a position from which recovery can only be effected through the application of *g*-forces outside the airplane's design limits. For example, a smoothly executed loop at a safe altitude will generate maximum *g* when the pilot pulls up from the initial entry dive (see Figure 2.3), but at a very low altitude, the *g*-force required to pull out of the recovery dive could be even greater and might exceed the plane's controllability limits.

Military pilots may experience radial accelerations of a much higher order—possibly as high as +8 to +10 *g* for up to 60 seconds. Such forces would be quite damaging to the individual without protection. At +3 *g* (+2 *g* incremental, normal to the wings) a 200-pound pilot weighs 600 pounds, and it would be quite difficult to rise out of

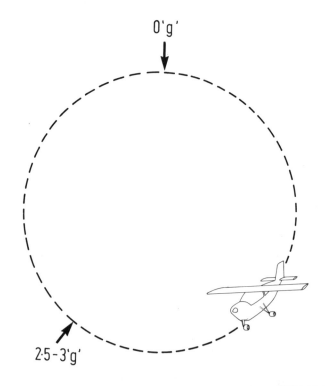

Fig. 2.3 In light aircraft aerobatics, *g*-forces are mild compared to those attainable in modern combat aircraft. The maximum *g* in a looping maneuver would be only two or three times normal gravitation.

the seat. Movements of the trunk and arms become progressively more difficult with increasing g and virtually impossible at +7 g. This is an important consideration in designing the location of an ejection-seat handle, for example.

The major effects of high positive and negative accelerations are on the blood flow to and from the brain and the eyes. A study involving one thousand naval aviators illustrates the effects of increasing levels of positive acceleration.[3] Blood is forced downward in the body, and an initial greyout period involving loss of peripheral vision occurs at a mean threshold of +4.1 g, followed by blackout at +4.7 g and loss of consciousness at +5.4 g. These are average values that conceal a wide range of individual differences in tolerance; in some subjects blackout occurs as low as +2.7 g and in others as high as +7.8 g.

It is also possible to experience negative accelerations in airplanes. Negative g is typically experienced in light planes when encountering a strong downdraft. All loose objects suddenly float upward, as will the pilot unless suitably restrained. The sensation is similar to that in an express elevator starting down. In fact, tolerance for negative g is much lower than for positive—as little as −2 g forces too much blood to the brain and retina, producing a redout effect typically described as unpleasant and alarming. Negative g can be experienced in a hard-over recovery from a stall, though hardly sufficient to produce redout. Only highly aerobatic planes can readily do that.

SPATIAL DISORIENTATION I:
THE SOMATOGRAVIC ILLUSION

CRASHED DURING MISSED APPROACH IN FOG

> *A Citation 500 was being piloted by the sole occupant on a private flight from Cardiff, Wales, to Jersey, Channel Islands. During an instrument approach at night and in poor weather the pilot discontinued the approach at 200 feet. During the ensuing missed approach pullup the aircraft struck the roof of a house and crashed. The pilot was killed. Using acceleration figures provided by the manufacturer, the Citation's pilot would have experienced a 14.6-degree displacement of the gravitational vertical from the true vertical while the aircraft was accelerating. Such an illusion could only be overcome or dispelled by total reliance on the flight instruments.[4]*

Although the brief outline of the Citation accident does not cover many aspects of the case that were undoubtedly relevant to the crash—the pilot's instrument flight training and previous experience, for example—the incident is by no means unique. We have already noted how the vestibular sacs serve as relatively sensitive accelerometers, conveying information about the rate of change of motion. The extreme sensitivity of the vestibular sacs to linear acceleration was demonstrated by Naval Aeromedical Research Laboratory (NAMRL) investigators in 1949.[5]

A blindfolded observer was carried in the rear of a light aircraft while the pilot maintained straight and level flight. The observer recorded his perceptions of bodily position as the pilot produced a variety of accelerations and decelerations. Very small accelerations were readily detectable—as little as 0.02 incremental g for positive vertical acceleration and -0.08 incremental g for negative acceleration. The important finding was that these small changes in acceleration produced very powerful sensations of climbing and diving; an incremental acceleration of only 0.1 g ($+1.1$ g total) caused a strong sensation of having pitched up into a 20 to 25-degree climb; a similar deceleration produced a sensation of having pitched down to a 15-degree dive.

Just why such accelerations should be interpreted as changes in pitch—in other words, as sensations of climbing and descending—can be understood as follows. In straight and level flight the pilot's weight acts in the direction of the earth's gravity—straight downward at 1 g (Figure 2.4). Under acceleration (Figure 2.5) there will be an effect of thrust at right angles to the true gravitational vertical. The resultant of these two forces will be as shown in Figure 2.5, corresponding to a sensation of force at the base of the spine. This will be felt in exactly the same direction as the force that would be produced if the aircraft were put into a moderate climb, although somewhat stronger.

In itself, of course, this sensation need not produce any hazardous results. However, if the pilot is simultaneously deprived of contact visibility and subsequently disregards or is misled by readings from flight

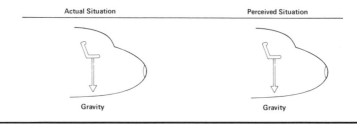

Fig. 2.4 In straight and level flight the force of gravity is perceived to be in alignment with the true vertical axis.

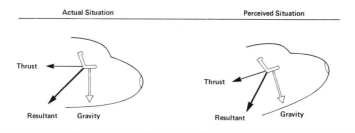

Fig. 2.5 When the aircraft accelerates forward, the combination of thrust and gravitational force produces a resultant force that is inclined backward from the local vertical. There is a tendency to perceive this resultant as the normally downward-acting gravitational force. The pilot can feel as though the aircraft has pitched up and make an inappropriate control response. Exactly the reverse can occur on deceleration, in which case the pilot can feel that the aircraft has pitched downward.

instruments (especially a reversed interpretation of the artificial horizon), the results can be disastrous. It seems probable that the frequency of accidents occurring during a missed approach procedure can be traced to the pitchup illusion following the sudden application of power.

The crash of a British Airways Vanguard in October 1965 was a typical case in which the sudden application of thrust following a go-around decision (and the associated lag in response by the altimeter and vertical speed indicator) could have caused the pilot to pitch the nose down, resulting in a sharp descent directly into the ground.[6] It is also easy to see how the pilot of the Citation could have experienced such a somatogravic illusion as a result of the acceleration produced by application of go-around power estimated at 0.26 forward g increasing to 0.33 g. This could have led the pilot to believe that the aircraft had already pitched up by as much as 14 to 18 degrees.

SPATIAL DISORIENTATION II: "THE LEANS"

We have already seen how small linear accelerations and decelerations are readily perceived as changes in pitch—normally associated with entering a climb or descent. In a second series of experiments at NAMRL, the perception of various degrees of turning was investigated, again using a blindfolded observer in the rear of the plane.[7] While maintaining a constant altitude, the plane was rolled into and out of turns with bank angles of 10, 18, 30, 40, 50, and 60 degrees. A steep turn is usually defined as one involving more than a 40-degree bank angle, so relatively steep angles of bank were included.

The observer's perceptions of tilting and turning were found to be quite unrelated to the true state of affairs.

- Small angles of bank went completely undetected. Even the 60-degree bank angle was not always noticed!
- The duration of feelings of turning were also poorly related to reality, generally beginning five seconds or more after the maneuver was started and disappearing one-third of the way through the maneuver.
- As with linear acceleration, there was a feeling of pitching up and down during the entry to and recovery from turns. In the case of the 60-degree steep turn, the sensation experienced was of a 45-degree climb!

In part, the inability to detect turn and bank in a cloud can be accounted for in much the same way as the false sensations of pitch under linear acceleration. Figure 2.6 shows the two forces in the turn with the resultant force acting straight down the vertical axis of the pilot's body. The feeling of weight acting straight downward may in fact be perceived as climbing straight ahead with wings level. A commonly encountered alternate version of this kind of spatial disorientation is referred to as the "leans." This consists of a false sensation of bank when the aircraft is actually flying straight and level.

The leans illusion typically occurs when the airplane has rolled unnoticed into a banked attitude at a rate below the pilot's threshold

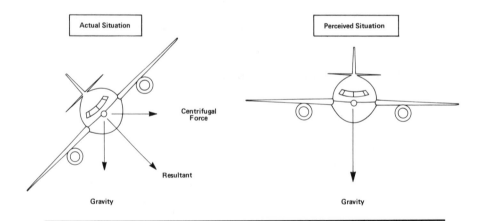

Fig. 2.6 A schematic representation of the somatogravic illusion. The resultant force created by radial acceleration during a prolonged turn can give rise to a false impression. The resultant is perceived as the apparent vertical and the aircraft attitude as wings level and climbing.

for detecting angular acceleration. Once the situation is noticed by reference to instruments, a more rapid roll will typically be initiated to bring the aircraft back to straight and level. Because the initial sensation was one of wings level, this subsequent above-threshold correction will be perceived as a roll away from wings level in the opposite direction. To overcome the effect, the pilot may lean toward the apparent vertical—that is, in the direction of the original roll—which gives this illusion its name. The majority of pilots have experienced this illusion in flight.[8]

The examples of spatial disorientation described so far appear primarily when no reference can be made to outside visual cues. In these circumstances the pilot has to rely immediately on the flight instruments. Because of the inherent lag in pressure instruments, it is only by quick reference to the gyroscopic instruments, such as the artificial horizon, that disorientation can be dependably avoided. Nevertheless the misleading sensations can be extremely powerful and long-lasting and have even been reported by pilots taxiing on the ground!

It is also possible for some forms of disorientation to occur when outside visual cues are available, the best known example being the "lean-on-the-sun" illusion that occurs when flying in clouds. Naturally, a cloud will appear brightest in the direction of the sun and darker elsewhere. In normal circumstances this will serve to orient the pilot correctly, because the brightest area will generally be the uppermost cloud layers. Should the sun in fact be low on the horizon the pilot may fly in a wing-low attitude in reference to this apparent vertical.

Another source of powerfully misleading sensations in flight can occur following movements of the pilot's head when the aircraft is turning or climbing. One form of this illusion typically occurs when a pilot is undergoing a moderate acceleration of 2 to 3 g or more. A movement of the head produces feelings of a change in attitude—that is, the aircraft seems to be climbing or diving. In military aircraft pulling out of a steep dive, the resulting sensation can be a powerful one of tumbling forward.

A more commonly occurring illusion takes place when the head is moved in an aircraft that is simply turning without any high-g being experienced. Because the semicircular canals are arranged in planes approximately at right angles to one another, a movement of the head changes the orientation of the canals with respect to the existing plane of the turn. Because the canals signal rotational acceleration, taking a canal out of the plane of the turn will cause a corresponding sensation of turning in the opposite direction.

This will be coupled with a new sensation of turning from one of the other canals that has just been brought into the plane of the turn. The result of this crosscoupled stimulation will be extremely confusing and can disorient the pilot. This phenomenon was found to be the cause of a series of crashes with a particular military aircraft. The design and location of the avionics required the pilot to bend forward and turn his head as the aircraft was turning onto the final approach to a landing.

STUDENT PILOT T-38A CRASH

> *A student returning from a solo night crosscountry exercise was reentering the circuit following one attempted landing. Slower traffic ahead caused the pilot to enter a climbing left-hand turn away from the runway. The runway supervisor asked the student for a fuel check 9.7 seconds into the climbing turn. To check his fuel, the student would have rotated his head at least 110 to 120 degrees to the right and 20 to 30 degrees forward. Six seconds later the aircraft struck the ground at 360 knots.*[9]

The circumstances of the T-38A accident in which the aircraft struck the ground under power and at relatively high speed are strongly suggestive of spatial disorientation. The head movements that the student pilot would have had to make to check the fuel gauges are precisely those that could have induced a crosscoupled or Coriolis stimulation of the semicircular canals as described above.

As with the visual phenomena discussed in the previous chapter, the vestibular illusions we have considered are best viewed as the results of a sensory system having to deal with forces in a novel three-dimensional environment not encountered in a two-dimensional environment for which we are well adapted. The illusions we have considered are relatively pure vestibular illusions, involving only the mechanisms of the semicircular canals and the vestibular sacs. The following example involves both the vestibular organs and the visual system. This will lead appropriately to a consideration of the unwelcome question of motion sickness.

SPIN RECOVERY: THE SOMATOGYRAL ILLUSION

There has always been debate over the merits of training pilots in spin recovery, and practices have varied from one country to another. It is probably sufficient to say that the spin and spin-recovery phases of training are initially regarded by students with either excited anticipation or apprehension. The British Civil Aviation Authority in 1983 dropped the full-spin recovery from the private pilot syllabus, bringing it in line with the U.S. Federal Aviation Administration by not introducing spinning until the more advanced stages of training.

The spin is essentially a condition in which the aircraft rotates about the rolling, pitching, and yawing axes simultaneously. It is therefore quite a different maneuver from a steep spiral dive, particularly in the fact that speed remains fairly constant during the spin, whereas it builds up rapidly in a spiral dive. For this reason pilots have been known to choose to spin out of a difficult situation such as being caught inadvertently in a cloud or in powerful rising air currents along one side of a mountain range ("spinning down the cone of silence"), rather than risk loss of control and a spiral dive with its attendant likelihood of structural damage in pulling up.

Needless to say, the pilot must be sure that there exists sufficient height below a cloud base to effect a recovery from the spin, because the characteristic that makes a spin hazardous is the extremely rapid altitude loss. Much effort in initial flight training is therefore devoted to training pilots to recognize the flight conditions likely to lead to the inadvertent development of a spin at low altitude.

The most pronounced movement in a spin is rotation about the aircraft's longitudinal axis. Both this and the steepness of the nose-down attitude vary widely from one aircraft type to another but may be as rapid as one revolution every three seconds in a near-vertical attitude. The acceleration into the spin causes the fluid in the semicircular canals to signal a rotation in the appropriate direction. However, because the semicircular canals only provide information about acceleration, these sensations will slowly disappear as the spin continues. This may take 15 to 30 seconds—much longer than would normally be spent in a spin.

The pilot, to recover, has to determine the direction of the spin and apply rudder against the direction of rotation. This may be done by reference to the directional instruments when outside visibility is obscured. Once the rotation is halted, the effect on the semicircular canals is to produce the sensation of an angular acceleration in the opposite direction. The potential effects of this illusion are easy to imagine—the pilot may attempt to prevent the apparent spin in the opposite direction by reversing the application of rudder. This will be likely to cause the aircraft to reenter the spin in the original direction. The combined effects of the original rotation and two reversed accelerations are likely to disorient the pilot completely.

Unfortunately, the situation is made potentially worse by the fact that the semicircular canals have nerve endings that connect in the brain with nerves to the muscles surrounding the eye. Movement sensations from the semicircular canals result in a reflexive movement of the eye muscles known as nystagmus. The rotation associated with a spin will produce a movement of the eyes quickly in one direction followed by a slower movement in the opposite direction. As we noted in Chapter 1, for clear, sharp vision to occur, a stable image must fall on the narrow foveal portion of the retina.

The effects of nystagmus will therefore be to degrade vision by moving the whole retinal image at the crucial moment when the pilot is attempting to overcome the misleading vestibular sensations produced by the semicircular canals. For several seconds, then, the pilot may be deprived of adequate visual input while experiencing thoroughly misleading vestibular sensations. This may account, in part at least, for the fact that once a pilot without training in instrument flight becomes engulfed in a cloud, loss of control and disorientation follow swiftly and inevitably.

In one experiment, 20 private pilots who flew into simulated weather all lost control.[10] The time before this occurred was extremely short, ranging from 20 seconds to 8 minutes, with an average of just 3 minutes. The time before loss of control was shorter when the aircraft was in a turn. Disorientation accidents form a significant part of the total toll in military operations as well as in private flying. However, in the latter case, the disorientation is usually the direct consequence of judgmental errors that allow the pilot to become entrapped by weather in the first place. In military operations disorientation may be induced by the severity of conditions encountered regardless of the pilot's experience and judgment.

The inbuilt nervous system connection between the vestibular organs and the eyes is also relevant in accounting for other phenomena that may on occasion have disastrous results. We are all familiar with the pressure changes in the ear encountered on descent in a commercial aircraft. The practice of issuing sweets for passengers to chew on is designed to help in equalizing the pressure in the middle ear to outside pressure changes. The same result with less detriment to the teeth can be achieved by yawning, swallowing, or by holding the nose and gently blowing.

Pressure is equalized through the Eustachian tube connecting the middle ear with the mouth (see Figure 2.1). One of the reasons why pilots are advised not to fly with colds is that the functioning of the Eustachian tubes may be impaired to the extent that pressure equalization becomes difficult with consequent pain and damage to hearing. If a sudden pressure change occurs within the middle ear, a condition known as pressure vertigo can result. The effects can include impairment of vision, and at least one recent airline accident is thought to have resulted from it.

AMERICAN AIRLINES 727 ACCIDENT, ST. THOMAS, VIRGIN ISLANDS

> *On 27 April 1976, an American Airlines Boeing 727 made an apparently normal approach in daylight and light gusting winds to the airport at St. Thomas in the Virgin Islands. The aircraft leveled off a few feet above the runway and failed to touch down until insufficient runway remained. The captain attempted to go around but aborted this attempt when he realized that insufficient runway remained. The aircraft overran the runway and was subsequently destroyed by fire with the loss of 37 lives.*[11]

There is evidence from the cockpit voice recorder that on the descent a rapid and painful pressurization occurred. Because of the interaction between the vestibular and visual systems referred to above, it is thought that this may have led the pilots' eyes "to overaccommodate, blurring their vision and causing the runway initially to appear further away and then higher relative to the wheels of the airplane than it actually was. This could cause the pilot to level off high and fail to land where both he and the copilot expected the airplane to touch down."[12]

Another important interaction between the visual and vestibular systems occurs as a result of the ingestion of alcohol. In one experiment, subjects were required to fixate on a point of light that rotated with them during accelerations of 5 deg/sec^2 for 12 seconds. Normally, subjects are able to suppress the nystagmus following the acceleration and subsequent deceleration, thus maintaining a stable retinal image. In contrast, after drinking 2.5 milliliters of 100-proof spirit per kilogram of body weight, subjects were unable to suppress nystagmus experienced during the acceleration and braking. The light appeared to move jerkily, and strong sensations of vertigo were reported by most subjects.[13]

MOTION SICKNESS

Airsickness is a significant problem for certain military crew members, in particular navigators in high performance aircraft. It can also afflict experienced pilots changing from one type of aircraft or task to another and is common among student pilots. A survey of flight cadets at RAF Cranwell revealed that three-quarters of these student pilots had experienced some degree of motion sickness during training. Figures from this and other surveys suggest that about 15 to 20 percent of student pilots experience sufficiently severe sickness to result in the abandonment of at least one training flight.

The incidence of motion sickness is probably lower for civilian student pilots but is still likely to affect 40 to 50 percent at least once. Individuals vary greatly in their susceptibility, and it is probable that the most susceptible do not volunteer for flight training. Nevertheless, at least 5 percent of would-be aircrew are likely to drop out of training through excessive susceptibility. It is common for individuals to experience some of the symptoms of motion sickness on first exposure as a passenger in a light aircraft on a gusty day.

At first thought the cause may seem to be fairly obvious. It has long been known that individuals without functioning vestibular organs are not susceptible to motion sickness. It would appear reasonable to assume therefore that excessive stimulation of the vestibular organs—for example, by continuous rolling and pitching movements in a ship at sea—would lead to the symptoms of motion sickness. This would be a plausible explanation were it not for the fact that it is possible to produce motion sickness in the complete absence of any form of motion whatsoever!

A 180-degree cinema of aerobatic maneuvers, roller-coaster rides, and even speeded-up car chases can produce strong symptoms of motion sickness and cause people to lose balance. The same phenomenon has recently been observed in flight simulators with realistic visual displays. Several studies involving a helicopter simulator produced the surprising finding that the more experienced pilots were more susceptible to this visually induced motion sickness than inexperienced pilots. This is in contrast to the facts noted earlier that motion sickness is a greater problem with student pilots than with experienced aircrew.

This finding, that motion sickness can occur in the absence of any stimulation of the vestibular organs, has led to the development of a quite different approach to the understanding of the causes and prevention of airsickness.[14] The key lies in the discovery that sickness can be provoked when there is a mismatch between the current sensory input and what would be expected to occur on the basis of previous experience. This illustrates how it is possible for individuals to adapt or grow accustomed to sickness-inducing stimuli.

Aircrews flying regularly rarely experience airsickness, whereas those flying again after a break frequently do. The fact that susceptibility declines as people get older is also compatible with this view. The "neural mismatch" theory makes sense of the numerous different ways in which motion sickness can arise. More specifically, the mismatch can arise because of contradictory information being supplied by the visual and the vestibular systems or, alternatively, when information is provided by one of these systems in the absence of compatible information from the other.

Another source of neural mismatch can arise between signals from the semicircular canals and the vestibular sacs. Again, this might be due to contradictory information from the two organs (as in the case of crosscoupled, or Coriolis, stimulation) or the absence of information from one or the other. A summary of these mismatches is provided in Table 2.3, and the following practical recommendations have been offered.

- For passengers, lying prone or in a reclined position reduces sickness. Head movements should be restricted as these set up further signals from the vestibular system that are liable to increase the mismatch between the current sensory input and the individual's expectations.
- Again, for passengers, various drugs are available that reduce susceptibility. However, those curently available all have side effects and are not suitable for use by aircrews.
- Careful exposure to sickness-inducing situations can build up adaptations. This follows the principle of graded exposure or systematic desensitization commonly used to treat phobias.
- Mental activity may be helpful in reducing the severity of the sickness. This is likely to be more applicable to passengers who are totally unoccupied than to pilots and navigators who already have a considerable workload.

CONCLUSIONS

It should be clear that the operations of our spatial senses are taken very much for granted until unusual circumstances lead to disorientation or sickness. At all levels of proficiency and experience, pilots are warned against flying "by the seat of the pants" and are expected to develop sufficient skills in instrument flying to overcome the misleading sensations provided by the vestibular organs. A summary of some of the conditions leading to disorientation, most of which have been considered in this chapter, is given in Table 2.4.

Spatial disorientation and motion sickness are particularly powerful sensations that cannot be dependably eliminated by concentration, training, or good judgment. "Remember, nearly all disorientation is a normal response to the unnatural environment of flight."[15] The effects can, however, be minimized through such factors as cockpit design and aircrew training. These two important topics form the basis of the next two chapters.

Table 2.3.   Sources of Motion Cue Mismatches

Type	Visual–vestibular mismatch	Semicircular canal–vestibular sacs mismatch
Contradictory information	Looking at the ground through binoculars from a moving aircraft	Crosscoupled (Coriolis) stimulation
Absence of information from one source	Simulator sickness in a fixed-base simulator with realistic visual display	Pressure vertigo
	Unable to see out of aircraft in motion	Low-frequency linear oscillation caused by turbulence

Source: Adapted from Benson (1978a).

Table 2.4.   Summary of Problems in Spatial Disorientation

Type of Flight	Special problems
Instrument flight	Misleading impressions provided by vestibular cues
Overshooting without visual reference	Sensation of pitching up (somatogravic illusion)
Turning without visual reference	Failure to sense turn (the leans)
	Crosscoupled stimulation when combined with head movements leading to erroneous sensations of rotation and aircraft attitude
Spinning	After stopping original spin, strong sensation of spinning in reverse direction (somatogyral illusion)
Rapid descent	Pressure vertigo leading to visual impairment
Turbulence	If mismatched with visual scene, sickness can result

Source: Adapted from Benson (1978b).

FURTHER READING

Spatial orientation and disorientation are discussed extensively in several chapters of *Aviation Medicine: Physiology and Human Factors,* edited by G. Dhenin (London: Tri-Med Books, 1978). A more psychological treatment is presented by J. Reason and J. Brand in *Motion Sickness* (London: Academic Press, 1975). A more popular account of disorientation, the vestibular illusions, and motion sickness is provided by J. Reason in *Man in Motion* (London: Weidenfeld & Nicolson, 1974). A good coverage of the vestibular system is given in *The Senses,* edited by H. Barlow and J. D. Mollon (Cambridge: Cambridge University Press, 1982).

Training and Design

[3] Training Environments: Instruction and Simulation

TRAINING EVERYWHERE at this time was carried out solo, on "broomstick" gliders with insensitive controls and little performance. They were bungey-launched by a rubber rope, stretched out by as many people as the instructor reckoned the circumstances required. For early launches the glider was only intended to slide along the ground while the pupil tried to keep the wings level. Sometimes it slid along the ground, but sometimes it did not. Instead, it would shoot into the air, so that the pupil shut his eyes and hung on waiting for the crash. When this came and the noise and dust had died down, the pupil would be surprised to find himself un- hurt, but horrified to discover the wings collapsed and on the ground.

ANNE WELCH, *The Story of Gliding*

INTRODUCTION

As anyone who has ever attempted to learn to fly will testify, the initial stages of learning to guide such a complex machine as an airplane through an ever-changing, three-dimensional environment can be full of difficulties and frustrations. We have seen in earlier chapters that our physiological capacities that serve us well as two-dimensional ground dwellers can become quite limiting in the new three-dimensional environment of the air. Most national and international aviation organizations are increasingly accepting the position that flight training, particularly in general aviation, is a problem.

Although massive advances have taken place in flight simulation

61

technology since the 1940s, as they have in aircraft and systems development, comparable progress has not taken place in the basic training programs for pilots or flight instructors. Even a cursory examination of flight training curricula shows a process that has changed very little from methods used to produce pilots in World War II. As one senior pilot has reported, "The training has not changed very much over the years. The exercises, the instructor's patter, the techniques are much the same as they were when I first took my training (in England) in 1946."[1]

At the outset of World War II, the Empire Air Training Scheme was born. It met the immediate need for rapid training of pilots to defend the cities against the devastating bombing raids and was largely copied by the U.S. Army Air Corps and Navy and by the Allies in Canada, Australia, and New Zealand. The postwar boom in aviation was fueled by the abundance of experienced returning pilots and inexpensive surplus equipment. Inevitably, military thinking would dominate civil aviation, with the transfer of slightly modified training and certification procedures by ex-military personnel forming the civil aviation authorities.

Although airline training departments have greatly advanced the use of flight simulators, with few exceptions general aviation pilot training is almost unaltered despite the mountain of research material supporting the conclusion that the system in place is outdated and no longer appropriate. Educational and aviation research and the lessons learned from accident investigation provide ample evidence that our modern-day pilots need to know much more about the environment and the system in which they operate, if we wish to maintain if not improve the safety record.

Flight instruction is expensive, yet ways to reduce this expense are available. The successful use of interactive computer programs, part-task trainers, and simulators is an accepted fact. Prominent airlines around the world conduct 95 percent and more of their training with these devices, yet recognition of their use in elementary training is resisted by aviation authorities who continue to issue certification largely on experience requirements rather than criterion-based competency. While it is reasonable to expect that experience measured in flight time will have some effect on performance, no longer is it appropriate to allow experiential learning to substitute for education.

There is an often unrecognized but important distinction between *training* in skills and procedures and the judgmental *education* of a professional airman. Traditional general aviation training is concentrated on the former with little attention to the latter. There is a growing belief that the education process should at least parallel the training and that an appreciation of the essence of airmanship should precede the student's introduction to the airplane. As things stand, most civilian pilots' first exposure to structured education in airmanship occurs when they join a major airline.

Despite the difficulties involved, many thousands regularly embark on the long process of acquiring the necessary formal qualifications to become commercial pilots. The training needs of large organizations, such as the major airlines and air forces of the world, have been influential in directing attention and resources to studying the initial recruitment and subsequent training of pilots at all stages of their progress. In conjunction with the design of aircraft systems and equipment to make them easier and safer to fly, the study of learning and training procedures has occupied the efforts of many employed around the world as aviation psychologists.

This is understandable because these two areas represent major opportunities for psychologists to influence in a significant way the ease and safety of flying. Compared to the cost of major technical advances, these efforts may be significantly cost-effective. In practice, the greatest interest has been centered on the question of the effectiveness of simulator training. We will discuss research in this area in some detail, with particular attention to the question of simulator realism or fidelity and training efficiency, and the important place of part-task trainers and automatically adaptive display augmentation.

ANALYZING FLIGHT PERFORMANCE

Training programs can range from periods of on-the-job experience or apprenticeship to formally structured instruction. The most common approach to developing a structured program of instruction has been by the method of task analysis. This consists of breaking down the whole task into a series of simpler tasks. The task requirements consist of an observable sequence of actions leading to the accomplishment of some immediate goal. This approach can be useful for tasks that can be unambiguously defined (e.g., industrial assembly tasks) and the elements of which can be expressed as a sequence of subtasks.

Many complex skills do not lend themselves to this kind of analysis because of the difficulty of unambiguously defining the desired outcome. In addition, if there are many different ways of achieving the end result, it may be impossible to break the task into a sequence of simpler tasks. This is readily apparent in the case of pilot training for which the desired outcome is to produce a pilot with the skills, attitudes, knowledge, and judgment to operate a particular aircraft safely and efficiently. These might be regarded as necessary, though not necessarily sufficient, components of "airmanship."

The application of task analysis to flying has resulted in training programs in which certain desired outcomes are specified in terms of behavioral objectives. The key characteristic of behavioral objectives is that they are specific statements of desired performance, such as "to return the aircraft to straight and level flight from . . . turns, dives, and climbs."[2] For the student, the statement of objectives in these terms removes any uncertainty about the aims of the exercise and also provides clear standards for the evaluation of performance by both the student and the instructor.

The task analysis approach also is applicable to display requirements.[3] The adequacy of any display can be evaluated by the degree to which it supports the necessary discriminations and manipulations. The magnetic compass, for example, does not provide a direct representation of direction because corrections must be applied for variation, deviation, drift, acceleration errors, and so on. Thus supplementary information is required to determine whether the aircraft is heading in the intended direction. Principles of display design will be covered in Chapter 4. For the moment, note that training problems can be induced by inadequate design; as A. C. Williams observed,

> If a pilot overshoots a landing field or stalls out of a steep turn, we may be sure it was not done intentionally; the error occurred because the pilot failed to respond or responded in the wrong way to information that was present and could have been used properly. Lack of training may account for the failure in one sense, but, had the critical information been presented in an unmistakable manner, requiring little or no interpretation, and in a manner that demanded a proper response, the error could have been prevented.[4]

The limitations of the task analysis approach are apparent from the difficulty encountered in specifying the task elements that contribute to the training objective of airmanship. It is apparent that elements of judgment and situational awareness need to be included with the perceptual-motor skills usually considered. More sophisticated analyses of the elements of airmanship have been used to develop a comprehensive testing and selection battery.[5] An alternative approach to the design of flight training has been developed as the basis of a major revision of the flight training and certification system in New Zealand.[6]

The needs-assessment approach emphasizes the importance of learning rather than teaching.[7] Training should provide the most effective environment within which learning can take place. Rather than break the overall objective of airmanship into a series of separate tasks, the emphasis is on defining what the learner needs to know to accomplish a particular objective. This approach also generates a hierarchy of competencies but from the top down rather than from the bottom up. One of the advantages may be that the subsequent instructional objectives have more generality than traditionally derived behavioral objectives.

Competency specification. For each maneuver or procedure required for each pilot license, a set of performance criteria must be met for certification. Exit criteria for each successive license are increasingly stringent to insure the necessary knowledge, skills, and discipline for safe flight operations within the permissive limits of that license. Thus, although the numerical tolerances for continuous control variables are similar for the various license categories, to qualify for the successive licenses, an applicant must demonstrate criterion performance levels for increasingly complex operations under increasingly demanding operational conditions.

Criterion-referenced performance scoring (CRS) can be either quantitative (e.g., beyond twice tolerance, within twice tolerance, within tolerance, within one-half tolerance, within one-fourth tolerance) or categorical (e.g., hooded recovery from an unknown attitude within ten seconds and with no control reversal—yes or no; checklist compliance without omission or transposition—yes or no; and so on). Scoring the student's performance on continuous variables in multiples and fractions of the criterion values provides an indication of progress toward criterion and beyond. For categorical items, progress is indicated by the consistency of compliance with a procedure. Thus, if the student performs all procedural items correctly on one of three trials, some progress has been made, whereas three of three shows a higher level of mastery.

The criterion performance tolerances for continuous control variables and the categorical items of compliance are specified by the applicable national regulatory agency and are reasonably consistent internationally, as are the permitted operations and operational conditions associated with the various licenses. Thus, using a five-point scale, with a score of three representing, for example, the specified altitude control criterion of $\pm$ 100 feet, a deviation of 200 feet or more from desired altitude would yield a score of one, whereas holding altitude within 200 feet, but not consistently within 100 feet, scores a two; within 50 feet, a four; and within 25 feet, a five.

The differences in achievement levels for the various licenses, ratings, and entitlements are reflected in the conditions under which an individual can maintain criterion control and procedural compliance. For example, to be released for safe solo, an ab initio student must demonstrate the requisite skills at criterion levels on a clear day with little air turbulence or crosswind, whereas the commercial pilot with an instrument rating must consistently demonstrate the ability to control the airplane at criterion levels under all legally permitted conditions. Thus, the extent of the subjectivity in scoring maneuvers and procedures is an assessment of whether the test conditions are representative of the limits within which the pilot will be permitted to operate. In many cases, such conditions can best be created in a simulator.

TRAINING RESOURCE MANAGEMENT

In the preceding section the importance of applying a learner-centered rather than a teacher-centered approach to flight training is evident. In this section we will review some of the variables that are important in creating the most effective conditions for learning.

NO ROOM FOR RECOVERY

> *A Cessna 152 was being flown on a low-altitude exercise near Nelson, New Zealand. The aircraft commenced a steep turn at a height of approximately 200 feet, then lost altitude slightly before rolling rapidly in the direction of the turn and diving vertically into the sea. Causal factors were the instructor's failure to take timely action after the aircraft was mishandled by the student, the nature of the exercise attempted relative to the student's ability, the instructor's inexperience, and the standard of supervision of the instructor's training methods.*[8]

The flight instructor. A basic ingredient in the success of any training enterprise is the quality of instruction. This is as true in the use of multimillion dollar simulators as in the one-to-one pupil-instructor relationship at a flying club. Many people have been launched on successful aviation careers through the particular talents and enthusiasms of some individual instructor or club member. In general, it is possible to encounter the full array of human personalities in the instructing role, although professional pilots tend as a group to be somewhat different from other occupational groups in terms of certain traits or characteristics.

On the whole, professional pilots tend to be above average on traits such as stability and calmness, alertness, discipline and orderliness, self-reliance and pragmatism, and relaxed composure.[9] These qualities seem to encompass the necessary approach to the working environment of the professional pilot and the "hours of boredom punctuated by moments of stark terror." Rather than necessarily being the innate bearers of such qualities, one would be inclined to suspect that pilots who have become successful in professional aviation have developed or acquired some of these characteristics during the course of their training.

The instructing role requires even more from the professional pilot than flying skill and some of the temperamental qualities outlined above. The instructor has to relate to a wide cross section of individuals, from 17-year-old students to 70-year-old retirees, and attempt to teach them a complex skill largely in the confines of a noisy, cramped, and distracting classroom. No attempt will be made to analyze the ideal instructor. Such a creature probably does not exist any more than ideal leaders exist.

In fact, research has shown that good leadership is contingent on an interplay of certain factors, such as knowledge of the topic or task, assertiveness, social acceptability, and the particular situation at hand. To be effective, the type of instruction must also be contingent on the needs and abilities of the student in conjunction with the requirements of the particular syllabus or task. Although we may not be able to define an ideal instructor, it is possible to draw on psychological studies of learning and teaching to suggest some principles that may be used in successful and effective teaching.

Instructing style.   Most prominent among the different aspects that make up an individual's teaching style is a tendency to use positive rather than negative reinforcement, commonly taking the form of praise and reproof. A study of instructor behavior showed that verbal patterns of comment and guidance could be classified in 11 basic categories as shown in Table 3.1.[10] By far the most common were instructional cues followed by direct commands. The instructors differed widely, some using acceptance and praise (positive reinforcement), others applying both general and specific scolding (negative reinforcement). The great variability in the behavior of even a small number of instructors is evident.

The effects of these different styles of instruction were vividly demonstrated by an analysis of the stress level experienced by each student after each lesson in the simulator. This was ascertained by measuring the excretion of catecholamines (a stress response—see Chapter 6) in urine samples collected after each lesson. Students taught by the positive instructors showed significantly lower stress levels than those taught by negative instructors. Because stress is known to have detrimental effects on the performance of newly learned or not fully consolidated skills, it may be supposed that the

Table 3.1. Categories of Instructional Behavior

Behavior	Examples
Instructional cues	Giving facts, opinions, ideas, primes, clarifications, prompts (e.g., Make sure that your pitch and power are appropriate for landing.)
Commands	Giving orders or directions that result in immediate student responses (e.g., Make a right turn. Let's work on touch and go's.)
Correction	Pointing out an incorrect student response without criticism, ridicule, sarcasm, or emotion (e.g., Set your trim. You're too high.)
Questions	Asking questions that force the student to think or respond (e.g., How fast should we be going?)
Acceptance	Affirming that the student's response is correct (e.g., O.K., that's correct.)
Praise—general	Making positive statements that do not carry specific information (e.g., Very good, good work.)
Praise—specific	Making positive statements that carry information about a student's response (e.g., Very good, you kept your airspeed right at 70.)
Scold—general	Rejecting a student's response with criticism, ridicule, or sarcasm (e.g., That was terrible.)
Scold—specific	As above, only containing specific information (e.g., That was terrible, you let the nose drop too much.)
Modeling—positive	Showing students how to do something the correct way (e.g., assuming control and demonstrating a crosswind technique)
Modeling—negative	Showing students what they did wrong or how they did it wrong (e.g., assuming control and performing a turn too fast or too slow)

Source: Adapted from Krahenbuhl et al. (1981).

higher stress levels produced by the negative instructors would not be helpful, at least in the early stages of learning.

There is no doubt that flight training is inherently stressful for most student pilots, and the instructor is the pivotal influence in increasing or reducing this stress level. It should be said that stress is primarily associated with the pace, workload, and lack of familiarity with the view from the air and the difficult environmental conditions of light aircraft rather than with a fear of physical danger.[11] There may, of course, be other circumstances, particularly in the military setting, in which it is desirable to increase trainees' stress levels. Because of the importance of these topics in determining pilot performance, we will look at them in more detail in Chapters 6 and 7.

On the whole, positive reinforcement has been shown to be more effective in shaping behavior than punishment. Unfortunately, it can often appear to the instructor that the reverse is the case. Extreme responses such as an outstandingly good landing or a particularly poor attempt at a steep turn are likely to be followed by less extreme responses—a less than perfect landing or a slightly better steep turn, respectively. This is a purely statistical effect known as regression to the mean.

If the good attempts were praised and the poor ones punished by the instructor, then it could appear that punishment leads to improvement and praise to deterioration in performance. In fact, the changes in performance have occurred in spite of the instructor's praise or blame. In the long run of any sequence of events—heights of parents and children, for example—extreme events such as very tall parents are likely to be followed by less extreme ones—relatively shorter offspring. The same will be true of any variable series of events, such as learning to land an airplane.[12]

TRICKY T-TAIL

> *The pilot of a PA-38 Tomahawk was attempting to take off from a 300-meter snow-covered stubble field. On the second attempt he held the control wheel fully back until reaching 45 knots, at which point the airplane pitched up steeply, stalled, and crashed. The pilot had been cautioned during training that the T-tail configuration produces a sudden increase in elevator effectiveness as the aircraft accelerates. This warning was evidently forgotten.[13]*

Guiding principles. Piloting an airplane is the constant repetition of one process, recognizing and reducing differences between what is happening and what is needed: in technical terms, nulling the indices of actual and desired performance for each successive mission subgoal. Thus, from moment to moment the pilot must determine the desired attitude, altitude, heading, and speed to fly and the actions needed to maintain the functional effectiveness of the airplane's systems and other crew members and passengers. Matching actual performance to the desired indices requires skill in command and control, the right stuff for safe and effective flight operations.

Skill in the various phases and modes of flying is acquired in three overlapping stages: the *cognitive* stage, in which the student pilot learns the indices of desired performance that have to be discriminated and the effects of control inputs; the *associative* stage, in which practice develops skill in matching actual to desired performance indices; and the *automatic stage,* in which discrimination and manipulation functions become so overlearned that they are carried out smoothly and precisely with little if any conscious attention. When discrimination and manipulation become virtually automatic, conscious attention is made available to cope with unpredicted events and stressful situations.

For each phase or mode of flying training, each stage of learning has its optimum learning environment. The cognitive stage should be achieved almost completely on the ground—in the classroom, at the chalkboard, by reading, watching films and videos, and by using computer-based instructional systems and part-task simulators. An airplane cockpit is a terrible environment for learning the indices of desired performance for a maneuver or procedure. In the associative stage, skill is acquired through hands-on manipulation in the simulator and in the airplane. The automatic stage of discrimination and manipulation must eventually be achieved in the airplane, but its acquisition is speeded by continued practice in the simulator.

The choice of the optimum environment for the various stages of learning in the various phases of flight training is based on cost as well as training effectiveness. Hours in the airplane are several times more expensive than hours of ground instruction and simulator training. Airplane time, as well as that of the instructor and student, is virtually wasted by demonstrations, "follow-me-through" exercises, and subtle, often unconscious, manual control inputs by the instructor. Learning in flight is maximized when the student already fully understands the indices of desired performance of a maneuver or procedure *and is in full control of the airplane.*

As training progresses, each new maneuver or procedure is introduced on the ground and demonstrated in the simulator with detailed verbal explanation. The student then attempts the task in the simulator with verbal guidance by the instructor as needed. As the student's skills increase, the need for verbal instruction decreases, and the opportunity for positive, reinforcing feedback increases. It is helpful, where appropriate, for the student to verbalize what is being attended to and adjusted moment to moment, whether in the simulator or the airplane.

In the matter of flight control, the instructor should restrict his or her role to that of a safety pilot; any necessary assumption of control by the instructor should be complete, as should resumption of control by the student. Rather than helping the student through small, subtle control inputs, the instructor should point out what the student is doing correctly as well as the cues that are being missed or how to adjust the timing and amount of control inputs. However, even such verbal assistance should be carefully screened. If students have mastered their cognitive groundwork, the main thing they need in the air is a chance to practice with minimum distraction.

As the various presolo maneuvers and procedures are mastered to the specified performance criteria in the simulator, the student is allowed to practice them in the airplane. Further demonstration of procedures and airwork maneuvers by the instructor should be unnecessary, although some students may want to see the instructor make one landing before attempting the maneuver. By making optimum use of the simulator and other ground training aids, presolo dual instruction can be held to a minimum. Demonstrations in the airplane are given only if it is apparent that the student does not understand some index of desired performance.

Curriculum design. Designing a curriculum refers to the planning of the instructional delivery to maximize the effectiveness of learning. The research we will draw on here has been conducted almost exclusively on the learning of perceptual-motor skills. Consequently, the results may not be generalizable to learning the full range of competencies underlying the notion of airmanship.

Psychologists have been investigating the learning of perceptual-motor skills for more than a century.[14] Until fairly recently it was thought that practice promoted skill through a process of strengthening the association between stimulus and response. More recently, skill acquisition has been described as a closed-loop system in which learning occurs as the result of feedback regarding the success or failure of previous attempts. A common example of a closed-loop system is the household thermostat used to control a heating or air-conditioning system. The reference mechanism is a key part of a closed-loop system.

The thermostat provides a simple example of a reference mechanism. It has to receive some input from the environment in the form of a temperature reading. This then has to be compared with the criterion (the desired temperature). If the actual temperature is lower than the criterion, the mechanism will switch the heating on until the criterion level is reached. The key element in a closed-loop system is feedback. Unless there is a means of passing back information about the current state of affairs, the system will not be able to detect errors or discrepancies from its reference of correctness. In the case of the central heating system, with no thermostat the house could be freezing or unbearably hot.

To operate effectively the system must know what to look for in the environment (e.g., a landing aimpoint), know how to recognize correctness or error (assessing whether the direction of movement of the aimpoint signifies undershooting or overshooting), and finally know what action to take to correct the error (apply or reduce power, etc.). In addition to identifying key elements to attend to in the surrounding visual world, instruction should therefore be aimed at establishing the appropriate reference of correctness for each task.

These references of correctness are frequently referred to as the "indices of desired performance." Controlling an airplane is the continuous matching of the "indices of actual performance" to those desired. This matching process can depend on visual information (nose position in relation to the horizon in a level turn), auditory information (sound of the airflow as the stall approaches), tactile information (prestall buffet), position of the controls and muscles (stick held hard back on landing), and so on. Learning will be more efficient if the student is given explicit guidance in establishing a reference of correctness and a means to detect deviations from the reference.

Discrepancies between actual and desired indices of performance provide the intrinsic feedback essential to any type of continuous control and hence are essential to learning to fly. However, learning can be further facilitated by the extrinsic feedback provided by the instructor's comments as to what the student is doing correctly and what needs to be done differently. Unless there is a means of passing back information about the current state of affairs in one form or another, a system will not be able to detect errors or discrepancies from its reference of correctness.

Other factors that can affect learning include the length and distribution of training sessions. Such questions are not easily answered because the many variables in the training session interact in complicated ways.[15] For example, the performance of a flight maneuver or procedure may appear to deteriorate rather than improve during a brief training session in which a student is exploring the effects of alternative control techniques to gain a basic understanding that will lead to superior performance in later sessions. Unfortunately, the simple laboratory experiments on the distribution of practice cannot be generalized to the complex, noisy, fatiguing, and potentially dangerous flight training environment.

A possible advantage of distributed practice is that the spacing between sessions may allow further consolidation of skills through mental practice. This refers to rehearsing the task by imagining the discriminations and manipulations involved in the skill. One study undertaken by the U.S. Air Force showed that mental practice while sitting in a cockpit mockup was effective in improving the landing skills of a group of student pilots.[16] These subjects listened to tape recordings giving detailed instructions of the actions to be performed as the aircraft flew around the circuit. Later tapes gradually withdrew those detailed cues, providing only very general instructions.

Students who had gone through these practice sessions were found to perform better on the next session of circuits and landings than other pilots who continued with routine training. Of course, it is likely that the experimental student pilots were more highly motivated than the controls and, more importantly, may have gained a better concept of the task as a whole through listening to the tapes. It is apparent that such skills are learned through the development of an internal scheme or picture that organizes the indices of desired performance so that errors in actual performance can be more readily detected and corrected without instructor input.

Instructional patter often provides this scheme in outline form, particularly when preparing the student for a new maneuver. It is important, however, that this patter establish detailed behavioral objectives for the task rather than a vague and ambiguous frame of reference. Less and less overall detail should be provided on each subsequent attempt at an exercise, the instructor concentrating on providing specific feedback on the student's actions. The development of overall competence will, it seems, be increased if guidance is kept to a minimum.

Guidance can be verbal, but it can also take the form of physically controlling or limiting the student's responses. This may be helpful early on to set up the appropriate mental picture in a simulator and in avoiding gross errors that could in fact be dangerous in flight. Too much guidance, however, prevents the student from learning the appropriate reference of correctness or benefiting from intrinsic tactual feedback. An interesting variation on this problem occurs in tandem-seated aircraft, particularly gliders and military trainers, where the instructor sits behind and out of sight of the student.

If the instructor is providing guidance without the student's awareness, this will effectively distort the tactual feedback from the task. However, it is more common for the student to suspect that guidance is being supplied when in fact it is not. In terms of the processes we have been discussing, the effects will be the same as an overapplication of guidance. The solution is a matter of communication, with the instructor dividing responsibility for parts of each task and explicitly assigning the student control authority for those parts to be practiced.

One of the most important issues in training curriculum design is that of part-task versus whole-task training. This refers to a choice between training on the full task (e.g., flying a complete mission in a simulator) and repeated practice on some component of the mission only (e.g., starting the engine or landing). Part-task training might be desirable for several reasons:

- To provide training at a lower cost than can be provided by whole-task training. This is particularly applicable to the field of simulation to be discussed in more detail below.
- To provide additional training in individually critical tasks; for example, in aircraft carrier landings.

- To provide training in new task elements to pilots with considerable previous experience; for example, in type conversions.
- To provide recurrent training in infrequently encountered maneuvers and procedures; for example, in failed-engine landings.[17]

It would be desirable if there were some design criteria on which to base the decision to adopt a part-task training procedure. Unfortunately, such guidance is not generally available. With regard to the manual tracking aspect of pilot skill, a review has suggested that there are at least three approaches.[18] The first is to simplify the task, for example, by modifying a simulator's response dynamics. A second possibility is to separate a task into subtasks; for example, flying an ILS approach might be divided into independent glideslope and localizer control subtasks. The third approach is to divide the task into a sequence of task segments.

In one study at the U.S. Naval Training Systems Center in Orlando, Florida, undergraduate students were trained to make simulated aircraft carrier landings.[19] Two of the three strategies described above were compared. Some subjects received a simplified version of the carrier landing task in which the normal lag between control input and aircraft response was reduced. A second group was trained on progressively longer segments of the landing task, starting at 2,000 feet out, then from 4,000 feet out, and finally from 6,000 feet out. A control group made all approaches from 6,000 feet out with normal simulator dynamics.

After training, all subjects were tested on the whole-task in the simulator. Those who were trained on the segmented part-task were better at the whole-task than the other two groups, including the group trained on the whole-task. This suggests that suitably designed part-task training may be the most effective way of promoting the learning of the task as a whole. At least with a manual tracking task, the procedure of practicing segments of the task seems to be most effective. As found in an earlier experiment, simplifying the control dynamics was counterproductive.[20]

PREDICTING PILOT PERFORMANCE

Not surprisingly, the aviation psychologist's role has been heavily slanted in the direction of improving selection test batteries. This effort was established quite early—in 1917 in the United States and 1920 in Germany, for example. These early efforts were directed at testing the kinds of abilities that seemed to underlie the performance of perceptual-motor skills, such as reaction times, motor coordination, perception of equilibrium, and so forth.

One early test that was thought to discriminate well between successful and unsuccessful pilots was reaction to a sudden loud noise, such as an unexpected pistol shot behind the head! In addition to this test of so-called emotional stability, the perception of tilt and mental alertness were also correlated with early flight training performance.[21] Currently, even with more sophisticated test batteries, about 75 percent of the variance in pilot performance at advanced stages of training is not predictable.

One measure that initially showed some ability to differentiate successful from unsuccessful pilots was developed with trainees in the Israeli Air Force.[22] The test measured success at dividing attention between two messages presented simultaneously, one to each ear. Flying an aircraft and controlling air traffic (see following sections) depend, among other things, on an ability to perform several tasks concurrently. An air traffic controller, for example, must simultaneously monitor a radar screen, communicate with several aircraft, maintain a continuously updated mental picture of the dynamically changing traffic situation, and formulate predictions of potential traffic conflicts.

Clearly an ability to switch from one task to another without losing track of the overall picture is essential for this kind of performance. Both cadets at a pilot training school and pilots on regular flying duty (mostly on high-performance aircraft) were tested on their abilities to switch attention between simultaneous messages. Performance was found to be significantly correlated with progress in flight training for the cadets and to be higher for the operational pilots. However, subsequent validation studies have failed to show comparable predictive power.[23]

Another promising approach is to use more complex measures of time-sharing capacity as predictors of flight performance. In one study, student pilots performed a primary tracking task and a secondary choice reaction-time task concurrently.[24] A cross-adaptive logic was used to keep performance on the primary task relatively constant. Performance on the reaction-time task was used as an indicator of the subject's "spare-capacity" or residual attention left over from the primary task. Multiple correlations were calculated between the reaction-time performances and ratings of the student pilots' progress after 10, 20, and 30 hours of flight training. These correlations proved to be reasonably high (0.59 to 0.68) and to increase with increasing flight training.

In contrast, measures of perceptual-motor skills and general intelligence show decreasing correlations with performance during training. Thus, it has been particularly difficult to predict performance in advanced flight training and in operational flying. Assuming that time-sharing skills are progressively developed as a consequence of flight training, dual-task measures should show an increasing correlation with flight performance. This finding was replicated in a further study of student pilots.[25]

Despite the apparent difficulty of the prediction problem, crew members know what to expect of fellow crew members under stress, which ones to trust and which not to trust. Subjectively identified, the predictive variables include attention left over to take care of the emergency while not losing control of the routine, being able to estimate quickly probable outcomes for different courses of action, having a sense of relative values that allows rapid reordering of priorities as situations deteriorate or improve, and decisiveness of action in the face of indecision by others.

Few would question the relevance of the variables just listed to crew selection; the problem is how to measure them. Despite the difficulties, the quest for early predictive indices of future operational performance goes on and has been accelerated by the advent of the microcomputer. For example, during the early 1980s the USAF Human Resources Laboratory developed a portable battery of basic attributes tests (BAT). This PortaBAT system is being validated, as is the MICRO-PAT system developed by Bartdale, Inc., in England. High test marks with either system depend on cognitive information processing involving time-shared attention allocation as well as the more traditional perceptual-motor and intellectual factors.

Thus, it would appear that some of the basic human abilities attributed to operationally effective pilots are now being assessed with higher predictive validity than previously enjoyed. However, one human attribute that most pilots consider the essence of airmanship remains elusive. During the 1980s the pilot selection and training community has become increasingly concerned about pilot judgment, both as to what it is and whether it can be measured and taught.[26] Judgment has both cognitive and motivational aspects that characterize the personality trait of airmanship, "the ability and the tendency to define the relevant aspects of an aerial problem or opportunity."[27]

BURNED OUT ENGINE

> *An example of airmanship occurred in Okinawa in 1945. A pilot taking off in a heavily loaded C-46 lost power from one engine just as the plane became airborne and the end of the runway passed below. Holding altitude caused a rapid loss of airspeed. Advancing the good engine to full power, feathering the prop and closing the cowl flaps on the dead engine, and retracting the landing gear were not sufficient. The airman went against the book and closed the cowl flaps on the good engine! This gave him five more knots, just enough to circle and land—with a burned out engine but a safe airplane, crew, passengers, and cargo.*

The airman had defined the aerial problem correctly and seized an unanticipated opportunity. To the extent that a pilot forms a veridical mental picture of the problem and opportunity, the course-of-action selection becomes relatively trivial, and virtually automatic in the case of a well-trained pilot. The critical attribute or trait to be measured as a pilot selection (or, more accurately, rejection) criterion would thus appear to be the facility with which one searches for, evaluates, and correctly integrates information from diverse sources, some of which may be highly improbable (an engine coming off the airplane during a take-off in Chicago) and much of which may be probabilistic (the weather in Antarctica).

A modern airman, in his or her emerging role as a manager rather than flier, must search for, evaluate, and integrate information not only about the status of the various aircraft subsystems but also about the myriad other physical facts of flight. It is our thesis not only that the situational awareness just described is the essence of airmanship but also that the human characteristics that facilitate situational awareness can be measured by creating complex physical problems involving multiple information channels, all fighting for the airman's limited pool of attention.

FLIGHT SIMULATION

The use of simulators in flying training depends on two considerations: their training effectiveness and their economic effectiveness. Much of the awareness of flight simulation has come to center heavily on expensive, high-technology systems. Early attempts at flight simulators were extremely simple, even crude, devices. With the development of powerful microcomputers, it is now practical to provide simulator training systems that are both sophisticated and relatively cheap and therefore attractive to general aviation as well as to the traditional users—the airlines and the military. In either case, the study of the training effectiveness of simulators leads to some principles for maximizing the overall economic effectiveness of pilot training.

The first ground-based training devices designed to mimic some aspect of flying an aircraft were developed surprisingly early. Between 1910 and 1920 several devices, including the Eardley Billing Oscillator, had been designed to facilitate the development of the basic psychomotor skills used in flying. However, an application of major significance did not occur until the development between 1927 and 1929 of the first successful pneumatic flying trainer by Ed Link (of the Link Piano Company). Subsequently, many versions of the Link trainer were developed and have been used by several generations of pilots. The latest offering from Link Systems, a division of CAE of Canada, is the Boeing 767 simulator at around ten million dollars!

The major advances in simulation technology during the 1950s, 1960s, and 1970s were fueled primarily by the needs of aerospace research and development rather than training. In contrast, the design of simulators in the 1980s has been guided by the desires of the marketplace, unfortunately still with little regard for the real needs of pilot training. Simulation has become big business, as witnessed by the attendance of 1,582 paid registrants, including 752 government representatives and 800 engineers and marketing managers from industry, at the 1986 Interservice/Industry Training Systems Conference in Salt Lake City. Annual sales are counted in the billions of dollars!

The widespread use of complex training simulators by the airlines and the military has been advanced on the basis of three considerations: their safety relative to training in airplanes, their ease and flexibility in controlling the training situation, and their relative cost-effectiveness. The trade-offs among these three factors approach infinity, but their resolution is based more on what degree of apparent fidelity is technologically possible at the time than on training needs as determined by objective indices of training effectiveness.

It is obviously safer to practice potentially dangerous operations in a ground-based device than in the air. Engine-out performance is notoriously poor in some twin-engined aircraft, and practice of particularly critical flight stages may incur real hazards. Second, it is possible to produce a whole range of unlikely events when one has control over the complete situation. Conditions that would not likely occur in millions of hours of flying can therefore be simulated, for example, an engine fire and concurrent hydraulic failure amid a tropical thunderstorm. This sort of control lends itself particularly to the training of the procedural aspects of flight, including instrument flight and emergency drills.

Finally, cost is a major consideration, at least in the civilian sector. With the high cost of fuel and any loss of revenue-bearing service, airlines in particular have found it easy to justify their investment in simulator technology. With the costs of training in, say, a Boeing 747 of several thousand dollars an hour, even a complex, high-fidelity, motion-base simulator is cost-effective. Surprisingly little experimental attention has been given to the question of whether 6 degrees of motion and photo-quality, wraparound visual scenes are essential to the effectiveness of simulator training. There is increasing operational evidence that neither contributes sufficient incremental transfer to be cost-effective.

In contrast, there is impressive experimental evidence that low-cost flight simulators (Figure 3.1) that provide simplified flight dynamics, instrument indications, and cartoonish image animation can yield high transfer of initial training in instrument flight, contact flight including landing approaches and touchdowns, communication

Fig. 3.1 Example of a low-cost, microcomputer-based general aviation flight and navigation trainer. Figure courtesy of Massey Aviation Institute, Palmerston North, New Zealand.

and navigation, and emergency procedures. Although the expensive, high-tech image of simulators has slowed their application at the general aviation level, a variety of relatively inexpensive single and light-twin simulators are available. Typically these devices do not include costly motion bases or high-fidelity out-of-the-cockpit visual presentations. Later in this chapter, we will look specifically at the contribution of these two ingredients to training effectiveness.

Transfer effectiveness. The entire edifice of simulated flight training is based on the notion that what is learned in the simulator will transfer to the actual flying of the aircraft. It will be helpful to make a distinction between three areas of flying skill: (1) perceptual-motor skills, (2) procedural skills, and (3) decisional skills. We can note right away that simulators have been used primarily in the first two areas and in rehearsing the recognition of and correct response to a wide variety of emergency situations by already experienced aircrews. Prior to the 1980s, little use was made of simulators in the teaching of decisional skills.

Exactly how effective are simulators in teaching skills in the first two areas? The early simulators were primarily designed to provide familiarity with the perceptual-motor components of flying. The earliest studies were carried out in the late 1940s with a variety of Link trainers, using later performance in real airplanes as the criterion of effectiveness. Several of these studies showed that students with prior training in the simulator were more proficient at the required flight maneuvers.[28] This was encouraging, but unhelpful in answering the important question of how much simulator training was needed to save a certain amount of actual flight time.

During the 1970s several investigators attempted to measure this transfer effectiveness rather more precisely. In one study, students who received 11 hours of instruction in the then new Link GAT-1 were found to require an average of 11 fewer hours in the air to pass the Private Pilot flight check in a Cherokee 140.[29] Pilots without simulator training required 45.5 total flying hours to pass the test, whereas those trained on the GAT-1 passed the same test after 34.5 hours. The transfer effectiveness can be calculated using the simple formula:

Transfer effectiveness = $(X - Y)/Z$

where

X = flying hours to reach proficiency in the airplane with no prior simulator training,
Y = flying hours to reach proficiency in the airplane following simulator training, and
Z = training hours in the simulator.

Dividing the 11 hours saved in the air by the 11 hours invested in the simulator yields a transfer effectiveness ratio of 1.0. Even the old Link "blue box," also evaluated in the experiment, yielded a transfer effectiveness of 0.82, saving 9 flying hours for 11 hours of simulator training.

Overall transfer effectiveness provides only an approximate guide to the actual value of each hour of simulator training. This is because the value of each additional hour in the simulator turns out to be less than the value of the preceding hour. It is easy to appreciate how the first one or two hours of simulator instruction might save several hours in flight, where much time is wasted in explanations and demonstrations by the instructor in a noisy, cramped, and strange environment to the student. It is equally easy to appreciate that after quite a few hours in the simulator, each additional hour would contribute somewhat less to the future saving of time in the airplane. This is known as "incremental transfer effectiveness" and can be calculated in a similar way to the overall transfer effectiveness.[30]

In studies of flight training using groups of students who spent, respectively, 3, 7, and 11 hours training in the GAT-1, it was found as expected that the transfer effectiveness of the first two hours in the simulator was greater than unity, with successive hours saving progressively less airborne training time.[31] The incremental transfer effectiveness of the eleventh hour was less than 0.24. In fact, the eighth through the eleventh hours in the simulator each saved only about 15 minutes of flight training time. Whether this is cost-effective or not depends on the actual costs of simulator and aircraft operation.

The ratio of simulator to airplane costs will obviously tend to decrease as the size and complexity of the airplane increase (and hence its cost of ownership and operation), but not as rapidly as one might expect because complex airplanes have complex simulators. Thus, if the cost of owning and operating a Boeing 747 were ten times the cost of its counterpart simulator (as it approximately is), it would be cost-effective for the airlines to continue simulator training until the incremental transfer ratio dropped to 0.1, a saving of six minutes in the air for the final hour in the simulator. To continue simulator training beyond that point would not be cost-effective, although it might be justified for some logistic reason such as equipment availability.

At the other end of the spectrum, ab initio training, the transfer effectiveness ratio has to be quite high for simulator training to be cost-effective (or the cost of the simulator quite low), because the cost of training in the airplane is lower. Fortunately, ab initio training in microprocessor simulators and teaching machines can yield high transfer if these devices are programmed intelligently, namely, if the branching logic of the training scenarios adapts automatically to whatever response the individual student makes, as does the hypothetical ideal flight instructor.

In deciding when to use simulators in training, it is important to note that the cost-effectiveness crossunder point might have been reached for one aspect of training—say the learning of basic perceptual-motor skills such as stall recoveries and landings—but simulator training may become highly effective at a later point in training when new skills are being taught, such as instrument flying, navigating, emergency procedures, and air traffic control phraseology! It is in the teaching of such procedure-based skills that simulators and part-task devices have shown the greatest effectiveness.

Part-task teaching machines. An approach that shows great promise involves the use of a teaching machine with inexpensive computer graphics and a hand controller to teach the tricky computations for planning and flying a holding pattern in the presence of crosswinds. This is a precise maneuver, normally performed in instrument meteorological conditions (IMC weather), that requires the pilot to fly a "racetrack" course of two legs of a certain length with turns at either end, usually referenced to a ground-based radio navigation aid, such as a VHF omnidirectional radio (VOR) or a nondirectional beacon (NDB). Flying the pattern can be a relatively difficult task when the need for adjusting to different wind conditions is taken into account.

Nevertheless, a study involving fairly inexperienced private pilots (none had more than 170 hours of flight time) showed considerable success for this kind of simulation.[32] No attempt was made to simulate any aspect of aircraft performance other than the task at hand. One group of students was told to fly the pattern by reference to the navigation instruments simulated on the screen. At the end of each attempt, detailed feedback was provided via the computer. Another group of students received conventional training in the Link GAT-2 simulator.

Although both groups showed the same high transfer of training relative to a control group, as later assessed in the airplane, there was a large advantage to the computer-trained group in terms of cost-effectiveness because no attempt was made to provide a realistic overall simulation of the task. Rather, the strategy was to isolate the cognitive part of the task and to provide practice and, importantly, feedback on that aspect. Unaccountably, this demonstrated effectiveness of computer-based, part-task training has not been taken up by the training industry.

A procedural area where part-task training is commonly used in early flying training is in radio communications. Clearly this aspect of flying can be neatly separated from the overall task of controlling the aircraft, and two headsets and microphones and a cassette player providing extraneous background noises and interference are all that is needed for an effective simulation. There is obviously nothing very realistic about sitting in an armchair practicing emergency calls. This is, however, an effective way of simulating the key elements of the task.

Unfortunately, there is a powerful tendency to assume that greater realism (and higher cost) must promote greater training transfer effectiveness. It is important to keep this in mind because it bears on the crucial question of how faithful to the airplane simulations need to be to function as effective training devices. There is no question that procedural items, to the extent they are included in a simulation, need to be represented faithfully. To do otherwise can actually result in negative transfer. The two debatable (and fiercely debated) issues are what motion cues are needed, if any, and what extracockpit visual cues should be provided.

Motion.   To obtain a valid assessment of the effects of cockpit motion, it is first necessary to distinguish between flying performance in the simulator and subsequent transfer to performance in the airplane. Numerous experiments have shown that both the presence and the type of motion cues can affect performance in a simulator. There is no doubt that angular accelerations above a pilot's vestibular threshold can be used by the pilot with an apparent improvement in performance, and high vertical accelerations (rough air) can make a simulator harder to fly. With one inconclusive exception favoring no motion,[33] the only experiments that have shown any differential effects of cockpit motion have been restricted to performance in the simulator.

One experiment in 1976 by the U.S. Air Force involved the measurement of transfer to flight from training with and without cockpit motion in the Advanced Simulator for Pilot Training (ASPT) at Williams Air Force Base in Arizona.[34] Four student pilots were trained with the full 6 degrees of motion (yaw, pitch, and roll and lateral, longitudinal, and vertical displacement), and four were trained with the motion system turned off. The presence of motion had no apparent effect on subsequent performance in flight. Of course, in an experiment with so little statistical power, no conclusive answer could have been expected. Evidently the issue was not considered sufficiently in doubt to warrant a conclusive experiment.

Nevertheless, six more transfer of training experiments to evaluate cockpit platform motion were conducted at Williams Air Force Base during the next three years. In reviewing these studies, and all others involving cockpit motion prior to 1981, Waag concluded: "Studies to date have failed to demonstrate that platform motion cueing enhances the effectiveness of simulator training. In no instance was performance in the aircraft significantly enhanced as a result of simulator training with platform motion. . . . The failure to demonstrate improved transfer for tasks in which force information serves as a primary cue seriously questions the value of platform motion."[35]

The investigators conducting the Visual Technology Research Simulator (VTRS) program at the U.S. Naval Training Systems Center in Florida completed two large, sophisticated, multifactor transfer experiments to assess the contributions of various simulated visual cues to field carrier landings and bombing accuracy, respectively.[36] In neither experiment was cockpit motion included because they had long since dismissed it as an unimportant experimental variable on the basis of earlier in-simulator, quasi-transfer experiments. In fact, the motion system of the simulator had been disabled to reduce maintenance costs and allow greater flexibility in the study of visual systems.

The following experiment illustrates how insensitive transfer of training is to extreme distortions of simulator motion cues.[37] A Link GAT-2 with 2 degrees of motion (roll and pitch/heave) was modified so that its direction of roll could be randomly reversed, thereby being in agreement with the attitude and turn instrument indications half the time and diametrically opposite half the time. Independent groups of students were also trained with normal cockpit motion and no motion. All groups showed positive transfer relative to a control group trained only in the airplane, but the amount of transfer did not differ significantly among groups. Amazingly, no student in the first group ever noticed the reversed motion!

A curious argument has been advanced in connection with this experiment, namely, that the reason the normal cockpit motion did not yield significantly higher transfer was because it, too, was not as faithful as possible; surely a 6-degree-of-freedom (6-DOF) system would have provided higher fidelity and hence higher transfer. The argument goes on to say that even the best 6-DOF systems to date may not yield the maximum transfer possible, and thus even larger buildings allowing ever greater distances for linear accelerations would be cost-effective if this put the finishing touches on a combat pilot.

Surprisingly then, given the enormous cost of building and maintaining moving-base simulators, the question of what contribution, if any, various kinds of movement cues make to transfer effectiveness remains essentially unanswered. The technical advances that have resulted in moving-base simulators with six degrees of movement have not been accompanied by a clear understanding of the specific importance of any of these cues. Meaningful transfer experiments involving complex motion systems simply have not been done. Nevertheless, the arguments in favor of moving-base simulators include the following:

• It is only in a moving-base simulator that pilots can learn to disregard acceleration information and to depend entirely on their instruments.

• In some flight conditions—sustained low-level flying, for example—movement simulation is vital in providing exposure to conditions that would degrade performance in the air.

• Motion has a generally alerting function and thus produces more realistic training and, therefore, more effective transfer.

• Moving-base simulators are generally "felt" by pilots to be more realistic and are much preferred by pilots to fixed-base models.

It is probably the last point that has been most responsible for the complex, 6-degrees-of-motion systems in airline and military full-mission simulators (the USAF's A-10 simulator is a notable exception). This is because the final judges in the procurement of training systems are the senior company vice-presidents and the generals and admirals who will be company vice-presidents in a year or two. In the absence of objective evidence of any transfer value attributable to cockpit motion, subjective judgments are necessarily based on other considerations, some of which have nothing to do with training effectiveness, one way or the other, as will be discussed later in this chapter.

Surprisingly, but true, with modern computer-animated visual systems, cockpit motion can be turned off without the pilot's realizing this has happened, and it is routinely done in many cases. However, it is certain that full-motion systems will remain a part of simulator design as long as they are required by regulation for zero-time type-rating training. It is now possible for pilots transitioning from one type to another comparable type (e.g., DC-10 to B-747) to obtain the new type rating solely on the basis of simulator time without any time in the actual aircraft.

Extracockpit visual cues.   Whereas pilots are taught to disregard angular acceleration cues, the reverse is true for visual information. The maneuver most difficult to perform initially is landing, and its performance depends heavily on outside visual information. Curiously, landing an airplane at night when most visual cues are no longer available is not as difficult as expected. For example, the minimum flight time required for a night rating addition to the private pilot license in the United Kingdom is only five hours. In the United States it is even less—three hours of dual instruction at night including ten takeoffs and landings.

This suggests that, although the overall amount of visual information is greatly reduced at night, some particularly salient or useful cues remain. One of these seems to be perspective. This is the familiar method of depicting size and distance—the far end of a runway will cast a narrower projection on the eye than the near end. The illustrations in Figure 1.7 (see Chapter 1) all rely on this use of perspective. However, the most critical phase of the landing maneuver is the flare, or roundout, where perspective becomes imprecise and other cues such as motion parallax and texture become more important (when the green turns to grass, it's time to flare). During the flare and in the landing roll, the runway centerline cue becomes primary.

Although the night approach is flown in much the same way as the daytime approach, some changes in technique at the flare to touchdown are required to compensate for the absence of the normal cues at this point. These observations can be used to suggest what essential visual cues should be provided in a simulated out-of-the-cockpit view. The earliest attempts were primitive indeed, consisting of a pseudoperspective drawing of a runway on a blackboard. The instructor could alter the apparent perspective by tilting the blackboard as the student pilots flew the adjacent Link trainer. Not surprisingly, the researchers noted that few flight instructors could be persuaded to take this procedure seriously.

However, a device not much more complex than the tilting blackboard was used to teach the landing task to ab initio students with a resulting saving of 61 percent of the trials required by a group who did not receive this part-task training. This device consisted of a closed-loop silhouette of the runway perspective with centerline and aimpoint

Fig. 3.2 An example of a high-fidelity, computer-image-generated (CIG) visual scene. This is the Rediffusion SP-X visual system. Reproduced by permission of Rediffusion Simulation Ltd.

projected on a screen in front of a Link SNJ/T-6 simulator.[38] A reluc-
tance to accept part-task trainers has undoubtedly hindered the use of
such devices in ab initio training. If the instructor clearly points out
the similarities and differences between the part-task as practiced in
the simulator and the whole-task, such simple simulation can be
highly effective.

Just as there has been a clear trend toward increasingly complex
and expensive moving-base simulators, so also has there been a similar trend toward high-fidelity computer image generation (CIG) with
wraparound views. These provide the pilot with amazingly realistic
moving scenes (see Figures 3.2 and 3.3). Although stubbornly ignored,
the distinction between performance in a simulator and its transfer to
performance in the air is as important in evaluating visual simulations
as it is in the case of cockpit motion. For example, a simulated visual
cue not present in the real world might make a simulator easier to fly
while actually reducing transfer, although the overall transfer effects
would almost surely still be positive. Two experiments will illustrate
the point.

Fig. 3.3 A CIG visual system combined with a wide-angle display can produce scenes of astonishing realism. Reproduced by permission of Rediffusion Simulation Ltd.

In the first experiment, static images of various combinations of visual cues were projected briefly on a display screen viewed through the windscreen of a Link GAT-2. Some similar cues are shown in Figure 4.7 (see Chapter 4). All of the simulated cues were representative of prominent real-world airport features save one, a computer-generated highway-in-the-sky showing the desired flight path to touchdown. Pilots were asked to judge their positions and attitudes relative to a proper final approach, and not surprisingly the unreal-worldly highway-in-the-sky proved by far the most effective cue in making these perceptual judgments.[39] If augmenting a visual display in this way can improve performance so greatly in a simulator, why not employ it as a training aid?

In the second experiment, a dynamic, closed-loop, skeletal airport scene (similar to that in the first experiment) was computer-animated and presented on the same screen in front of the GAT-2. As expected, the highway-in-the-sky made flying an accurate final approach much easier, but what would its effect be when the student had to land without it? Would an acquired dependency on the display augmentation interfere with transfer of skills learned in the simulator? Would there be a weaning problem? To cope with this possibility, an automatically adaptive display mode was included in the experiment; the "highway" symbology appeared only when the student exceeded predetermined error limits and disappeared as soon as the proper correction was made.

The adaptive logic worked like magic. Early in simulator training when large errors are made, the display augmentation guides the student immediately in the right direction without help from the instructor (evidently very important). As correct responses are made early in the training sequence, the training wheels come off; only the skeletal real-world cues remain for guidance, and weaning occurs rapidly because the synthetic guidance cues do not appear once the student is consistently flying the simulator within preset limits. There was high transfer to the airplane from all simulator conditions, including the full-time augmentation, but the adaptive augmentation was the superior strategy.[40]

The fact that extremely skeletal visual cues with automatically adaptive guidance and performance feedback can be easily animated by a relatively inexpensive computer may be threatening to the visual simulation industry, but it is certainly good news for general aviation. The key may be found in the basic literature on transfer of learning under the heading of "stimulus generalization." It seems that stimuli quite different from the originally adequate stimulus (in this case, a contact daylight view of the airport) can serve to elicit the desired response (an accurate approach to a smooth simulated landing).

At the other end of the visual simulation research spectrum was a program at the U.S. Naval Training Systems Center from the mid-1970s through the late 1980s. Not only were the Visual Technology Research Simulator (VTRS) facilities highly sophisticated for their time, but so was the research. Among its many findings, the program showed clearly that it is meaningless to ask, "How much visual fidelity is enough?" This is because visual fidelity is not a unitary factor but rather the composite product of many design variables. It is not even possible to answer in isolation how much of any individual variable—say resolution, shades of contrast, or field of view—is necessary and sufficient because of its complex interactions and trade-offs with the many other design variables in a visual system and the various flight operations to be taught.

To cope with the impossibility of sorting out the effects of costly design features one at a time, the VTRS investigators advanced a holistic research strategy, featuring economical multifactor experiments in which many independent variables are studied simultaneously, first to identify which features have large effects on performance in a simulator and then to pin down how those critical design variables interact to produce high transfer to the airplane.[41] It is a sequential strategy that also includes quasi-transfer experiments to measure in the simulator the transfer of training from relatively simple, and hence less costly, configurations of simulated visual features to the most complex and costly available at the time.

In the long run their economical experimental methodology will no doubt have a greater impact on subsequent research than their specific findings will have on simulator design. For example, in a single experiment, they measured the performance effects of 11 variables under 1,024 experimental conditions including 128 different simulator configurations. The more expensive versions of some equipment variables such as the field of view of a visual system and its scenic content do result in better performance in the simulator and, for some flight maneuvers, higher transfer. However, these differences are always small in comparison with differences among pilots, how much and how the simulator is used, task environment variables, and the introduction of automatically adaptive display augmentation as discussed earlier.

Nevertheless, the effects of some design variables are not trivial. Within the ranges of the design features that might reasonably be considered for procurement, it was evident that an 80 × 160-degree field of view was quite adequate for carrier landing and air-to-surface weapon delivery in the simulator, whereas a 36 × 48-degree field clearly was not, thereby adversely affecting performance on "field" carrier landings and bombing accuracy when transferring to the airplane. Similarly it was shown that a simple grid pattern representing the surface of the earth resulted in poor bombing performance and little transfer, whereas only a slightly more complex scene with some skeletal buildings (with far less detail than is now available) yielded large improvements in both performance and transfer.

In terms of potential economic impact, it is not only important to find out what is needed in a simulator but also to find out what is not. Although the effects that design features have on performance in the simulator are poor predictors of their transfer value, the quasi-transfer experiments in the simulator seem to provide a better basis for prediction. It would appear reasonable that if skills acquired in training with a degraded configuration of a given feature transfer intact to the more complex and costly version, then those skills might also be expected to transfer well to performance in the airplane, just as night-landing practice transfers to daytime performance.

Only time and further transfer experiments will tell, but on the basis of the quasi-transfer experiments to date, the following reductions in complexity would have no measurable effect on transfer of training, although some would adversely affect performance in the simulator:

- Reducing the TV line rate from 1,025 to 525 Hz
- Reducing engine update rate from 30 to 7.5 Hz
- Increasing visual transport delay from 117 to 217 milliseconds
- Changing the seascape background from a wave pattern to a homogeneous gray
- Reducing the maximum brightness of carrier detail from "dim" to "very dim"
- Eliminating six degrees of cockpit motion.

Buying fidelity.   At any given time, the fidelity requirements for training simulators procured by the military are defined by the limits of the current states of the hardware and software arts. In the United States, only research by universities and the navy's VTRS program has provided a reasonably objective experimental basis for specifying design requirements for effective training, and the results of these efforts have had little visible impact on procurement policies (the notable exception being the fixed-base A-10 simulator). The reigning philosophy is, "If you're not sure what's important, play safe and buy the most fidelity possible; surely something will work."

The situation with the airlines is on somewhat firmer ground, and the difference is mainly a reflection of motivation. The airlines are profit oriented, and their simulators have to be cost-effective, which still leaves a lot of room for unnecessary "bells and whistles" and counterproductive motion systems. The military's motivation is more subtle: they want the best training simulators money can buy, but even more they want flying time in real airplanes, which translates directly to fuel budget. If military flight simulators were allowed to save as much training time as the airlines' simulators do, current peacetime fuel budgets would be hard to justify.

The airlines also have done a better job than the military in "selling" simulators to their pilots (and to the FAA). To do so they emphasized apparent fidelity, buying simulators that look, feel, and smell like airplanes. Ironically, this highly successful campaign has had a bit of an economic backlash. The pilots have so fallen in love with the concept of high simulation fidelity that they are asking for more and more, and the FAA is insisting on it through regulation. The airlines' training managers know they can turn off their motion bases with no measurable effect on training, but not when the FAA is around.

The concern that poor crew coordination and communication mitigation in the cockpit have been heavily implicated in major airline disasters has justified the involvement of the National Aeronautics and Space Administration in Cockpit Resource Management (CRM) and Line-oriented Flight Training (LOFT) discussed in Chapter 8. These programs, in turn, have supported the requirement for so-called full-mission simulators. In a circular fashion, the fact that simulators having full-mission capabilities were available, including all manner of system failures and other emergencies, no doubt provided timely support for the notion that CRM and LOFT were good ideas. Although costly, these programs offer the airborne passenger, and the families of the crew, comfort in the knowledge that situational awareness and good pilot judgment get their finishing touches in the full-mission scenarios of CRM and LOFT.

So long as even the most expensive simulators remain cost-effective, the strategy of maximizing fidelity is understandable and even good management, given all the complex human relations involved. Nevertheless, there is room for huge savings without sacrificing training effectiveness, but such savings are likely to go begging. Instead, the next generation of military training simulators will no doubt have even larger and faster motion bases and computer-animated high-resolution, full-color, head-mounted virtual-imaging displays that fill the entire visual field.

In general aviation the situation is quite different, because the lower cost of flying time dictates that simulators and part-task devices must be cheap to be cost-effective. Here it is critical to identify and simulate only those cues that are necessary and sufficient for high transfer of training and to capitalize to the fullest on automatically adaptive display augmentation with highways-in-the-sky, frequency-separated flightpath predictors, and as a finishing touch, simple pictorial indicators to give the student immediate performance feedback.

FURTHER READING

The topic of skill learning is well covered by R. A. Schmidt in *Motor Control and Learning* (Champaign, IL: Human Kinetics Publishers, 1982). A more behavioral approach to training is presented by W. Becker, S. Engelmann, and D. R. Thomas in *Teaching: A Course in Applied Psychology* (Chicago: Science Research Associates, 1971). The topics of psychology and flight training are treated in detail by R. A. Telfer and J. Biggs in *The Psychology of Flight Training* (Ames: Iowa State University Press, 1988). An early and still best analysis and explanation of the art of flying was presented in 1944 by W. Lange-wiesche in *Stick and Rudder* (New York: McGraw-Hill, 1944; copyright renewed 1972).

[4] Human Factors in Cockpit Design

SO THE CREW fly on with no thought that they are in motion. Like night over the sea, they are very far from the earth, from towns, from trees. The motors fill the lighted chamber with a quiver that changes its substance. The clock ticks on. The dials, the radio lamps, the various hands and needles go through their invisible alchemy. From second to second these mysterious stirrings, a few muffled words, a concentrated tenseness, contribute to the end result. And when the hour is at hand the pilot may glue his forehead to the window with perfect assurance. Out of oblivion the gold has been smelted: there it gleams in the lights of the airport.

ANTOINE DE SAINT-EXUPÉRY, *Wind, Sand and Stars*

INTRODUCTION

The cockpits of the early jet transports were clearly from the same stable as the crowded and cluttered flight decks of the World War II transports. In contrast, those of the latest passenger jets seem less cluttered than single-engine trainers. The most obvious change is the replacement of numerous individual mechanical instruments with a small number of cathode-ray tube (CRT) screens that can provide, on command, any of the required navigational displays or instrument indications. The advanced Boeing 747-400 flight deck, for example, contains five CRTs presenting flight and navigation instruments and engine-indicating and crew-alerting systems (see Figure 4.1).

Although the technological developments that have occurred

Fig. 4.1   The engineering cab used during the design and test phase of the 747-400 flight deck. The Electronic Flight Instrument System (EFIS) consists of an Attitude Director Indicator, Horizontal Situation Indicator, and an Engine Indication and Crew Alerting System. The displays appear on five color CRTs. Reproduced by permission of Boeing Commercial Airplane Company.

should not be undervalued, to a great extent many of the changes reflect a relatively recent recognition of the importance of human factors in design. This refers to the intentional effort to design new products with the characteristics of the user firmly in mind rather than as an afterthought to engineering convenience. The need for human factors considerations to be given prominence in design is more widely recognized partly as a reflection of the growth in computer technology and the need to make such systems "user friendly."[1]

THE DESIGN OF FLIGHT CONTROLS AND DISPLAYS

The initial contribution of human factors in aviation was to advance some general principles governing the design of cockpit displays and controls. The control layouts in World War II aircraft had been particularly haphazard, leading to many accidents and near accidents caused by someone misidentifying or misoperating a control, such as a copilot retracting the undercarriage instead of the flaps after landing. These kinds of operating errors were routinely put down to pilot error and left uncorrected, although a few psychologists managed to recommend some fixes that were implemented late in the war.

A more satisfactory approach was to examine experimentally the design and layout of controls and instruments in conjunction with an analysis of the demands and workload placed on the operator, the pilot or copilot in the case of airplanes. Since World War II, scientific principles of display and control design have been developed and have influenced the design of modern cockpit systems. Most of the control and display design principles were discovered in the 1940s and 1950s and validated in the 1960s and 1970s as first analog and then early digital computers made such experimentation possible. However, it was the small, reliable, and cheap microcomputer that enabled their wide application.

THE OPTICA TRAGEDY

> *The first production Edgley Optica was orbiting the town of Ringwood, England, when the aircraft was seen to descend slowly from about 800 feet to between 150 and 100 feet and enter a steep but apparently controlled turn to the right. A few seconds later the bank angle suddenly increased to about 90 degrees, and the aircraft spiraled steeply into a wood, killing both occupants. The balance of available evidence suggests that the pilot was forced to descend by a partial or transient power loss, either occasioned by mishandling of the fuel tank selector or some other cause. A contributory factor could have been the ease with which a misselection of the fuel tank selector can be made in certain circumstances.*[2]

Basic principles. The obvious first principle—that controls and displays should be accessible and legible—is among the most often violated. Frequently used instruments should be placed where they can be most easily seen. Although the main field of vision extends up to ±30 degrees vertically and ±80 degrees horizontally to the line of sight, the area that can be comfortably scanned by eye movements alone is about ±30 degrees to the line of sight. A common violation of this requirement can be seen in the location of the vital fuel on/off indication on many light aircraft. On one common type this is placed by the pilot's left ankle, and on another it is entirely out of view so that its position must be confirmed by touch.

The extent to which fuel selector design has contributed to engine failure accidents is well documented.[3] Nearly 20 percent of general aviation engine failure accidents are caused by fuel starvation. The design of the fuel selector valve contributes significantly to the occurrence of fuel starvation accidents. A comparison of airplane models with a "both tanks" selector position and those models in which one tank or the other must be selected showed that, although there were twice as many aircraft in the former category, there were seven times as many fuel exhaustion accidents associated with the latter group.

In general, the layout of instruments should be determined by each instrument's importance, its relative frequency of use, its similarity to other instruments, and any requirements governing sequence of use. Evidence for the last requirement has been obtained from early experiments involving eye-movement recordings of pilots' visual fixations. Using motion picture cameras to record eye position and later relatively crude head-mounted devices to film the instrument panel and track the pilot's eyes simultaneously, information about the typical pattern of instrument fixations was obtained.

Among early findings, the artificial horizon was the most looked-at instrument, occupying more than half of all fixations in a turn and a third in a climb.[4] The next most fixated instrument was the directional gyro. The current standard basic instrument layout places the modern derivatives of these two instruments above and below each other in the center of the panel. The airspeed (and Mach) indicator and the altimeter, located to the left and right of the upper instrument, form the standard "T" primary instrument arrangement. The gyro horizon has become a flight director indicator that presents aircraft attitude and flight path guidance, below which is the horizontal situation indicator that presents heading and navigation guidance.

Data from the same study show that the length of individual fixations varied between approximately 0.3 seconds and 0.6 seconds. The limit on the uptake of new information through the visual system appears to be approximately two fixations per second. This is certainly a low rate of sampling compared to that attainable by electronic systems and underlines the need to maintain a systematic scanning strategy of the key instruments. There is evidence that experienced pilots are able to maintain this sampling rate even under high workload, whereas less experienced pilots are prone to make fewer fixations of longer duration under the same circumstances.[5]

Some less frequently used displays and controls that are less centrally located nevertheless need to be used quickly in an emergency. Shape and color coding may be effective in such cases. The displays should have high contrast between the figures and the background. Some trade-offs may have to be made to assure that such displays are visible under a wide range of illumination. Color coding can be used to emphasize particular operating ranges, as in the green areas for RPM, engine temperatures and pressures, and so on.

Being able to distinguish controls by touch alone can be critical in routine operations as well as in an emergency. There are only a few guidelines for designers to follow. It is clearly good practice not only to make critical controls tactually discriminable but also to shape them to be readily identified with what they control. The most notable and effective example is the universally used wheel-shaped head on the control for raising and lowering the undercarriage. Meaningful shape coding can also be applied to switch knobs, but care must be taken to assure that the shapes used do not themselves induce missettings.

The importance of control design, location, protection, and operating logic is recognized in the FAA's Code of Federal Regulations.[6] These generally follow established principles with regard to shape discrimination and compatibility of movement between the control and the part being moved. Figure 4.2 illustrates the required shapes of several cockpit controls.

Displays are closely linked to control actions. Sometimes the displayed information may come too late for effective response as in the case of extreme wind shear on approach. One solution in this case lies with the development of devices that can measure the airflow some distance ahead of the aircraft and thus provide the pilot with sufficient advance warning of the presence of pronounced shears. However, there are other important considerations that can dramatically affect the occurrence of correct control responses.

As with visual displays, discriminability is of vital importance. When several actions are required in rapid succession (for example, extending flaps, slats, and undercarriage on approach), not only must the control levers be clearly distinguishable by touch alone, but also the direction of movement must be compatible with the direction of movement of the controlled object. In other words, a lever should move up and down, respectively, to retract and extend the flaps or undercarriage. Lack of spatial compatibility in layout leads to slower responses and increases the incidence of reversal errors.

One of the earliest human factors studies was concerned with the confusion that frequently occurred between the throttle and propeller controls in military aircraft.[7] Nearly 50 percent of the operating errors uncovered in this investigation were actuations of wrong controls. The

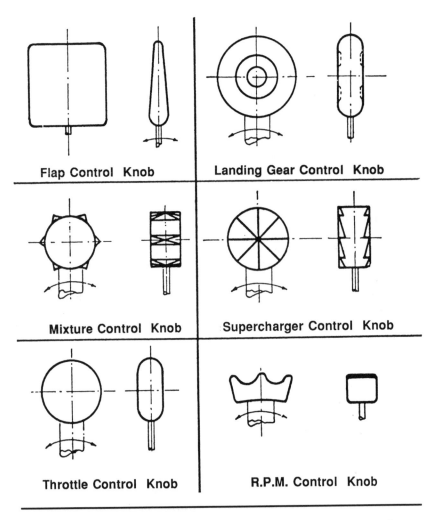

Fig. 4.2 Federal Aviation Administration requirements for cockpit control knobs (14 CFR, Ch. 1, Section 25.781).

most frequent confusions involved the engine controls, the most serious of which were reducing manifold pressure or cutting the fuel mixture shortly after takeoff when the throttles or mixture controls were mistaken for the propeller pitch controls. From Table 4.1 it is easy to see why this occurred.

In addition to this lack of uniformity in spatial arrangement, the controls were typically too close together and difficult to distinguish by

Table 4.1. Control Placements on Three World War II Airplanes

| Aircraft | Control sequence on throttle quadrant | | |
	Left	Center	Right
B-25	Throttle	Propeller	Mixture
C-47	Propeller	Throttle	Mixture
C-82	Mixture	Throttle	Propeller

Source: Adapted from Fitts and Jones (1947).

touch alone. Subsequent research on the design of controls has produced a substantial body of information to guide the designer in producing controls and displays that operate efficiently together. Certain relationships appear far more natural, or at least more typical, than others, such as rotating a knob clockwise to increase the displayed numerals on a radio receiver. However, even this rule is subject to compromise depending on whether the control knob is to the left or right of the number readout.

Designers have to be careful to assure that strong general response tendencies, known as *population stereotypes*, actually hold for the people who will be operating the equipment. A common example is the difference between American and European stereotypes concerning the direction a switch should be moved to turn a light on. This is downward in Europe and Australasia and upward in the United States. Although some color associations are highly stereotypic for most groups (for example, red for danger), even these can have different associations for some groups such as the Chinese, who associate red primarily with good fortune rather than danger.[8]

Many other examples of such relationships can be found. However, from time to time there may be a conflict between two population stereotypes. For example, instrument A shown in Figure 4.3 would be a less desirable arrangement than instrument B. Both can conform to the "clockwise to increase" stereotype, but only instrument B satisfies another seemingly natural stereotype, that the display should move in accordance with the movement of the part of the control nearest to the display. With arrangement A, no matter which way the knob turns to increase the display indication, one stereotype or the other will be violated.

In this example, the two stereotypes lead to opposite expectations of the direction in which the control should move in arrangement A. Of course a pilot can soon learn which will be the case with the instrument in question, but there is always the danger of confusion, and hence instrument B would be the preferred design. Instruments that fail to conform to such stereotypical relationships will be more difficult to operate and, more importantly, will give rise to operating errors, particularly in conditions of stress or fatigue.

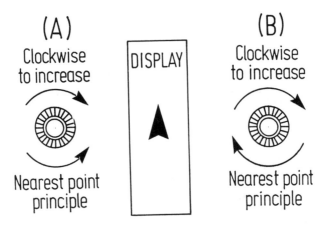

Fig. 4.3 Two population stereotypes are associated with this control-display relationship. According to the "clockwise-to-increase" principle, the control should be turned clockwise to increase the values on the display. In (A) this conflicts with a second stereotype that the indicator should move in the same direction as the nearest point on the control. Both principles lead to the same direction of movement in (B) however.

One of the most important flight instruments is the altimeter. Pilots are required to have a good working knowledge of this instrument and its sources of malfunction. For many years the design of altimeters violated the basic principles of display design. The three-pointer design (see Figure 4.4) was one of the clearest violations of the principle that design should minimize errors in interpretation. Errors in-

MISREAD THE ALTIMETER

A British European Airways Viscount had departed London Heathrow at 8:40 P.M. to collect a group of passengers at Prestwick in Scotland and return to Heathrow. The pilot commenced a descent from 18,500 feet and was cleared to 8,000 feet. Shortly after the report "passing 11,000 feet" the aircraft struck the ground at Tarbolton, Ayrshire. The cause of this controlled-flight-into-terrain accident was that the captain had misread the altimeter's shortest pointer by 10,000 feet, and the copilot had made the same error—or realized they had passed through 8,000 feet and was afraid to speak up![9]

Fig. 4.4 (left) The three-pointer altimeter with the largest hand indicating hundreds of feet, the medium-sized hand indicating thousands of feet, and the smallest hand indicating tens of thousands of feet. This design made it particularly easy to misread the aircraft's altitude by 10,000 feet. The counter-pointer design (right) is clearly superior, providing both a precise digital readout and a rate of change indication.

duced by this design have been responsible for countless accidents, many but not all fatal.

Early experimental investigations of the errors made in reading altimeters of various designs showed clearly that the three-pointer altimeter took longer to read than other designs and led to more errors.[10] It might be thought that a digital presentation of altitude would provide the most accurate and least error-prone method. When a single reading has to be obtained and altitude is not changing rapidly, a digital instrument is fine. The moving-pointer design, however, permits more accurate reading when altitude is changing and provides additional information about the rate of change.

The generally adopted solution is to embed a digital display within a moving-pointer altimeter and remove the third moving hand. This change of design eliminates most of the altimeter reading errors and preserves the advantages of the two forms of presentation. Accidents still occur from missetting the barometric pressure scale, and we will consider some of the factors that most commonly lead to such errors in the next chapter on air-to-ground communication. In the field of cockpit design, even such seemingly innocuous members as windshield posts can have profound consequences.

Windshield design and visibility. As we noted in Chapter 1, visual cues obtained from the external environment and the aircraft's instruments are of paramount importance in flying. It follows that the pilot's view of the instruments and the external view through the cockpit windows should be of optimum design. Although structural requirements may dictate the positioning of certain members, any given design cannot be specified by either optical or structural parameters alone; its acceptability must also take into account the pilot's legal responsibility to see and avoid other aircraft whenever possible.

WINDSHIELD DESIGN RESTRICTED VISIBILITY

> *A Rockwell Commander 560 and a Cessna 182 collided at 2,000 feet and crashed, killing the three occupants of the two aircraft. Both aircraft were operating in visual meteorological conditions in controlled airspace. A cockpit visibility study indicated that during the 45 seconds before the collision the visibility of the C182 was obstructed by the windshield centerpost in the vision envelope of the Rockwell Commander's pilot.*[11]

In a study of judgments of the distortions present in F-111 fighter aircraft windscreens, expert judges were shown to be highly sensitive to the overall optical quality of each windshield.[12] Secondary imaging and "rainbowing," although serious defects, cannot be adequately evaluated by any optical means, and hence quality control depends on expert judgment. Furthermore, any aircraft windshield must represent a compromise between visibility and impact resistance. Some older designs of jet aircraft, such as the Boeing 727 and the DC-9, have severely limited visibility. This was at least one of the contributing factors in the midair collision between a PSA 727 and a Cessna 172 over San Diego, California, in 1978.[13]

The role of cockpit windshield design in obstructing the visiblity of external traffic had been suspect for many years. During the early 1970s the DC-9 was involved in at least four midair collisions in which the otherwise clear visibility of the intruder from the pilot's reference eye position was obstructed by a window post. A fifth occurred over Zagreb, Yugoslavia, in 1976 between a British Airways Trident and an Inex-Adria DC-9.[14] Neither crew took any evasive action although the collision occurred in broad daylight and in clear air, and the two planes were on a stable collision course for almost three minutes. The conspicuity of the Trident was increased by the presence of a 7-mile-long contrail (a condensed vapor trail) that would be visible from 60 kilometers or more!

However, for each pilot, the DC-9 has forward and side windshields separated by posts with a projected width of more than 12 centimeters, almost twice the distance between our eyes. The layout of the DC-9 windshields is shown in Figure 4.5. The effect of the oversized window post, relative to the 6.35-centimeter (2.5-inch) standard of the FAA, is an 11-degree obscuration of binocular vision, sufficient to conceal the Trident and its 7-mile-long contrail from the pilot until the final second before impact. But the problems caused by oversized window posts do not stop there.

In addition to the tendency of the eyes to lapse to their dark focus, objects within the cockpit trap the focus of the eye at a short distance. If pilots were to look directly at a window post, focus would be drawn even closer than the normal dark focus distance. In fact what pilots do when scanning is to look to one side of a post and then the other so that the right eye (as well as the left) can see past the left edge of the post, and similarly the left eye can see past the right edge. This places any intruder (or its contrail) near the post far into the periphery.

The United States court dealing with the subsequent litigation over the collision accepted the evidence that the DC-9 crew's ability to detect the Trident might have been impaired by the design of the windshield. However, the court did not find the design negligent or a proximal cause of the accident because, in the absence of admissible evidence, it had not been proved that the pilot was actually looking through the windshield at all, and therefore the design deficiencies might not have been the cause of the failure to observe the other aircraft!

Transient factors, such as rain on a windscreen, can also create distortions that cause errors in visual perception. Some of the difficulties of night approaches have been referred to in Chapter 1, including the diffusion of light caused by raindrops on a windshield and their focus-trapping potential. In the Pan American Boeing 707 accident at Pago Pago on 30 January 1974, an additional illusory effect was produced by the passage of a severe rainstorm that was moving toward the aircraft as it was descending on final approach.[15]

The effect of the rain cloud would be to obscure the true horizon, and the forward movement of the rainstorm would make it appear as if the horizon were simultaneously moving lower. In the absence of any other indications, this might be interpreted as a pitch-up of the aircraft resulting in a pitch-down response from the pilot. In the Pago Pago incident, the aircraft was rapidly descending at this point in a strong wind shear, and the pilot was unable to arrest the rate of descent before impact with the ground 1,000 meters short of the runway.

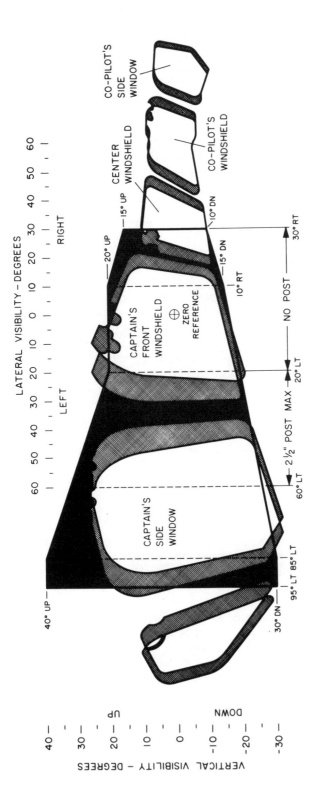

Fig. 4.5 Comparison of actual visibility from the captain's seat on a DC-9 with the standard FAA requirements indicated. Solid dark areas indicate that binocular visibility is obscured; shaded areas indicate additional obscuring of monocular visibility. From S. N. Roscoe and J. C. Hull (1982). *Human Factors, 24, 662.*

Dynamic displays.   The design of dynamic displays representing such things as aircraft attitude and position involves the solution of problems that may be even more complex. Perhaps the most critical of these is the design of aircraft attitude displays. To portray the attitude of the aircraft in relation to the horizon, three motion relationships are possible, as shown in Figure 4.6. In the first, a symbol representing the horizon could be made to rotate against a fixed airplane symbol. One alternative is a fixed background representing the horizon against which the airplane symbol rotates. Less evident perhaps would be to have both symbols move in a "frequency-separated" mode.

Although the fixed airplane and moving horizon arrangement was originally adopted and is still retained, there is considerable evidence that this is the least favorable arrangement. The moving airplane symbol against a fixed background is a greatly superior presentation, and the frequency-separated arrangement is better yet. Experiments with experienced and inexperienced pilots have shown more precise performance with fewer control reversals using the alternative systems.[16] The most serious problem with the moving horizon display is that pilots can mistake the horizon bar for the wings of the airplane and reverse the direction of their aileron control inputs.

For example, a pilot may inadvertently roll into a slight left bank while attending to some cockpit procedure. When the angled horizon bar is noticed, the pilot is likely to make an abrupt control input in the correct direction to level the wings. However, because of the properties

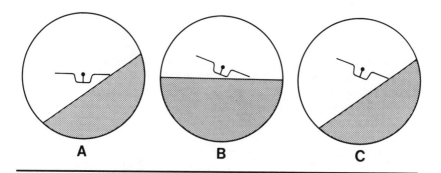

A   **B**   **C**

Fig. 4.6   Three solutions to the problem of representing aircraft attitude are shown. (A) A conventional representation in which the airplane symbol remains fixed and the horizon line rotates counter to the direction of roll. (B) A simple alternative in which the horizon line remains fixed while the aircraft symbol rotates in the direction of roll. (C) A better solution in which both the airplane and horizon move. This is known as a "frequency-separated" presentation in which the airplane symbol moves rapidly in the same direction as control inputs while the horizon line moves more slowly in accordance with aircraft attitude changes.

of the vestibular system (see Chapter 2), the pilot may experience this as a sudden rotation into a turn to the right, abruptly reverse the earlier control input, and roll into a left bank. The steeper the bank, the harder the disoriented pilot will hold the ailerons and rudder in the *same* direction the airplane is rolling. There can be many variations of this scenario.

AIR INDIA BOEING 747 CRASH, 1978

> *The Boeing 747 had departed Bombay for Dubai with 210 persons on board. Shortly after takeoff, at an altitude of just under 1,500 feet, the aircraft rolled into a 14-degree bank to the right. Over the next 13 seconds the aircraft gradually returned to wings-level. Then it continued to roll, slowly, into a 9-degree left bank. At this point the captain made an abrupt left-aileron input, momentarily reversed his input, then went to hard-over left. The pilot held hard left rudder and ailerons until impact with the sea less than 30 seconds later with the aircraft in a 108-degree left bank and the airspeed in excess of 300 knots.*[17]

The moving part. Compatibility of direction of control and display motion has taken on the status of a design principle. It is known as the principle of the moving part; namely, the part of the display that moves in immediate response to a control input should move in the same direction as the control input. The continuing use of the conventional attitude display that violates this principle can perhaps be attributed to the conservatism of the aircraft industry and its reaction to the public readiness to litigate against aircraft manufacturers.

As mentioned previously, there is a third solution to the problem of representing aircraft attitude that combines elements of the moving aircraft and moving horizon presentations. A moving airplane symbol responds immediately to control movements in the same direction as the control input. Rotating the control yoke to the left will cause the aircraft symbol to roll left immediately as the real airplane starts to roll left. The artificial horizon bar rolls more slowly in the opposite direction as the airplane assumes a banked attitude. The advantages and disadvantages of this kind of attitude display were carefully investigated in a series of studies involving both experienced and inexperienced pilots.[18]

One group of inexperienced pilots was tested in a Link GAT-2 simulator and another group in a Beechcraft C-45H. Each subject was tested with the moving airplane display, the conventional moving horizon display, and the combined presentation known as the frequency-separated display. Tracking was more precise, recoveries from unknown attitudes were faster, and there were fewer control reversals with the frequency-separated display than with the conventional moving horizon display. Professional pilots, tested both in the simulator and the Beechcraft, adapted quickly to the modified display. The investigators concluded that the frequency-separated attitude display is ideally suited for all levels of pilot experience.

Although the possibility of a mechanical failure of the attitude indicator cannot be positively ruled out as a cause of the Air India crash, the circumstances of the crash are entirely consistent with the control reversal phenomenon studied in the laboratory and in flight. We noted previously the importance of control-display compatibility and the desirability of having display elements that move in the same direction as the control movement. This principle favors both the moving aircraft and frequency-separated attitude displays over the conventional instrument.

Pictorial integration.   From experience, pilots know that navigating by reference to radio aids that require considerable mental gymnastics is difficult to learn and hard to fly without error. This is because conventional displays do not give the pilot an exact idea of position and the heading to fly to track toward a particular position. The original fixed-card automatic direction finder (ADF) for homing on a ground-based nondirectional beacon (NDB) is a simple device in which a pointer continuously indicates the relative bearing of the NDB. In practical use, the ADF requires additional mental computation to find the heading to fly to the NDB that will offset drift caused by the prevailing wind.

In contrast, map-type navigation displays show the position of the aircraft in direct relation to surrounding radio navigation aids, airways, and airfields. Experiments have shown map displays to yield tremendous improvements in a pilot's ability to maintain geographic orientation, plan complex routes, and control position precisely. Such displays, in conjunction with the global positioning system (GPS) and the microwave landing system (MLS), will allow increased density of traffic without compromising the safety of the overall system. In addition to providing a more realistic picture for the pilot, this kind of display demonstrates another important principle of display design, namely that of display integration.

Pilots navigating with conventional general aviation equipment have to assimilate direction and distance information from a variety of separate radio and gyroscopic aids and combine this with the aircraft's altitude, airspeed, and heading obtained from another set of instruments. Integrated pictorial displays combine information from several sources in a common framework. Such displays are now commonplace in such forms as the Horizontal Situation Indicator (HSI) that eliminates many of the difficulties associated with the presentation of a variety of information in quite different frameworks but still falls short of the integration in map displays.

Although some display principles appear almost self-evident on close acquaintance, it must not be forgotten that early equipment designers did not make use of them. The enormous growth in the number of instruments in the cockpit has made the integration principle one of the most important in current equipment design. The introduction of CRTs has assured the demise of the clockwork cockpit. It provides an opportunity for rethinking display formats and offers new degrees of freedom in their execution.

It is only by a process of systematic experimentation to establish generalizable design principles, testing pilots of varying experience performing a variety of critical flight tasks in simulators and in flight, that one can build a sound body of knowledge on which to base future designs. Such experiments as those involving the presentation of aircraft attitude and navigation information have suggested other, more ingenious principles.

Flight path prediction.　Most conventional flight displays provide the pilot only with information about the current discrepancy between the aircraft's position and where it ought to be. For example, the deflection of the ILS crosspointer bars tells the pilot that the airplane is above or below and to the left or right of the glidepath and localizer beams. Predictive displays, on the other hand, show the pilot the future effects of present control inputs. Such predictive displays will be vital to the effective use of the new microwave landing system (MLS) that will supercede the ILS by the 1990s. Figure 4.7 shows an example of a predictive MLS display.

The predicted descent path is shown by the series of aircraft symbols and the perspective view of the runway. In one experiment professional pilots flew simulated approaches in a Link GAT-2 simulator with computer-animated CRT presentations.[19] Pilots were able to fly a variety of predictive displays with high accuracy even under simulated conditions of severe wind shear. These experiments demonstrate that precise manual flight path control on curved MLS approaches under adverse flying conditions is possible but only if unconventional display systems are used.

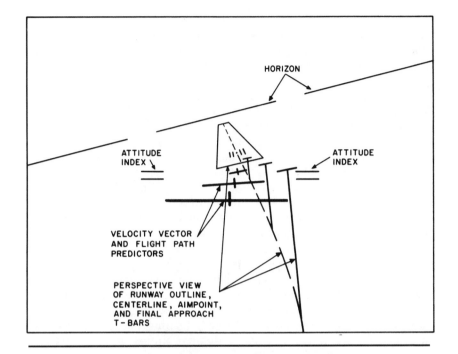

HORIZON

ATTITUDE
INDEX

ATTITUDE
INDEX

VELOCITY VECTOR
AND FLIGHT PATH
PREDICTORS

PERSPECTIVE VIEW
OF RUNWAY OUTLINE,
CENTERLINE, AIMPOINT,
AND FINAL APPROACH
T - BARS

Fig. 4.7 An example of a predictive display that might be used in conjunction with the microwave landing system (MLS). The airplane is to the left and slightly above the localizer and glidepath T-bars and descending. These kinds of predictor displays are needed if the curved, decelerating approaches made possible by MLS are to be flown accurately and safely. From *Aviation Psychology* by S. N. Roscoe. Copyright 1980 by Iowa State University Press.

The predictive contact analog display shown in Figure 4.7 is similar to those used in the MLS landing experiment but calls for a straight-in rather than a curved approach. The display embodies all of the principles referred to in this section and demonstrates the dramatic improvements that can be made. Another display that affords an opportunity to apply the principles of display integration, pictorial realism, flight path prediction, and frequency separation is the cockpit display of traffic information described in the next section.

Cockpit display of traffic information. An important application of new technology to appear on flight decks of the future is the cockpit display of traffic information (CDTI). The form this finally takes will depend on research studies of pilots' responses to the various possible kinds of displays. As we will see, the design principles applicable to other dynamic displays will also have an impact on the CDTI. Without expert attention to human factors, the introduction of such technology could induce new pilot and controller errors of its own and thus diminish rather than improve the safety of the air traffic system.

There are also, for example, important considerations concerning the transfer of responsibility for traffic separation and collision avoidance from ground-based controllers to flight crews. On the whole though, the evidence tends to favor such steps as improvements to flight safety. In a similar vein, the introduction of the ground proximity warning system (GPWS) has significantly reduced the number of inadvertent collisions with the ground, despite problems with false alarms. During the five years preceding its introduction in 1975–76, there were 17 controlled-flight-into-terrain accidents involving U.S. air carriers; during the following five years there were only 2.[20]

One generalization demonstrated by the design of the CDTI is that the involvement of the user (the pilot) in experiments during the early stages of design can help ensure that the goals of the system and the capabilities and limitations of the user are compatible. The computer industry was slow to learn this lesson, unleashing machines on the general public that required appreciable technical know-how to operate successfully. In this highly competitive industry, designers have developed powerful new ways of presenting and manipulating information through the use of icons—pictorial symbols that represent commonly used functions.

Instead of forcing people to think in computer terms, such efforts adapt the technology to existing human stereotypes and thought processes. Such criteria have been applied from the early stages of development of the CDTI. It is important, however, to treat expressed preferences for various kinds of display symbols and formats with caution. A well-established finding in psychology is that judges overestimate the number of cues that they are actually using in making their judgments. There may be a tendency, therefore, to express a preference for more complex displays than are optimum.

A group of 23 airline pilots was briefed on the concept of CDTI and asked to respond to a large sample of possible displays with various alternative methods of representing terrain, weather, and local traffic.[21] A variety of different symbols for own and other aircraft was included. Recognizing that pilots' opinions concerning new displays depend greatly on their prior use of older displays and that their assessments can shift dramatically with experience using new displays, the investigators nevertheless found reasonable consistency among these pilots on the following recommendations:

• Primary navigation aids and airports should be displayed symbolically.

- A digital display of own track, speed, and map scale should be included.
- Significant terrain features should be displayed with labeled heights.
- Weather display should not be included.
- A chevron symbol is preferred for own aircraft.
- Some information about other aircraft in the vicinity, in the form of digital data tags, should be available on command.

A variety of experiments were then undertaken in which airline pilots viewed CDTI displays based on these preferred characteristics. These were simple simulations of the CDTI display in which the pilots viewed sample displays depicting encounters with another aircraft approaching either 33 knots faster or slower than own aircraft and on different angles between courses. Different kinds of predictors were assessed. The most useful was a curved predictor that plots the future flight paths of own and other aircraft in the next 30 to 60 seconds. An example of a CDTI display is shown in Figure 4.8.

It was found that pilots have the most difficulty in assessing the likelihood that two aircraft are on a collision course when the two flight paths are curved and when the other aircraft is approaching from a large relative bearing. The addition of a predicted flight path based on each aircraft's current rate of turn was a significant aid to performance.[22] It was observed that pilots show a strong tendency to turn toward the conflicting traffic (except when collision danger is thought to be high) and to execute maneuvers in the horizontal rather than the vertical plane.[23]

Both tendencies may be design induced in that the display emphasizes the horizontal layout of traffic rather than vertical separation. To support this point, pilots' avoidance maneuvers were compared between a plan-view display and a perspective display in which vertical separation was also represented.[24] The perspective display had a pronounced impact on the use of vertical avoidance maneuvers. In addition to executing more vertical maneuvers (climbs and descents), the pilots decided on a maneuver faster with the perspective display. These design induced differences are of concern in the introduction of the Traffic-Alert and Collision Avoidance System (TCAS).

Other factors to be considered include previous visual flying experience in which turning toward other traffic has the advantage of keeping the intruder in sight for a longer period. There may also be a population stereotype of the kind discussed in relation to control movement and display presentation. In one study, nonpilots showed a consistent tendency to turn left to avoid a head-on collision.[25] More surprisingly, one American pilot in four also turned left in contravention of the FAA regulation requiring a right turn in such situations.

The suggestion is that the apparently more stereotypical left turn-

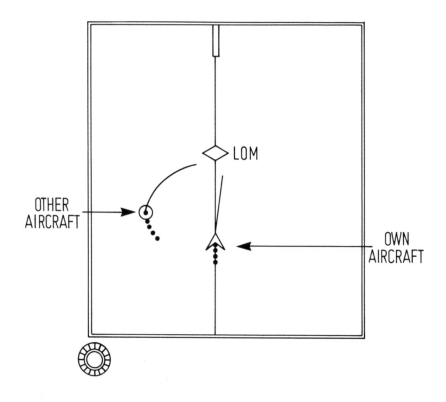

Fig. 4.8 A sample cockpit display of traffic information (CDTI). The addition
of flightpath predictors, as shown here, significantly increases the speed and
accuracy of most responses. The four dots behind each symbol represent the
distance traveled during the preceding 16 seconds. A curved predictor path is
displayed for the other aircraft (circular symbol) and a straight predictor for
own aircraft (chevron symbol). From S. G. Hart and L. L. Loomis (1980).
Human Factors, 22, 598.

ing tendency may appear in some situations despite the pilots' knowledge of the regulation. It is obviously important that pilot behavior
with systems such as CDTI and TCAS be studied carefully before they
become standard operational equipment on flight decks. In contrast
with World War II equipment design, there has been some progress in
incorporating a human factors perspective in the original design of
equipment. Such a perspective is more critical than ever with the increasing tendency to automate the flight deck.

FLIGHTDECK AUTOMATION

The impact of technological advances in aircraft design can be most clearly seen in the gradual reduction in the number of crew members needed to operate passenger jets. The introduction of extremely precise inertial navigation systems that direct the aircraft over a predetermined course rendered the position of flight navigator totally redundant. Advanced automation has so reduced flightdeck workload that two rather than three pilots are used to operate the Boeing 747 in its latest version. Significantly it has also changed the nature of that workload.

Rather than eliminating the need for human factors considerations to be taken into account, advanced automation changes the nature of the questions that need to be asked and answered. If the flight crew is to remain effectively "in the loop" as part of the system, then it follows that the interface between pilots and computers is crucial in keeping the pilots informed of the operation of the system and, conversely, keeping the computers informed of the condition and behavior of the pilots. The sophistication of modern avionics requires considerable ingenuity to ensure that pilot workload and opportunity for error are not actually increased by the new systems.[26]

Important issues are raised by the complex question of automating flightdeck functions. Automation itself is by no means new. Autopilots were introduced before World War II and are now commonly found on most classes of aircraft. The autopilot provides a good example of the fact that, even though automation exists, the pilot may in fact choose not to use it. The reasons for this may include such things as the wish to spare the passengers a rough ride in air turbulence or possibly a preference to exercise manual control to maintain skill, particularly during the approach and landing phase of flight.

This simple example raises issues that need to be addressed as technological developments make it possible to automate practically every aspect of a flight. At first sight a majority of aircraft accidents involve some element of pilot error. In many cases information was available to the crew that could have been used to avert the accident but was ignored or misinterpreted. As we have already seen, many incidents were induced by such design defects as haphazard control layout, displays that violate population stereotypes, and oversized window posts.

These accidents may be correctly regarded as design induced, and this topic will be discussed further in Chapter 7. Nevertheless, a major goal of automation has been to reduce the opportunity for human error by automatically monitoring the pilot's management of aircraft systems and flight control and providing a warning to the pilot in the event of an apparent failure or hazardous state. Horns indicating gear up with reduced power, stall warning buzzers, and stick shakers are early and relatively simple examples of automated monitoring of the pilot's actions and inactions.

A second goal of automation has been to optimize flight performance and manage fuel consumption. Continuously monitored and computer-calculated throttle settings and flight paths can achieve significant fuel savings that are passed on as greater profit margins and, in some cases, lower fares. Thus major advances in automation have already been introduced in current airliners. However, there are unanswered questions concerning further applications of flightdeck automation. These can be divided into two categories.

The first, which has received primary consideration by human factors engineers and the aviation community, deals with immediate human-machine interactions.[27] What happens in the event of computer failure, for example? What mechanisms can be devised to ensure that only correct information is entered into the flightdeck instrumentation? The second group of questions deals with the longer-range human consequences of high levels of automation. If the pilot becomes an inactive systems monitor instead of a direct controller, will this result in an unacceptable decline in manual skills? Will the pilot become increasingly bored and underloaded and possibly less effective in an emergency?

Because of the relatively low failure rate of automated systems, the human controller may be inadequately prepared to deal with the automatic system when failures do occur. This has been found experimentally in investigations of the ability of professional marine engineering officers to cope with failures in a high-fidelity supertanker engine-control-room simulator.[28] A substantial proportion of the observed errors were attributable to a lack of knowledge of the basic system and the automatic controllers. Further effects on the ability of operators who are monitoring rather than actively controlling the system will now be considered.

The sequence of errors that came close to precipitating disaster at the Three Mile Island nuclear reactor in Pennsylvania in 1979 highlighted the design and use of warning devices in highly complex operator-controlled systems. It seems regrettably apparent that human factors considerations had been relegated to a very low priority by the designers of nuclear power plants, with the result that operators confronted with an undiagnosed equipment failure have to deal with bits of information from literally hundreds of sources.[29] It was a failure to diagnose the underlying problem that brought the Three Mile Island reactor critically close to a meltdown.

Warning systems: Lights that glare and horns that blare.
The proliferation of warning devices on the modern flight deck raises design questions similar to those discussed in relation to other controls and displays. Although the aircraft industry has given human factors considerations a much higher priority than have the nuclear power plant designers, there are still areas of concern.[30] One is the problem of false alarms in warning devices. There are insufficient data for an accurate estimate of the prevalence of false alarms in flight warning instruments, but an impression may be obtained from Table 4.2—a list of false alarms obtained from a single issue of a major airline's flight safety review.[31]

Table 4.2.   Sample of False Alarms Noted in a One-month Period of One Airline's Operation

Aircraft	Type of false alarm	Number of reports
Boeing 747	Fire warning	1
Boeing 747	Stall warning	1
Tristar	GPWS/overshoot	3
Boeing 757	GPWS/overshoot	4
Boeing 737	GPWS/overshoot	1
Boeing 737	GPWS/in cruise	1
BAC 1-11	GPWS/in cruise	1

Source: Adapted from "False Alarms," *British Airways Flight Safety Review* (November 1984).

From another source, one first officer claimed that 20 percent of his movements in the cockpit dealt with "inhibiting lights that glare or horns that blare."[32] The unacceptably high rate of false alarms was one of the original causes of flight crew disenchantment with the ground proximity warning system. Too high a ratio of false alarms can, of course, lead to crew complacency and a failure to respond to a genuine signal—the "cry wolf" phenomenon.

From a human factors point of view, it is clear that the GPWS has been admirably designed in certain respects. The synthesized voice signal is easily detectable and highly prioritized—that is, it should command the pilot's attention ahead of the usual array of warning lights and tones. Under conditions of stress or distraction, however, this may still be insufficient to mobilize the appropriate response. In the case of Eastern Flight 212, there were considerable distractions in the form of a heated exchange of views on various topics occurring within the cockpit, and the existence of a low, patchy fogbank beneath the aircraft's flight path partially obscuring the runway.

EASTERN DC-9 CRASH, NORTH CAROLINA

> On 11 September 1974, Eastern Airlines Flight 212 crashed 3.3
> miles short of the runway at Charlotte, North Carolina. The air-
> craft had prematurely descended through an altitude of 1,800 feet
> before reaching the final approach fix. The terrain proximity
> warning sounded in the cockpit signifying that the aircraft was
> 1,000 feet from the ground. Evidently the crew was not so alerted,
> because the descent continued. "It appears that the crew's disre-
> gard of the terrain warning signal in this instance may be indica-
> tive of the attitudes of many other pilots who regard the signal as
> more of a nuisance than a warning. If this is indeed the case, the
> Board believes that airline pilots should re-examine their atti-
> tudes toward the terrain warning alert."[33]

Auditory warnings can also be too loud.[34] A loud, insistent warning can impede cockpit communication, and dealing with the warning
can be given higher priority than tackling the indicated fault. The U.K.
CAA has developed guidelines for the design of auditory warning systems.[35] These recommend no more than six different warning sounds.
A warning should begin at a clearly audible level and then be repeated
as a background reminder. If the fault is not rectified, the signal returns to its original level. Pitch and pulse rates should indicate levels
of urgency, with rising pitch and increasing pulse rate indicating increasingly urgent conditions.

Although the introduction of the ground proximity warning system has been accompanied by a large reduction in controlled-flight-
into-terrain accidents, the effect of another warning device—the altitude alert system—is questionable as originally implemented. The
altitude alert system simply provides an aural or visual warning when
a set altitude is not maintained. Because of the proliferation of warning
systems in the cockpit, the signal is sometimes simply not detected,
particularly when some additional distraction, such as new ATC instructions, is present. Another source of error lies in missetting the
desired altitude in the first place.

The increasing use of keyboard data entry for navigational systems has raised the possibility of errors arising from incorrect entry of
coordinates. Missetting the barometric altimeter has always been one
source of accidents, and missetting the altitude alert system is likewise
easy to do. The operation of the crew self-monitoring system is, of

course, designed to detect and prevent any such errors. The fact that most failures of the altitude alerting system are first detected by controllers rather than the pilots suggests that crew monitoring may not be operating as effectively as it might be in this area.

AVIATION SAFETY REPORTING SYSTEM

> *Much information on errors and incidents in the U.S. aviation system comes from a confidential, anonymous reporting scheme known as the Aviation Safety Reporting System (ASRS). The program has been administered by NASA since August 1975. The aim of ASRS is to encourage the reporting of safety-related incidents without fear of recrimination. By July 1979 more than 17,000 such reports had been submitted. To disseminate this information, a news sheet entitled* Callback *was initiated. In its ninth year of publication it had a circulation of 45,000, and the ASRS had received more than 70,000 reports.*

The most commonly reported hazardous events are altitude deviations. Nearly half the reports submitted to ASRS are concerned with this problem. One of the long-term dangers of increased automation— that of overreliance on the automated system—has been well illustrated by the history of the altitude alerting system. In fact, a reasonable case can be made that pilots' altitude awareness "has been adversely affected by the altitude alert system."[36] The effect of complacency in the operation of automated systems is further illustrated in the following section.

Human-machine interactions.   A list of some as yet unanswered questions is shown in Table 4.3. The key problem is how to divest the pilot of monitoring and controlling functions without compromising safety in unusual or unforeseen circumstances. Although automated systems can monitor a large number of system variables better than a pilot can, there has been relatively little success in producing automated decision making for unpredictable events. One danger has been ever-present since autopilots have been routinely used. Because autopilots have proved extremely reliable, pilots tend to become complacent and fail to monitor them.

Table 4.3. **Some Problem Areas in Human-machine Interaction and Flightdeck Automation**

Category	Sample questions
Equipment design	What safeguards should there be against inadvertent activation or deactivation of systems?
	How should the pilot monitor the state of the system?
	How much knowledge should the pilot have of the system?
	Should the system automatically correct errors without notifying the pilot?
	When should the system be manually overridden?
	How will unforeseen circumstances be dealt with?
	How can entry errors, such as missetting waypoints in a navigational computer, be averted?
False alarms	What principles should be applied in providing alarm-validity checks?
	Should a computer determine the priority of alarms?
	Why are alarms sometimes ignored (the "cry wolf" phenomenon)?
Failure to monitor	How can overreliance on automatic systems be prevented?
Flexibility	How much modification of the system should be possible in flight?

Source: Adapted from Boehm-Davis et al. (1983).

DESCENT INTO THE SWAMP

> *On 29 December 1972, an Eastern Airlines L-1011 Tristar overshot Miami airport following an indication that the landing gear had failed to extend satisfactorily. The crew became entirely preoccupied with checking the nose gear and the warning instrumentation. At some point the autopilot disengaged and the aircraft descended into the Everglades 19 miles WNW of the airport. The probable cause of this accident was the failure of the flight crew to monitor the flight instruments during the final four minutes of flight.*[37]

Lest it be thought that this well-publicized accident was an isolated example, the NTSB report of an accident involving a runway overrun by a Scandinavian Airlines System DC-10 at New York's JFK International Airport in 1984 also cited overreliance on an automated system as a contributory cause.[38] In this case, it was the crew's reliance on an unreliable autothrottle speed-control system that contributed to the accident. Perhaps the most extreme example of unwarranted faith in automated systems comes from this example reported in the ASRS *Callback:*

Log entry from pilot: Autoland carried out. Aircraft landed firmly and left of centerline. Most unsatisfactory.

Engineer's entry: Autoland not fitted to this aircraft.

Monitoring versus controlling.   Skills such as flying an airplane or riding a bicycle are continuous processes involving manual input, control-element output, and vehicle-response feedback. For example, a pilot initiates some movement of the aircraft's controls that changes the state of the aircraft in some way. Information about this change may be perceived directly or interpreted through the aircraft's instruments. The pilot uses this feedback to stop or continue the control movement. Such a system is referred to as a *closed-loop system* because there is a continuous process of action, feedback, comparison, and further action.

The involvement of the pilot in such a system is frequently referred to as being "in the loop." Far from being a passive observer or monitor, the pilot is playing an active role in the control of the system. Although a simple system, such as a central heating thermostat, can be thought of as having a single loop, most *closed-loop systems* have a hierarchy of loops, with a general planning and directing loop at the highest level and the direct manipulation of the aircraft's control elements at the lowest level. This is illustrated in Figure 4.9.

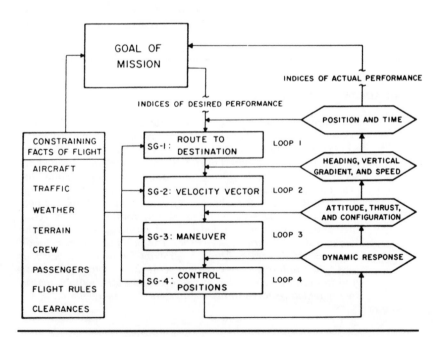

Fig. 4.9 A schematic representation of the hierarchy of loops in goal-directed aircraft guidance and control. From *Aviation Psychology* by S. N. Roscoe. Copyright 1980 by Iowa State University Press.

With automation it has become routine to remove the pilot from the lowest loop during most parts of the flight. The autopilot may be engaged for nearly all of the flight, removing the pilot from direct control. Psychologists at the University of Illinois have shown that the active controller who is fully in the loop is able to detect changes and errors in the system considerably faster than an inactive controller or monitor.[39] However, in another study involving 15 airline pilots in a Boeing heavy-jet simulator, performance at detecting gradual errors in pitch and heading was better for those who were simply monitoring the system than for those who flew a fully manual approach.[40]

In conclusion, there appears to be no simple answer to the question of the optimum distribution of control functions among crew members and automatic devices. A balance must be struck between the importance of detecting particular kinds of failures and the additional workload imposed by being more fully involved in the loop. In the operation of an aircraft, it is generally of more importance to detect and correctly diagnose navigational errors and system malfunctions than small disturbances of the flight control system. The consequences of being out of the flight control loop can, however, be extremely alarming.

In an admirable attempt to go beyond the finding that the captain lost control of the aircraft, the NTSB considered in some detail the human performance aspects of a China Airlines mishap.[41] Among the topics discussed were the disorientation of the crew and the effects of circadian rhythms on performance. Of particular relevance, however,

---

CHINA AIRLINES BOEING 747SP INCIDENT

The China Airlines flight from Taipei was over the Pacific about 300 nautical miles northwest of San Francisco at an altitude of 41,000 feet. Following a loss of power from one of the engines, the aircraft rolled right, nosed over, and entered an uncontrolled descent through clouds during which the aircrew became disoriented. The captain eventually regained control of the aircraft at a height of 9,500 feet above sea level. Only two of the 274 people on board were seriously injured, but damage to the aircraft included complete separation of large outboard sections of the horizontal stabilizers and elevators. The National Transportation Safety Board determined that the probable cause of this accident was "the captain's preoccupation with an inflight malfunction and his failure to monitor properly the airplane's flight instruments which resulted in his losing control of the airplane."[42]

---

was the delay that occurred in switching from the role of passive monitor to entering the flight control loop by disconnecting the autopilot.
There was a gap of almost four minutes from the failure of the No. 4
engine to the autopilot disconnect.

The experimental results of the Illinois study described earlier
would suggest that it might take a pilot using the autopilot up to five
times as long as a pilot already in the loop to diagnose an error correctly (in this case, an unusual bank attitude). Such estimates should
be regarded as highly speculative at this stage, because there has been
little experimental work on monitoring tasks that are accurately representative of flight tasks. In addition to these direct issues of human-
machine interaction, there is a second category of psychological problems that may be of equal or greater importance in the long run.

Psychosocial effects of automation. It is becoming increasingly clear that psychosocial factors have an important influence on
the operation of flight crews. We will look at this topic in detail in
Chapter 8. The introduction of highly automated systems may have
important consequences for the selection, training, status, and job
satisfaction of flight crews. Table 4.4 outlines a sample of questions
relating to these issues.

The highly automated flight deck calls for a quite different approach to flying than that associated with the traditional image of the
ideal pilot as portrayed in *The Right Stuff,* Tom Wolfe's account of the

Table 4.4. Some Problem Areas in the Psychosocial Effects of Flight-deck Automation

Category	Sample questions
Manual skills	How rapidly will manual flying skills deteriorate with dis-use?
	What training procedures will be required to cope with skill decay and facilitate transfer between aircraft with different degrees and kinds of automation?
Job status and satisfaction	Will the loss of direct control adversely affect satisfaction?
	Will the pilot become dangerously detached from the outside world?
	Will crews be understimulated, bored, and less able to react quickly in an emergency?
Selection and training	How should pilot selection criteria be modified to identify individuals best able to manage automated airplanes?
	Will pilots prefer to remain on older, less automated types rather than upgrade to automatic systems?
	Should pilots be trained in computer technology and programming?
Crew coordination	How should the automatic system be included in the crew-loop system of issuing callouts and challenges?

Source: Adapted from Boehm-Davis et al. (1983).

first U.S. astronaut program.[43] The reaction of these military test pilots to the totally automated Gemini capsule they were to ride into orbit was most unenthusiastic. As a result, various manual controls were added to the system to give these fliers something to fly. There may be increasing problems in upgrading pilots trained on traditional aircraft to the increasingly automated airline flight decks.

Selection may need to be oriented to those skills and abilities that are involved in operating complex computer systems rather than the high standard of psychomotor skills currently emphasized. All these suggest a fairly substantial change in the status and image of the professional pilot. This raises questions of legal liability of the pilot-as-monitor rather than the pilot-as-controller. However, the naval terminology of "captain" of a ship may be even more appropriate to this monitoring role.

Another more speculative possibility is that the substitution of automatic, increasingly abstract methods of control for direct, dynamic actions may have the effect of psychologically distancing operators from the results of their actions. This may be reflected in the use of the terms "Pacman" and "Atari" to refer to the CRT instruments in the modern "glass cockpit." Designers of weapon systems, of course, capitalize on this and allow an individual who would be incapable of inflicting direct personal violence to unleash enormous destruction at the push of a button.

It has even been suggested that a possible hazard of flightdeck automation may be that "the perception of the total environment will shrink to that of the cockpit, and in particular, to that of the display and keyboard interface."[44] It seems ironic that the increasing fidelity and use of simulators in training may actually be contributing to a loss of psychological contact with the real world on the flight deck.

All the questions raised so far deal with potential consequences of automation that need to be considered as the technology becomes more widely adopted. Aviation has been highly adaptable and flexible in the past to changes in technology. Sometimes the adaptation and learning have been in the nature of trial-and-error. With the costs in lives and dollars that can accompany errors, adapting to automation should be based on careful analysis and experimental evaluation of the questions in the safety and economy of flight simulation.

The future: The intelligent cockpit?   Much of the concern in automation to date has been with the question of which of the pilot's functions to automate and which to leave under manual control. By and large, the answer has been to automate the functions in the lower levels of the loop and to leave the planning, procedural, and decision-making activities under direct, unaided control. This has generally made good sense in that repetitive and rapid responses can easily be handled by automatic equipment, whereas higher-level skills are assumed to require a degree of knowledge and flexibility that only humans possess.

Since the late 1960s, enormous advances have taken place in the field of artificial intelligence and particularly in the practical implementation of this understanding in expert systems. This has entailed a rethinking of the simple division of human-machine capabilities. The extension of computerized intelligence to the cockpit is already underway, and the issue of automation has become a complex question of deciding whether planning and decision making can be enhanced by computer aiding rather than by completely computerized execution, as typified by the somewhat unreliable HAL of Arthur C. Clarke's *2001.*

Computer aiding can complement the human decision maker's skills by providing immediate access to information about the present and future states of the system. A simple example in flight management is a computer-based system for processing and displaying procedural information.[45] The system replaces written checklists that are normally carried on the flight deck. Input to the computer is provided by readings of aircraft instrument indications and by a keyboard for use by the crew. The computer can infer that a particular procedure has been completed or that the crew intends to branch to some other procedure.

A procedure could be displayed as in Figure 4.10. The completion of a particular action, such as switching off the fuel pump or raising the landing gear, would be marked by the automatic dimming of that line on the display. The system thus provides a check of actions already completed, a particularly important feature when a procedure must be interrupted to attend to a subsidiary procedure before returning again to the main procedure. This computer-aided system substantially reduced the number of unnecessary steps in aircraft systems management.

Computer aiding has been extended to the difficult functions of alerting and warning. Research on the F-18 fighter aircraft identified a number of deficiencies in the cockpit alerting system.[46] Traditional systems provide a fixed indication for a given condition regardless of the contingent circumstances. A computer-aided system can prioritize the indication according to circumstances. For example, if the aircraft canopy is unlocked but the engines are at idle, a low-level advisory is sufficient. An unlocked canopy with engines above 90 percent RPM would warrant a high-priority warning.

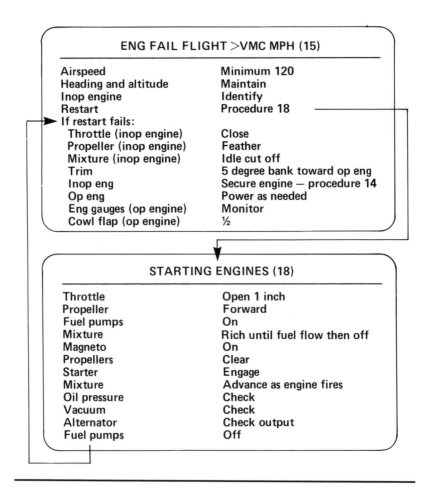

Fig. 4.10 An example of computer aiding in an engine-failure procedure. The computer-based information system keeps track of the status of the current procedure and, at step four, would display procedure 18 before returning to the original procedure at step five. The decision to branch to the new procedure would be indicated via the keyboard, but return to the appropriate step of the original procedure would be automatic. Adapted from S. H. Rouse, W. B. Rouse, and J. M. Hammer (1982). *IEEE Transactions on Systems, Man, and Cybernetics, SMC-12,* 455.

FURTHER READING

A useful introduction to human factors in system design is provided by C. D. Wickens in *Engineering Psychology and Human Performance* (Columbus, OH: Charles E. Merrill, 1984). A collection of papers on the design of displays and controls in the aviation context is presented by S. N. Roscoe in *Aviation Psychology* (Ames: Iowa State University Press, 1980). More general coverage of the human factors approach to design is offered by M. S. Sanders and E. J. McCormick in *Human Factors in Engineering and Design,* 6th ed. (New York: Mc-Graw-Hill, 1986) and most recently by J. A. Adams in *Human Factors Engineering* (New York: Macmillan, 1989).

Performance Factors

[5] Navigation and Communication

HE GLANCED at his altimeter: 1,700 metres. He pressed the palms of his hands against the controls to lose height. The engine throbbed wildly and the plane began to tremble. Fabien corrected the angle of descent, then looked at the map to check the height of the hills beneath him. 500 metres. To keep a safe margin he would fly at 700. He was sacrificing his altitude as one stakes a fortune.

ANTOINE DE SAINT-EXUPÉRY, *Night Flight*

INTRODUCTION

In comparison with certain animal species that are able to navigate over vast distances with unfailing accuracy, the human sense of geographical orientation is not well developed. Some individuals claim to have a much better sense of direction than others. Such people do, in fact, perform the task of pointing toward hidden locations more accurately than people whose self-proclaimed abilities are low.[1] Those individuals with a good sense of direction evidently are also slightly quicker at learning orientations in an unfamiliar environment. There seems to be no superiority, however, in pointing to compass north.

Although a good general sense of one's immediate environment is undoubtedly useful, it would be folly to travel in strange territory without some external aid such as a map or chart. The oldest recorded maps are those used by the Babylonians, dated at 2300 B.C. Maps come in just about every shape, size, and form but have the common defining characteristic of providing a symbolic representation of certain features of the world. Some characteristics have become conventions, the most common being the direction of north at the top of the map. (Another common convention has been to base world maps on a Eurocentric viewpoint. This is frustrating to some southern-hemisphere dwellers, who find themselves apparently falling off the lower right-hand edge of the world!)

More specialized maps and charts, of course, follow different conventions. Nautical and aviation charts require special knowledge of these conventions for their interpretation. Investigations of how people learn to use maps have shown that there are noticeable differences between good learners and poor learners.[2] Surprisingly, even very experienced users may be quite poor at learning new material. The difference between the two groups seems to lie in the use of particular strategies, with good learners adopting a much more systematic approach.

Dividing the map or chart into sections and then systematically focusing on the elements within each section was found to be the most effective strategy. The good learners proved to be much better at solving spatial relationships than the poor learners. One pilot was better at remembering the spatial arrangement of features on the map than at remembering the verbal attributes. In contrast, all the other subjects found it easier to remember the verbal attributes. This in turn seems to be related to visual memory ability. Evidently, people with better visual memory learn more rapidly to use the effective strategies to memorize spatial information.

Individuals seem to vary substantially in their abilities to perform tasks requiring the visualization of spatial relations. In a typical test, subjects have to judge which of five two-dimensional drawings matches a comparison figure. The five stimuli include one correct match obtained by rotating the comparison figure along with four mismatches created by rotating and reversing the original figure. Because performance of such a task seems to bear a strong resemblance to judgments called for in flying and navigating an aircraft, such tests have often been incorporated in aircrew selection procedures (e.g., the Royal New Zealand Air Force's space perception test).

Rapid advances in technology of the kind described in the previous chapter have rendered basic map reading virtually obsolete for the professional civil or military pilot. The vast majority of private pilots, however, are licensed to fly solely in visual meteorological conditions where navigation by reference to a topographical map remains the prime means of determining one's position. The same approach of human factors design that was described in connection with the design of cockpit systems and flight displays in the previous chapter can also be applied to the design of aeronautical maps and charts.

ERGONOMICS AND MAP DESIGN

CONTROLLED-FLIGHT-INTO-TERRAIN

> A TWA Boeing 727 crashed about 25 nautical miles northwest of
> Dulles Airport at Berryville, Virginia. The accident to Flight 514
> occurred while the airplane was descending in instrument mete-
> orological conditions. The NTSB said, "The probable cause of the
> accident was the crew's decision to descend to 1,800 feet before
> the aircraft had reached the approach segment where that mini-
> mum altitude applied. It does appear to the Board that there was
> a deficiency in the approach chart. The profile view did not depict
> the intermediate fix with its associated minimum altitudes. This
> information was available from the plan view of the chart, but it
> appears that the crew gave their primary attention to the pro-
> file."[3]

As with most accidents, the rule of multiple causation applies to
the crash of TWA Flight 514. The report clearly implicates a number of
factors including confusion and misinterpretation of ATC terminology
as contributory causes of this accident. Nevertheless, it is obviously
vital that maps and charts used in aviation be designed in such a
manner that the information required by the pilot is available in precise and unambiguous form. This is the same requirement as that
demanded for other forms of visual display described in Chapter 4.

Unfortunately, many of the design rules used in producing visual
displays have been found to have limited applicability to map design
for the aviation user. Furthermore, pilots have had to put up with
maps designed for multiple purposes with only secondary thought for
the particular needs of aviation. For example, charts used for visual
flight are often simply standard topographical maps overprinted with
additional aeronautical information (see Figure 5.1). It can be difficult
to locate vital information among the visual clutter of topographical
charts.

In the case of a Lear 24B that collided with a mountain 24 nautical
miles from the airport (see Chapter 8 for a description of the accident),
a critical warning was conveyed through the *absence* of a symbol on
the chart.

> The only notification that Palm Springs is a nonradar airport is
> the absence of an (R) immediately following the approach control
> frequency on the chart or airport plate. If the absence of an (R) as a

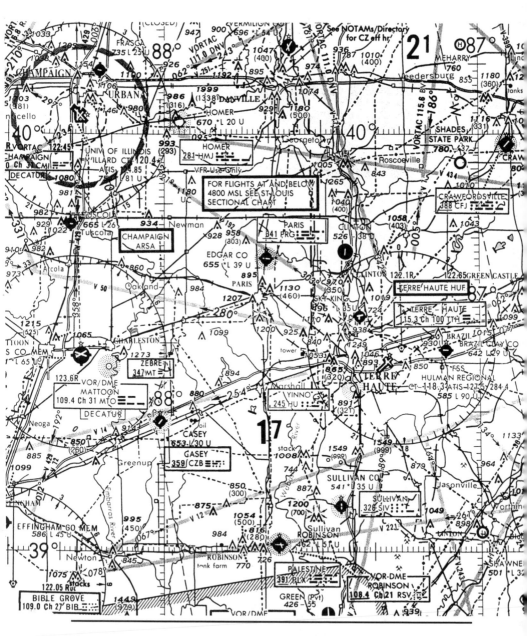

Fig. 5.1 Detail of a World Aeronautical Chart (WAC chart) used for visual flight. Aeronautical symbols and airspace information are overlaid on topographic data. This is from one of 12 at 1:1,000,000 scale covering the contiguous 48 United States. Published by the National Oceanic and Atmospheric Administration, Washington, DC.

warning device to alert pilots that something which they have come
to expect and take advantage of (radar coverage) does not exist is
evaluated, then this warning device would fail to meet accepted
safety standards. It would fail from the standpoint of a safety and
human factors engineering analysis. It would probably fail in a
court of law were a jury to deliberate over the question of the adequacy of that as a warning or alerting device.[4]

Most of the research on aviation map design has been driven by
the needs of the military, particularly with the emphasis on low-level
flight by high-speed combat aircraft. An important consideration is the
ease with which surface features, such as an airfield, forest, or lake,
can be located. Detailed topographical maps, such as the Ordnance
Survey maps used in the United Kingdom, contain large amounts of
information including place names, roads, railways, relief features,
and conventional symbols representing church spires, water towers,
and so on.

As explained in Chapter 1, the eye is so constructed that only light
focused on the central area known as the fovea is resolved in clear
detail. Nevertheless we are aware of what is going on elsewhere in the
visual field, particularly of movement. Although most of the available
light reaching the eye falls on the rods in the periphery, the relative
visual acuity of the eye declines sharply with increasing distance from
the fovea. At only 20 degrees out from the fovea, relative visual acuity
is only about 10 percent of foveal acuity. The map or chart designer
must therefore cater to two quite distinct aspects of visual information
processing.

The first aspect concerns the detection of information that falls
within the relatively narrow cone of foveal vision. There is considerable evidence that color coding of targets is particularly effective in
producing faster and more accurate search of a map.[5] The ability to
identify a target of a particular color is several hundred percent better
than for one of a particular size or shape, and search time is approximately 40 percent to 60 percent faster. Once a target has been located
on a map or chart, its meaning must be clearly apparent. The key
principle to be applied here is that the number of such symbols should
be limited to those specifically needed by the user.

The low-altitude combat pilot hardly needs the dense clutter of
symbols available on the standard 1:250,000 topographical map. Experimental studies have shown that for low-altitude, high-speed operations the key characteristics for maps are a highly distinctive representation of relief and an uncluttered appearance.[6] This combination can
be difficult to achieve. For example, wooded areas are frequently
marked by solid green that obscures height information represented
by color codes. Using other methods of representing woodland, such

as tree symbols, makes the map more difficult to search. The solution must be a compromise, perhaps only marking small or distinctively shaped areas of woodland that might be especially useful for navigation.

Another important factor in searching a map or chart is the information from the periphery of the eye that plays an important role in determining where the eyes will next fixate. This is most strikingly illustrated by studies of eye movements in searching pictures. Surprisingly, we do not search a picture from left to right or in any other systematic manner. Instead, eye fixations jump around the picture, pausing at areas of variation or unpredictability. This happens as soon as a picture is seen and so cannot be the result of carefully scanning the picture with foveal vision.

When searching maps or other complex displays, such as aerial photographs, the time taken to find a target is inversely proportional to the extent into the periphery at which the target can be seen.[7] Color cannot be distinguished in peripheral vision because the cones are mostly located in the fovea. Shape is poorly distinguished in peripheral vision because visual acuity falls off rapidly away from the fovea. Brightness contrast, orientation, and movement are the cues most likely to be detected in peripheral vision, and these were the cues shown to be of most significance in the detection of an external target on a collision course (see Chapter 1).

Individuals differ in their peripheral acuity, and there is a high correlation between peripheral field sizes and finding targets in aerial reconnaissance photographs.[8] Peripheral field size was derived from a measure of subjects' abilities to detect a gap of 15 minutes of arc in a circular target at a distance of 33 centimeters. This research, carried out by the Boeing Airplane Company, suggested that because individuals with wider peripheral fields were better at locating targets, a measure of peripheral field size might be a useful measure in the selection of aerial-photo interpreters.

Other investigators have examined the effects of various typographical variables, such as lowercase lettering versus capital, bold type versus normal type, and so on. One of the major effects was the faster and more accurate search times when the targets were printed in lowercase letters with an initial capital rather than in all capitals. The former also takes less space, leaving the map less cluttered and therefore preferable for aviation purposes. Unfortunately, despite their uncluttered appearance, the readability of approach charts in common use is compromised by the small size of some of the print, especially for older pilots.

Fig. 5.2   A typical airport approach plate depicting an instrument approach procedure. This is the ILS approach to London Heathrow Runway 23. Chart 11–6. Copyright 1984 by Jeppesen & Co. GMBH. Reproduced by permission.

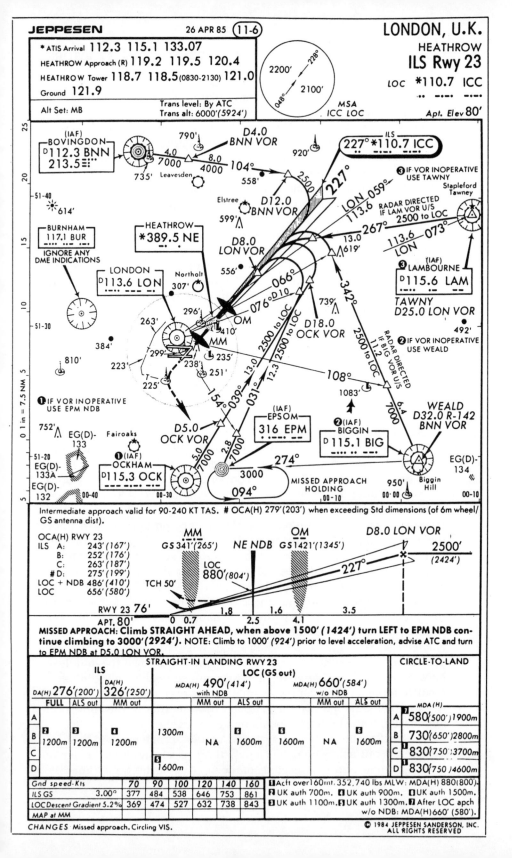

It has been shown experimentally that individuals with relatively poor visual acuity at short distances, who are within the acceptable limits for a private pilot medical certificate, may have severe difficulty reading commercially available approach charts. When the lighting conditions are dim, only those with 20/20 near acuity can read the chart numerals satisfactorily. The authors of this study, carried out by the FAA, conclude that pilots manage to make effective use of these charts through increased cockpit lighting, memory, and previous experience with the charts.[9]

This situation hardly seems satisfactory. The attention to human factors in the design of other displays has been directed away from simply training the user to cope with unsuitable configurations and toward catering to the abilities and limitations of the user from the outset of the design process. However, improving the legibility of paper charts would most readily be accomplished by increasing their size and hence the weight that pilots would have to carry aboard in their chart cases. A better solution is the use of large, panel-mounted, computer-generated map displays.

NAVIGATION DISPLAYS

Airborne navigation aids, such as area inertial navigation systems (AINS), have replaced the human navigator in modern airliners and have resulted in vastly improved navigational accuracy over enormous distances. An AINS is a self-contained system using gyroscopes to sense the aircraft's accelerations, from which its velocity vector and integrated position are computed. Once an initial starting point and orientation have been entered, the AINS can be programmed to guide the aircraft to any other point on the earth's surface (within the aircraft's range, of course). The accuracy of the system is therefore heavily dependent on the accuracy of the information in the computer.

We have already described the crash of Air New Zealand Flight 901 in Antarctica in circumstances that led the crew to fall victim to the phenomenon of sector whiteout (Chapter 1). This need not have resulted in tragedy had the longitude of McMurdo waypoint not been changed without the crew's knowledge. Whereas crew members expected the programmed course to lead them safely down the middle of McMurdo Sound, a change in the programmed waypoint coordinates resulted in following a course 25 miles to the east, directly in line with the 12,500-foot Mount Erebus. A point made earlier in the context of automation (Chapter 4) can be made again here.

Although automation may solve certain problems and lead to greater overall safety and efficiency, there is always the danger of creating a new and unexpected source of error at the same time. Because the AINS depends on the accuracy of the navigational data fed into it, typically with a keyboard entry device, it follows that the AINS must be subject to whatever errors arise in data entry. In defense of the crew of the DC-10 that crashed on Erebus, the altered coordinate data were entered accurately from the hand-held copy generated by the ground-based master computer for the Antarctic flight plan.

Unfortunately the company, up to that time, had not devised a system to safeguard against unnotified changes to a master flight plan. The crew members would have seen nothing to alert them to the fact that the current plan differed from that produced for the previous flights and for their flight briefing and map preparation. The crew's double check of the transfer of data from the master computer printout to the onboard computer would have done little more than lull them into a false sense of security, because they knew there was only one Antarctic flight plan held in the master computer.

KOREAN AIR LINES FLIGHT 007—A NAVIGATION ERROR?

> On 1 September 1983, a Korean Air Lines Boeing 747 was en route from Anchorage, Alaska, to Seoul, Korea. The aircraft was more than 300 nautical miles off course and had been flying inside Soviet airspace for about two hours. The aircraft was intercepted by Soviet fighter aircraft and shot down, killing all 269 on board. Several theories have been advanced to account for the presence of KAL 007 so far off course, including various circumstantial pointers to suggest that the aircraft was deliberately flown over Soviet territory to provide evidence for U.S. surveillance of Soviet radar and communications. An alternative explanation would be that the initial position at Anchorage was entered incorrectly in the AINS, resulting in a different course from the one assumed by the crew. Subsequent investigation suggested that a single misentered digit causing a 10-degree initial position error would have placed the 747 close to the observed track.[10] This hypothesis, of course, requires the assumption that the crew ignored or otherwise failed to make use of other sources of position information from the outset of the flight.

The cause of this disaster is not so clear as in the cases of the Mount Erebus and Bombay tragedies. Whether or not the keyboard-error theory is the correct explanation for KAL 007's waywardness can never be proved. Some pilots who fly the northern Pacific believe the KAL crew knew where they were and were intentionally taking a frequently used shortcut.[11] However, that an unintentional keyboard error led to the observed track of KAL 007 seems possible in light of empirical evidence on the frequency of keyboard errors made by typists.

Using a standard typewriter keyboard (the "QWERTY" layout), experienced typists have been shown to make approximately 11 errors per one thousand characters entered at normal typing speeds. For entering navigational data on the flight deck the QWERTY keyboard would be unacceptable because of space limitations and the need for single-handed operation. After some investigation, a quite different layout has been adopted for most airborne navigational systems.[12] An example is shown in Figure 5.3. Using keypads of this type results in a general accuracy in the region of 5 to 10 errors per one thousand characters. Obviously independent double checking is still required.

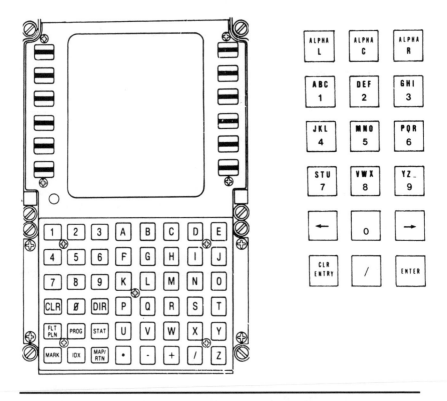

Fig. 5.3 An example of a keyboard interface for a modern flight management or navigation system (left) and a recommended keyboard layout following extensive tests of keying accuracies and speeds associated with different keyboard designs. From L. C. Butterbaugh and T. H. Rockwell (1982). *Human Factors, 24,* 522, 532.

Although comparatively rare, such errors can have tragic consequences. The prevention of entry errors is currently a major concern for airline operators, particularly where there is a high density of traffic as on the North Atlantic routes. Since 1977 monitoring of aircraft using a portion of North Atlantic airspace has been undertaken.[13] It has been reported that the majority of errors involving track deviations of 50 to 70 nautical miles from course have been the result of incorrect waypoint insertion or misunderstandings between ATC and the crew. The most common error in entering waypoints has been found to involve a mistake of one degree of latitude, or 60 nautical miles.

Unfortunately, the crew coordination process is itself subject to error. This will be discussed in Chapter 8. The Air New Zealand accident and the Korean Air Lines incident point up the need for an independently driven map display to guard against miscoordination of navigation procedures. The basic display could be driven in various ways because extreme precision is not needed for gross position checking. The Korean 747, for example, was as much as 365 nautical miles off course, and its AINS position relative to the planned course and any waypoints would have been immediately evident.

Experimental studies of navigational errors have shown that their likelihood varies according to the characteristics of the navigation and flight control systems and the workload sustained by the pilots. In one study, 16 instrument-rated pilots flew a simulated IFR task in a modified Link GAT-2 simulator.[14] In place of the more common VOR tracking technique in which the pilot flies directly from one VOR station to the next along predetermined airways, the simulator was equipped with area navigation (RNAV) capabilities. This freed pilots from following the set airways by allowing them to define waypoints along desired courses to destinations.

This system effectively allowed pilots to fly as though the VOR stations were located at some other position (the waypoint) and thus choose a more direct or otherwise preferable route. One of the key variables with the RNAV system is the number of waypoints that can be programmed and stored in advance. The pilot's primary workload at any given moment was assessed by presenting (to half of the pilots) a secondary task to which the pilot was to devote any spare capacity, or residual attention. This technique is discussed in more detail in Chapter 7. The results were quite clear.

The greater the number of waypoints that could be entered and stored in advance, the fewer the navigational errors committed. If a pilot were under a relatively high workload induced by the side task, this effect was even more dramatic. Although the opportunity for navigational errors is present in any system, their probability of occurrence can be greatly reduced by appropriate equipment design and attention to human operating characteristics. For example, the largest improvement in pilot performance in this experiment was brought about by the introduction of an augmented (reduced order) control system that allowed the pilot to command rate of turn and vertical speed directly.

THE AIR TRAFFIC CONTROL SYSTEM

The development of a safe and expeditious air traffic system required a ground-based control network to coordinate movements and ensure safe separation among aircraft. For many years the flight plan and progress of aircraft have been charted on thin rectangular "flight progress strips" passed from one controller to another as the aircraft traversed sectors. The introduction of radar and early forms of computerization greatly assisted this task without changing it in any fundamental way. The current issues in air traffic control are similar to those that were discussed in connection with the increasing automation of flightdeck tasks, namely, how to automate parts of the controller's task without jeopardizing performance in an emergency or during equipment malfunction.

ATC PROCEDURES INVOLVED IN TWA FLIGHT 514 ACCIDENT

The probable cause of the TWA Flight 514 accident was "the crew's decision to descend to 1,800 feet before the aircraft had reached the approach segment where that minimum altitude applied." The crew's decision to descend was a result of inadequacies and lack of clarity in the air traffic control procedures. The terminology in question was the phrase "cleared for the approach" issued by the controller, which was taken by the crew of Flight 514 to permit an unrestricted descent to 1,800 feet. This was not adequate for terrain clearance in the area. The misunderstanding was compounded by inadequacies in the approach charts used by the crew. The aircraft was destroyed in the impact, and all the occupants were killed.[15]

The introduction of new technology is not the only question of interest in connection with the psychology of air traffic control. The role of stress and the achievement of proper coordination among controllers and between pilots and controllers are of central importance. English is the international language of air traffic control, and its phraseology is necessarily highly standardized to eliminate imprecision of expression and to avoid ambiguities. Misunderstandings still arise from time to time, particularly among pilots and controllers whose native languages are not English. However, the crash of TWA Flight 514 considered earlier also involved a misinterpretation of air traffic control phraseology in clear English.

Although the vast majority of flights operate smoothly and without incident, misunderstandings between pilots have played a major part in a number of accidents, including several of the examples given in this book. A familiar example of ambiguity in communication is the instruction "takeoff power" issued by the pilot in command to initiate a missed approach procedure. In several cases this has been interpreted by the flight engineer or copilot as an instruction to reduce (take off) power. Such misunderstandings have led to the replacement of this phrase by the potentially less ambiguous "go-around power."

For the most part the language used by pilots and controllers today has evolved over sufficient time for such sources of ambiguity to be minimized. As long as there are human operators in the system, however, mishearing a clearance, incorrectly reading back a clearance, and failing to correct an incorrectly repeated clearance are potential threats. There are few studies of pilot-controller communication (with the exception of accident reports). One study of the effect of introducing bilingual air traffic control in Canada showed that in a simulated high-density terminal area, approximately 5 percent of transmissions contained some form of error.[16] More of these were produced by pilots than by controllers.

An area of concern with respect to the development of direct air-to-ground data transfer is the role of the party-line effect in detecting errors. At present, with clearances and readbacks given by voice over a common frequency, the crews of other aircraft on the same frequency have the opportunity to detect conflicting clearances or simply to detect errors in readbacks. An anonymous report in NASA's *Callback* gives an example in which a clearance to 16,000 feet was incorrectly read back as "Roger 6,000."[17] This was corrected by another pilot on the same frequency. In the absence of a correction there could have been disastrous results as there was nearby terrain at 6,500 feet.

Concern about the loss of the party-line effect has slowed the introduction of ground-to-air data links that would transmit clearances directly from an ATC center to a CRT display on the flight deck. In addition to removing a source of error correction, such a system might replace one category of errors (auditory) with another category (visual). NASA's Aviation Safety Reporting System (ASRS) is a valuable source of information to help resolve such issues. During one period of less than two years there were 1,801 reports of controller-controller problems and 5,402 reports of controller-pilot problems.[18]

As shown in Table 5.1, the errors that are most prevalent in the reports of controller coordination failures are largely attributable to the controller's failure to take into account information that was available. The importance of distraction and excessive workload in precipitating those failures is apparent from the reports. Distractions often arise in the supervision of an inexperienced controller by an experienced controller. Failure to use information that is actually available seems also to be characteristic of many crew operating errors.

The large number of reports of pilot-controller communication problems (almost 70 percent of the total number processed through the ASRS) suggests that this traditional means of oral communication presents hazards to safety. Table 5.2 summarizes some of the prevalent types of errors. Compared to the small percentage of problems caused by equipment failures, the role of human error is dramatically large. By far the most common problem is the failure to send a message at all!

Such an omission represents the first link in a chain of events that could have been organized differently. It is often concluded that a disastrous outcome could have easily been avoided if a single event, such as the transmission of an appropriate message, had been present.[19] This judgment may also be colored with the wisdom of hindsight. ASRS reports indicate that many instances of misunderstanding can

Table 5.1. Controller Coordination Failures

Type of failure	Percentage of reports
Perceptual error	33.0
Technique error	28.5
Nonrecall	9.0
Message inaccuracy	6.0
Failure to monitor or check	2.5
Misidentification	0.5
Other	20.5

Source: Adapted from Billings and Cheaney (1981).

Table 5.2. Controller-pilot Communication Failures

Type of failure	Percentage of reports
Appropriate message not sent	37
Contained, or based on, erroneous content	16
Originated too early or too late	13
Ambiguous phraseology	10
Recipient not monitoring	10
Incomplete content	6
Garbled or distorted	3
Loss of message—equipment failure	3
Confusion attributable to phonetic similarity	1

Source: Adapted from Billings and Cheaney (1981).

be attributed to the expectation factor (Chapter 1); that is, the recipient (or listener) hears what was expected. Pilots and controllers alike tend to hear what they expect.

FALSE EXPECTATION

> *The instructor pilot and the student both thought the controller told them to turn left to a heading of 010 degrees and descend to and maintain 10,000 feet. At 10,700 feet the controller requested the aircraft's altitude. The crew responded 10,700 feet. The controller stated the aircraft had been cleared to 12,000 feet, not 10,000 feet. "There are two contributing causes for this occurrence: 99 percent of all clearances from that area are to descend to and maintain 10,000 feet, and as the instructor I was conditioned to descend to 10,000 by many previous flights. The controller may have said 12,000 feet but I was programmed for 10,000 feet."[20]*

Appropriate expectancies allow us to interpret and respond more rapidly to incoming information than would otherwise be the case. Inappropriate expectations, however, can lead to false conclusions, but these can be minimized by careful design of the language of radio communication, the avoidance of potentially confusing call signs, and

---

NEAR-MISS BETWEEN HS748 AND F27, ROTORUA, NEW ZEALAND

> *A southbound Mount Cook Airlines HS748 passed within 60 meters vertically and 800 meters laterally of an Air New Zealand Friendship. The latter had been cleared to descend to the same altitude as the HS748 on its approach to Rotorua. The error occurred because the Rotorua controller mistakenly instructed "Newmans one one" to maintain 8,000 feet, intending that instruction for the Mount Cook flight designated "NM11" on the flight progress chart. The call was answered by Newmans Airlines Flight 108 that had just departed from Rotorua. The controller therefore mistakenly believed that he had instructed the Mount Cook flight to maintain 8,000 feet and subsequently proceeded to clear the Air New Zealand Friendship down to 9,000 feet. In fact, the Mount Cook flight was maintaining 9,000 feet.[21]*

---

crew monitoring of radio communications. It may be that an element of airmanship is the ability to use expectation to permit rapid responding, while maintaining a self-monitoring process that can catch the unexpected and correct errors of expectation.

The two-letter aircraft identifiers (e.g., NZ for Air New Zealand) are intended to provide a unique call sign for every flight. The controller at Rotorua was controlling three separate flights by three separate airlines whose identifiers were NZ (Air New Zealand), NM (Mount Cook), and NY (Newmans). The potential for confusion is evident, particularly as the NM for Mount Cook contained the two stressed consonants of Newmans. The choice of airline identifiers for use in oral communication must cope with the human factor of expectation, or mental set; neither the pilot nor the controller noticed the discrepancy between the initial reference to "Newmans one one" and the reply of "Newmans one zero eight."

The air traffic controller's job varies widely from one location to another in terms of volume of traffic and type of equipment in operation. The close relationship between controller and equipment makes it difficult to measure accurately the workload imposed on the controller by any given set of conditions. This complex interrelationship has resulted in a recognition of the necessity of dealing with the system as a whole. For example, the FAA maintains a system effectiveness information system (SEIS) with a data base that contains information on all reported controlling errors and miscommunications.

The causes of these system errors are classified in nine categories: attention, judgment, communications, stress, equipment, operations management, procedures, and external factors. More than 90 percent of the recorded errors involve human failures in the first three categories, most notably imprecision or ambiguity in communication of the sort that permitted the premature descent of TWA Flight 514 in response to the controller's phrase, "cleared for the approach."

Another approach is to classify the skills involved in the job of air traffic control.[22] Many of the input and output skills are similar to those of other occupations involving visual and auditory monitoring, the transmission of messages, and the manipulation of controls. The critical features of air traffic control are to be found in the handling of information between the input and output stages. Evidently important are the ability to "keep the picture" while alternating attention among different tasks and the prediction of future states—whether there will be a conflict between two assigned clearances at some future point, for example.

Controllers necessarily have to switch backward and forward in time to deal with several aircraft in the queue. This aspect of the controller's job contributes to the necessity of keeping the picture. This refers to the overall view, or mental model, of the situation based on the radar returns, data tags, and radio communications. Some of this information will be held in working memory, making the job of handing over to another controller during a busy period particularly difficult.

Keeping the picture is at the same time probably the most challenging and satisfying part of the controller's job and the most threatened by automation. Reducing the human to an inactive monitor of the computer could remove much of the intrinsic satisfaction from the task. It would also raise questions concerning the ability of the controller to recover the picture in the event of computer failure. The alternative for automation is to find ways of helping the controller keep the picture. The use of predictive displays may be promising in this respect.

Predictive displays. In the discussion of cockpit design, it was shown that predictive displays are helpful in improving performance. One automated aid that is likely to be useful in air traffic control is just such a device—computer-assisted approach sequencing (CAAS). Furthermore, there will inevitably be changes in the controller's tasks with the introduction of new approach aids such as the microwave landing system (MLS) with its greater variety of approach paths than permitted by straight-in ILS beams.

Two experiments involving eight professional controllers were carried out using a simulated control task involving an MLS approach to a high-density airport.[23] The controllers were allowed to use any normal control method (alterations of airspeed, radar vectoring, and holding patterns) to deal with the traffic. Some difficulty was created for the controllers in estimating ground speeds of the traffic on curved approach paths. As a result there was considerable difficulty in maintaining the required time separation between approaching aircraft. Controller and computer task allocation will have to be tailored to accommodate the flight path complexities of the MLS.

The controller's task is primarily oriented toward future states of affairs—that is, determining where conflicts might arise in the flow of traffic. Many large airports have parallel runways with several holding points where aircraft can be kept orbiting until cleared for final approach. Naturally, excessive use of holding procedures is costly in terms of fuel and salaries, annoying to passengers, and potentially dangerous in stormy weather. The aim of computer-assisted approach sequencing would be to assist the approach controller in vectoring inbound aircraft efficiently.

A similar tool for sector controllers is interactive conflict resolution (ICR), as shown in Figure 5.4. ICR provides a simulation of the trajectories of all aircraft passing through the sector. A zone is calculated around each aircraft consisting of the legal separation requirements based on navigational tolerances. The controller can use the ICR to check for potential conflicts at any future time, either for the whole system or for any particular aircraft. Before amending a particular clearance, the controller could assure that no future conflicts would be created.

ICR has been tried out in a simulation experiment using qualified operational controllers.[24] As in other questions of the effects of specific automation applications, it is difficult to obtain objective measures of the effectiveness of the overall system as well as the workload of the individual controller. The measures in this study were mainly subjective but seem to show a positive acceptance of ICR by these controllers and a substantial improvement in their ability to expedite the flow of departing aircraft.

Use of ICR allowed the controllers to clear aircraft to climb imme-

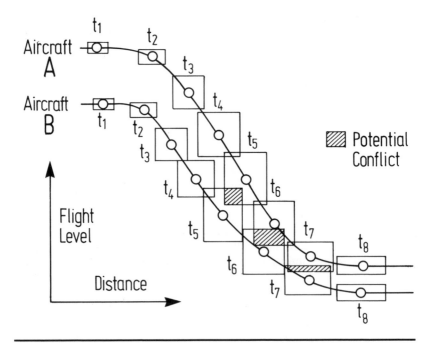

Fig. 5.4 The basic idea of interactive conflict resolution (ICR) can be seen in this elevation view of the projected trajectories of two descending aircraft at successive points t_1, t_2, and so forth. The boxes represent a "protection zone" to allow for navigational tolerances. The shaded areas represent points at which possible conflict might occur. Predictive displays have been shown to aid pilots in flying accurate, controlled approaches (see Chapter 4). Adapted from an original drawing, British Crown Copyright Reserved, by permission of R. G. Ball and the U.K. Ministry of Defence.

diately instead of holding them at lower levels following departure as was necessary with the standard departure procedures. There was some evidence that the use of ICR with higher traffic levels could outstrip the controller's ability to keep the picture. This might have serious implications for the controller's ability to take over the system safely in the event of computer failure, so highly redundant computing systems will be required to minimize the chance of such a failure.

Workload.   The increasingly automated air traffic system makes the measurement of controller workload vitally important because the consequences of underusing controllers may be as damaging for the overall safety of the air traffic system as having underused pilots in command of aircraft. Attempts to quantify workload have included such measures as rates of activity, errors and delays in dealing with the task, subjective estimates, and even physiological indices of stress (see Chapter 6). However, the indices evidently measure different aspects of workload because they are seldom highly correlated, and the subjective assessments are notoriously unreliable as well. Workload measures are discussed further in Chapter 7.

Part of the difficulty of relating objective measures of workload to job performance is that the controller can adopt different strategies for use in different circumstances. One simple example is that as the pressure on the controller's resources increases, the duration of each radio message decreases with some trimming of unnecessary wording. The performance of 15 approach controllers at Orly Airport in Paris was studied using a static simulation of traffic conditions involving low-, medium-, or high-density traffic (four, six, or eight aircraft, respectively). The experiment confirmed that controllers adopt different strategies for dealing with the different numbers of aircraft.[25]

Maximum information was processed with each aircraft in the low-traffic condition, allowing the most individual routing flexibility. As traffic levels increased, the operators reverted to standardized procedures for separating aircraft. The total amount of information processed was similar regardless of traffic. This is in accordance with a widely held view in psychology and ergonomics that people are relatively limited processors of information. The limited-channel-capacity model of human information processing is discussed further in Chapter 7. Such limits can be demonstrated quite clearly with pilot-controller communication experiments.

To the uninitiated, the exchange of clearances and readbacks on the aircraft radio can present a totally unintelligible babble. With experience, the pilot learns the standard phrases and anticipates the sequence of instructions contained in each message. This is necessary because the ability to hold numerous items in memory while performing some distracting task is not great. ATC clearances may contain several items (as in clearance for an instrument departure) that must be recorded and read back correctly. The pilot may also be occupied with some other task while this is being done.

An experiment with nonpilot subjects showed a rapid falloff in the number of instructions correctly remembered as the length of the message increased.[26] There is also a progressive decline in working memory over time, reaching an asymptote at approximately 15 seconds. Although standardized phraseology and a specially designed phonetic code are intended to minimize perceptual confusions, relatively little effort has been devoted to the problems of remembering transmitted information.

STRESS AND ILLNESS

It is easy to appreciate that the air traffic controller's job of handling large volumes of traffic under adverse weather conditions can be highly stressful. The inherent stress of the job can be further elevated in countries where controllers have been subject to imprisonment after a midair collision for which they have been judged responsible.[27] The long-term effects of occupational stress are presumed to be apparent through increased susceptibility to heart disease, hypertension, and ulcers in air traffic controllers.

One difficulty in determining both the short-term impact of stress and its longer-term effects is that there are enormous differences in workload and time pressure at a small country airport and a busy international terminal. Some studies have found physiological evidence of heightened stress levels in the latter group, but taken overall, air traffic control seems not to produce greater short-term physiological stress responses than many other occupations.[28] Most of air traffic controllers' negative feelings about their jobs seem to be related to pay and working conditions rather than to any inherent characteristics of their duties.

Nevertheless, significant long-term health effects were found in the medical records of more than four thousand U.S. controllers compared with similar records of more than eight thousand private pilots.[29] The clearest evidence for long-term stress was obtained from the incidence of hypertension or elevated blood pressure. The annual incidence of diagnosed hypertension was six times greater among the controllers than the pilots. There was also a slightly higher susceptibility shown by controllers who worked at high–traffic-density towers.

The mean age at onset of hypertension was significantly lower for the controllers (average age of 41 years) compared to the pilots (average age of 48 years). Similarly, the incidence of peptic ulcers was nearly two times higher among the controllers. The authors note that "controllers are at excessive risk of developing peptic ulcer, that they develop it at a younger age than others, and that these risks are related to the stress of the job." The differences in incidence rates for peptic ulcers and hypertension between the high-density locations and the low-density locations was particularly striking.

Despite these findings, it is still not certain what aspects of the controller's job are most responsible for these stress-related effects. A wide range of factors may be associated with the symptoms of occupational ill health.[30] These range from factors that are intrinsic to the job, such as being overloaded and working different shifts or in adverse physical conditions, to the person's role in the work organization. Problems of promotion, responsibility, relationships with colleagues, and personal decision making can all be involved in creating stress at work. The complex and elusive effects of both short-term and long-term exposure to stress and fatigue will be considered next.

FURTHER READING

The topics discussed in this chapter are developed further in several specialist publications. The ergonomics of map design are discussed by V. D. Hopkin and R. M. Taylor in *Human Factors in the Design and Evaluation of Aviation Maps* (Neuilly-sur-Seine: North Atlantic Treaty Organization, 1979). Problems arising in air-to-ground communication are detailed in *Information Transfer Problems in the Aviation System* edited by C. E. Billings and E. S. Cheaney (Moffett Field, CA: National Aeronautics and Space Administration, 1981).

[6] Stress, Fatigue, and Performance

TRAPPED this way in the first breaking waves of a cyclone that at sea level was blowing at the fantastic rate of 150 mph . . . whenever I seemed about to take my bearings a new eruption would swing me round in a circle or send me tumbling wing over wing. . . . Fear, however, was out of the question. I was incapable of thinking. I was emptied of everything except the vision of a very simple act. I must straighten out.

ANTOINE DE SAINT-EXUPÉRY, *Wind, Sand and Stars*

INTRODUCTION

Despite its common usage and popular appeal, the term "stress" remains one of the more confusing and controversial concepts in the psychological vocabulary. A variety of factors have been subsumed under this term, ranging from the long-term effects of significant life events, such as marriage, divorce, or illness, to the short-term effects of working in hot, cramped, or noisy environments or under mounting pressure of time or workload. A major source of confusion arises from the tendency to use the term to refer to both the external circumstances (e.g., high temperatures) and the effects that may result from exposure to these circumstances (e.g., irritability, illness, etc.).

It has sometimes been proposed to refer to those two categories as stress and strain, respectively. In terms of pilot performance we will be primarily concerned with the effects on performance resulting from exposure to stress. Our discussion of stress will be divided into four

parts: (1) the effects of working in stressful environments, (2) sleeplessness and fatigue, (3) other biological stressors, such as blood-sugar
levels, alcohol, and carbon monoxide, and (4) the effects of major life
events.

ENVIRONMENTAL STRESSORS

There is no doubt that working in hot, humid, noisy, cramped,
cold, or vibrating environments for any length of time can adversely
affect human performance. The extent of the impairment will depend
on the length of time spent in the environment, the nature of the task,
and the person's strategies for coping with the effects. Fairly extensive
guidelines are available to aid the designer in planning a suitable
working environment.[1] For example, humans are fairly sensitive to
temperature changes, although the use of specialized clothing can extend the range of tolerance.

Temperature.   If the ambient temperature lies above 30 or below
about 13 degrees Celsius, some impairment of performance can be
expected. As the temperature increases or decreases, the length of
exposure needed to produce impairment drops. The effects of heat
depend on other factors, such as humidity and wind, and a number of
indices have been developed to measure thermal discomfort.[2] Pilots
are seldom exposed to temperatures in the particularly sensitive range
above 30 degrees Celsius, although studies of helicopter cockpits have
shown temperatures as high as 56 degrees Celsius even with an outside air temperature of only 27 degrees. This is known as the "green-
house" effect of the large clear helicopter canopy.

Noise.   The effects of noise are rather more complicated because
what constitutes noise is subjective. Rock concerts and running water
can be perceived either as pleasant sounds or as irritating noises.
Some typical sound pressure levels were presented in Chapter 2. Objects generally considered noisy, such as vacuum cleaners, lawn
mowers, or chainsaws, typically produce sounds ranging from 60 decibels (quiet vacuum cleaner) to 115 decibels (noisy chainsaw) to 120
decibels (some jet aircraft at takeoff). In comparison with the DC-3,
with noise levels in the cockpit of 108 decibels, the noise levels within
modern jets are quite low.
    Both the sound pressure levels and the frequencies of the sounds
have to be considered in assessing the effects of noise. Chainsaws and
domestic tools produce relatively high-frequency noise (1,000 Hz and

above), whereas the sound produced by a jet aircraft overhead is predominantly low-frequency noise (50–500 Hz). Low-frequency noise can be felt as vibration that can directly affect performance. By and large, noise and temperature ranges for modern commercial air transport pilots are within comfortable limits. In contrast, the levels of these environmental stressors in helicopter cockpits and in some light aircraft may be beyond safe limits for the hearing receptors.

As with temperature limits, most countries have some scale of permissible noise exposure. Both the United States and United Kingdom have adopted the 90 decibel level as the maximum for average exposure in an 8-hour period. This drops to six hours for 92 decibels and four hours for 95 decibels. These standards take no regard of the complexity of the task that the operator is trying to perform. Average noise levels experienced by helicopter crews are estimated to be around 88–93 decibels.[3] The precise readings obtained depend on the weightings given to the different frequencies involved.

The values given above are all based on a standard that corresponds to the normal sensitivity of the ear to different sound frequencies. This gives less weight to the lower-frequency sounds present in typical engine noise. All the decibel values used here were based on this American National Standards Institute "A" scale. Using an alternative scale in which all frequencies receive equal weighting (the "C" scale) would produce higher values than those quoted above. As shown in Figure 6.1, helicopter crews are exposed to levels of noise that are at the outer limits of the normally acceptable range.

The noise in helicopters arises mainly from the gearbox and transmission and may be exacerbated by blade-slap caused by the rotor blades. One direct effect of vibration (below 50 Hz) can be to induce the pilot's body to resonate, that is, to vibrate at greater amplitudes than the initial vibration; the extent will depend on the size and build of the pilot and the design of the seats, which are notoriously uncomfortable and offer little postural support. The more common indirect effects of vibration are headaches, backaches, sleep loss, and other problems difficult to identify precisely.[4]

The effects of noise on both temporary and permanent hearing loss are easier to demonstrate. In the short term, exposure to noise produces a temporary partial deafness centered near 4,000 Hz. With longer exposure this loss becomes permanent and gradually spreads to lower frequencies. Studies of industrial workers, exposed to noise levels comparable to those in helicopters have shown hearing losses after ten years of approximately 40 decibels at 4,000 Hz.[5] Since normal speech consists primarily of frequencies below 8,000 Hz, such losses cause considerable impairment to ordinary communication.

Pilots working in particularly noisy agricultural or rotary-wing aircraft are likely to be equipped with noise-reducing headsets, but the

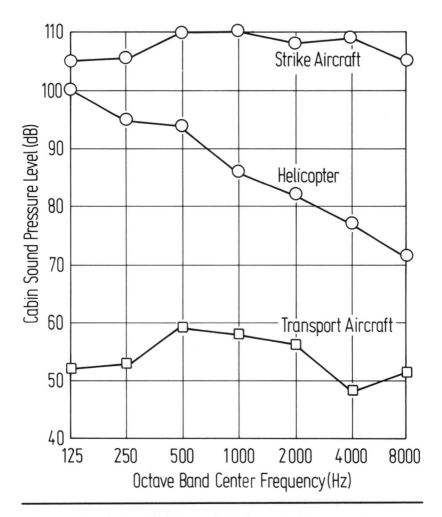

Fig. 6.1 Typical noise fields within the crew compartments of a strike aircraft, a helicopter, and a jet transport. The high levels of sound in the lower-frequency range are typical for the helicopter. From *Aviation Medicine: Physiology and Human Factors*, edited by G. Dhenin. Copyright 1978 by Tri-Med Books. Adapted by permission.

degree of protection offered by such devices is probably less than ideal. The problems posed by the combination of vibration, noise, and other stressors to helicopter pilots is just beginning to be recognized properly. While awaiting the outcome of further research on these topics, the British Civil Aviation Authority proposed reductions in the permissible flight-duty hours for helicopter pilots within any given seven-day period.[6]

Physiological responses to stress. A brief description of the main physiological terms involved will be helpful in understanding the research on stress and performance. Part of the nervous system is known as the autonomic nervous system. This regulates the automatic bodily functions, such as breathing, heartbeat, and digestion. The autonomic system has sympathetic and parasympathetic branches. These generate the nerve impulses that increase or decrease heartbeat, dilate or constrict the pupil of the eye, and so forth. The immediate response to any events that are novel, surprising, or generally arousing is for the sympathetic branch of the autonomic system to release noradrenaline into the blood stream.

This results in the well-known feelings of excitement, including elevated heart rate, as well as the effects of the sympathetic system on vision mentioned in Chapter 1. Because of the ease of measuring heart rate it has become one of the most popular measures of stress. It should be noted that many pleasant events can also give rise to increased heart rate, so that it is not a unique or specific measure of response to the kind of unpleasant environmental conditions discussed previously. Heart rate may best be thought of as a general indicator of autonomic activity.

A second bodily system, known as the endocrine system, is also involved in responding to stress. The endocrine system consists of glands located in different parts of the body. The pituitary gland in the brain and the adrenal glands located on the top of each kidney are of particular importance. The endocrine system sends signals by hormones, or "chemical messengers," rather than neural impulses. The existence of these hormones can be detected long after the events that triggered their release have passed.

One of the main biochemical responses to stress involves what are known as the adrenocorticotropic hormones.[7] There are a number of them released by the pituitary gland that can be detected in urine, thereby providing a method for measuring the extent to which a person has recently been under stress. These hormones have a resemblance to naturally occurring substances in the brain known as endorphins that in turn resemble opiates. The function of these hormones may be to prevent the body from being overwhelmed by extreme panic that would prevent an adaptive response to the source of the stress.

However, there may be a cost to the release of these hormones in terms of increased susceptibility to coronary disease. Research indicates links between their secretion and blood cholesterol, leading in turn to increased danger of damaged arteries and heart disease.[8] As with heart rate, the detection of these substances provides only a general indicator of activation rather than a highly specific measure of stress. This is an important point, because it is all too easy to equate the complex effects of stress with a single physiological measure. There is no doubt, however, that the task of flying an aircraft produces clear symptoms of increased activation as measured by both heart rate and hormonal excretion.

Several investigators have looked at the responses of students undergoing flight training.[9] Whereas a normal resting heart rate is approximately 70 to 80 beats per minute (bpm), the average heart rate of the flight trainees was found to be nearly 100 bpm. When students were training in a Link GAT-1 simulator, their heart rates were significantly lower than the heart rates of those training in a Piper Cherokee aircraft (84 bpm versus 95 bpm), a possible contributor to the efficiency of simulator training.

The hormonal indices also showed that all students were experiencing increased levels of activation in the airplane. Their levels of adrenaline and adrenocorticotropic hormones were considerably higher than those found in studies involving experienced pilots or busy air traffic controllers. As discussed in Chapter 3, even the difference between predominantly negative and predominantly positive instructing styles was reflected in the hormone levels found in the students, with the students under positive instructing style experiencing less activation.

The interpretation of heart rate as a measure of activation rather than emotional stress is strengthened by studies of experienced pilots in which a comparison can be made between the heart rates of the handling pilot and the pilot-not-flying. In one study of test pilots flying the Harrier jump jet, the safety pilot's heart rate remained at resting levels (60–75 bpm) throughout the takeoff, whereas the handling pilot's rose to approximately 115 bpm.[10] The same pattern was found regardless of whether the handling pilot was in the front or the rear seat. Several sets of results from civilian pilots show the same pattern.

With a BAC-1-11 two-pilot crew, the handling pilot's heart rate during approach and landing rose to approximately 100 bpm, while the nonhandling pilot's remained at around 80 bpm. When the pilots reversed roles, the difference between the heart rates of the two pilots also reversed. Since both pilots were experiencing the same physical sensations, the increased heart rate for the pilot doing the flying must be related either to the extra workload or to the additional responsibility, or to both. It is also significant that the heart rates of these experienced pilots flying standard approaches in commercial jet aircraft are usually below those of an average flight trainee in light aircraft.

Some quite remarkable data on heart rates of pilots flying bombing missions in North Vietnam were obtained by the NASA Flight Research Center.[11] Pilots of jet aircraft, including the A4 Skyhawk and F4 Phantom, were monitored during the takeoff, landing, and bombing phases of missions flown in various weather conditions and during both day and night. The overall average heart rate was a low 89.8 bpm. Even during the carrier takeoffs and landings, the average heart rates were about 105 bpm, and during the bombing runs, which included bad-weather ground attacks and high *g*-forces, an average of only 112 bpm was found.

There are, however, wide variations among individuals in the same situation. America's first orbiting astronaut, John Glenn, exhibited a remarkably low heart rate while awaiting launch (around 70 bpm) and only 110 bpm on liftoff compared to nearly 170 bpm for other astronauts in the same situation.[12] In addition to individual differences, there is some evidence that heart rate rises as the time-urgency or pacing of the task increases. We will discuss this in the following section on the psychological effects of stressors.

Effects of stressors on performance.   All of the environmental stressors mentioned above have been shown to impair people's abilities to carry out certain tasks. This has been demonstrated frequently in experiments that have measured the time taken to respond to one of several signals, the ability to detect an infrequently appearing signal (such as monitoring a radar display, for example), or perceptual-motor coordination. The presence of noise above 90 decibels was found to increase the time taken to respond and the number of errors produced in a task designed to mimic a simple machine-operating task.[13]

Using a similar task, other investigators have shown that subjects working in a warm room (38 degrees Celsius) performed more poorly than subjects working in more comfortable conditions.[14] This was true even when the subjects were tested in the tropics, where they had been living for at least the previous six months. When the task was one of detecting infrequently occurring signals, the effects of heat and noise were similar and again generally impeded performance. Apart from occasional extreme environmental conditions, such as those mentioned with regard to helicopter operations, it is unlikely that any of these effects will be of practical importance in the aviation context.

This is the case for the simple reason that it has been shown that such deficits can be largely overcome by the presence of sufficient incentive to do well. This may consist of monetary reward, praise and encouragement, or intrinsic desire to do well at a given task. Because pilots generally maintain a high drive to do well, it may be presumed that the effect of the environmental stressors on performance will be minimal in the short term. More significant effects on performance can be produced, however, by a class of stressors that may be regarded as more distinctly psychological. Individuals differ widely in their reactions to time pressure or danger.

For obvious reasons there have been few experimental studies of subjects exposed to real danger. One study, appropriately named "Project Rough Rider," involved four Royal Air Force test pilots who flew a series of storm penetration flights in a Scimitar interceptor aircraft.[15] In general, as the intensity of the turbulence reported by the pilot increased, so too did the amount of stress hormones found in subsequent urine analyses. The highest levels were produced by one pilot whose aircraft suffered a direct lightning strike and severe mechanical difficulties.

Unlike the heart rate measures, hormone levels seem to differentiate levels of stress even among highly experienced aircrews. This is supported by a study involving U.S. Air Force instructor pilots and their students.[16] Urine samples were routinely collected before flights over a 4-month period. Samples were again obtained following flights that were classified as emergencies or precautionaries. A comparison of different neurotransmitter substances showed that "the flight-line emergencies result in marked and measurable stress response in both students and instructor pilots."

In a study by the U.S. Army, a group of 15 soldiers were carried aboard a DC-3 aircraft that appeared to develop engine and gear problems necessitating a crash landing.[17] The scenario was quite realistic, with one engine shut down and its propeller feathered, fire engines and ambulances gathered below, and conversation about the gear problem. At this point the subjects were required to fill out two questionnaires, the first to record feelings of distress on a scale from 0 (wonderful) to 100 (scared stiff). The second required the soldiers to recall the emergency instructions given earlier. A flying control group responded to the same questionnaire during an uneventful flight in a DC-3. A third group was tested on the ground.

It would be reasonable to question the degree to which subjects in the experimental group were taken in by the whole performance. Five subjects saw through the situation immediately. Of the remainder, the average self-rating was between "timid" and "unsteady," or a rating of 60. This was significantly different from the average rating given by all of the control subjects, which was 43 ("didn't bother me"). Alternatively, this may not have been a true account of the experimental group's feelings (trainee soldiers are supposed to be macho), as suggested by their significantly higher adrenocorticotrophic hormone levels than those of the flying control group.

There were marked differences in subjects' performances on the memory test for emergency instructions and on a simple test of arithmetical reasoning also administered to the experimental subjects and the combined control groups. Subjects who were expecting the aircraft to crash-land made more errors and recalled fewer of the emergency instructions (average = 4.9 items) than did unstressed subjects (average = 8.8 items) and showed similar differences on the arithmetic test. The explanation for this may be found by examining experimental evidence obtained from subjects performing tasks in conditions of realistic threat or danger.

[Note that contemporary rules of ethical conduct would prevent such an experiment from being repeated today. The code of ethics followed by the American Psychological Association, for example, stipulates that experimenters should neither deceive subjects nor expose them to apparent danger or harm.]

Arousal and narrowing of attention.   Underlying the effects of stress on performance is the assumed operation of a mechanism called arousal, a general level of activation, measured on a scale from extreme drowsiness to frantic overactivity. The effects of arousal on performance can be accounted for reasonably well by assuming that we can perform a task best when we are somewhere between the two extremes. In other words, there is some optimum level of arousal for performance, and both greater and lower levels will impede performance. This is illustrated graphically in Figure 6.2 and is known as the Yerkes-Dodson law.

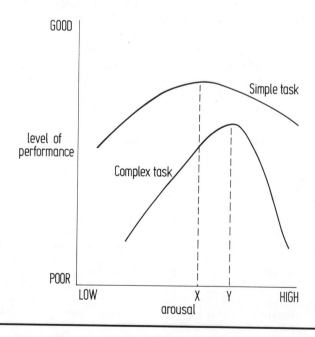

Fig. 6.2   The Yerkes-Dodson law relating arousal and task performance. The optimum level of performance for a complex task will occur at a higher level of arousal than for a simple task.

The law contains the further statement that the optimum level of arousal will be higher as the difficulty of the task increases. Thus the optimum level of arousal for a complex task, such as flying an ADF holding pattern, should be greater than for a simple task, such as checking a series of switch positions. In general, task difficulty is related to the extent to which memory is involved in a task. Consequently, reducing the memory required to complete a task reduces the task difficulty. The use of checklists at takeoff and landing is an example of the application of this rule.

The effect of stressors on performance is thought to be mediated by their effects on the subject's level of arousal. Although stressors frequently increase arousal beyond the optimum point and thus decrease performance, sleep-deprived subjects actually do better at some tasks in the presence of a stressor, such as loud noise. If it is assumed that a sleep-deprived person initially is at a relatively low level of arousal, the effect of stress will be to increase arousal and so improve performance, as shown in Figure 6.2. Once again, the difficulty of the task is important, with the effect mostly occurring on simple tasks requiring little memory.

Although it would appear that there is a clear explanation for the effects of stress on a person's ability to carry out a variety of tasks, two additional factors need to be considered. The first is the practical difficulty of arriving at a satisfactory measure of arousal. We have previously looked at heart rate and found this to be a useful index of autonomic nervous system activity. It is doubtful that it can be considered synonymous with arousal, however, because it varies with other factors, such as responsibility and workload. Indeed, it is often used as a measure of workload (see Chapter 7).

MIDAIR COLLISION IN THE CIRCUIT

Two student pilots flying Cherokee 180s were engaged in circuit training at Hamble. One aircraft was established on the final approach and was struck on its right-hand side from behind and above by the second aircraft, which was completing a right turn to final from the base leg. The traffic pattern around an airport is a dangerous area in which to fly, and great vigilance is required, even by experienced pilots. During the early stages of training, student pilots will be mainly concerned with the problems of flying the aircraft accurately. This is particularly so in the approach phase where concentration will be directed to the runway at the expense of foregoing an adequate scan for other traffic.[18]

Although several measurements have been used to assess arousal, it has been found that they do not all vary in perfect unison. Thus a person may seem to be aroused or activated based on one measure but not by another. This makes it difficult to translate the Yerkes-Dodson law into specific practical recommendations. The second point is that the effects of arousal on performance tend to be quite specific. Stress does not simply impair the general level of performance but qualitatively changes the type of attention given to different sources of information.

In a series of early studies, the so-called Cambridge Cockpit experiments, the effects of prolonged fatigue on performance were investigated, and marked changes in attention to different instruments was observed to occur over time.[19] As subjects became more fatigued, they tended to pay progressively less attention to instruments that were more peripheral, such as the fuel gauge, than to the centrally located artificial horizon, airspeed indicator, and altimeter. This does not occur because of some change in the pilot's peripheral vision but reflects a qualitative change in strategy, as shown in other studies involving a simulated underwater diving task.

In one such experiment, subjects were given a central task and an additional task of detecting the onset of a relatively weak peripheral light. Experimental subjects, tested in a pressure chamber, were led to believe they were in a pressure environment equivalent to a 60-foot dive. Control subjects carried out the same tasks outside the chamber. Subjects in the chamber reported feeling more anxious and had higher heart rates (10 bpm higher) than the control subjects. Whereas the experimental subjects performed as well as control subjects on the central task, they were almost 50 percent poorer at detecting the peripheral signal.[20]

Similarly, studies of pilots flying simulated low-level, high-speed missions have shown that the presence of low-amplitude vibration produces a decrement in performance of a subsystem monitoring task.[21] Using a task that is nearer to that of sampling various instrument indications in flight, investigators have shown that stressed subjects displayed a tendency to concentrate on the more central or frequently occurring signals and to neglect the sources of less probable information.[22] In the flight environment, this would be equivalent to restricting one's focus to primary instruments at the expense of a comprehensive instrument scan.

To overcome this narrowing of attention, emphasis in instrument training is placed on maintaining a comprehensive scan pattern and thus avoiding fixation on a single instrument. However, it is necessary to focus one's attention on any momentarily critical component of a task. In recovering from an unusual attitude, for example, it is essential to regain a normal attitude before attending to any other task. The danger arises when correct diagnosis of a problem is inhibited because less central, but nonetheless vital, signals are overlooked.

It appears that, in addition to its physiological effects, the immediate impact of stress on pilot performance is quite similar to the effects of an increase in workload. Both result in a decreased ability to attend to secondary tasks as attention becomes more narrowly focused on the central task. Further discussion of this can therefore be found in the section on workload in Chapter 7. For the moment, it is worth noting that operating under increasing time pressure gives rise to typical stress-related and workload-related effects.

An example from a study mentioned earlier can be used to illustrate these effects.[23] Test pilots flying relatively standard (4-degree) and steep (6-degree) approaches in a VC-10 four-engined commercial jet were found to show higher heart rates as the approach angle increased. Since the nonhandling pilot in the crew showed no such increase, the increased workload of flying a steeper approach must have been responsible for the elevated heart rate. Similar findings were obtained in a separate study in which pilots flew simulated ILS approaches.

SLEEP AND CIRCADIAN RHYTHMS

Both the loss of sleep and the disruption of sleeping patterns are subjectively stressful experiences that can lead to symptoms of drowsiness, irritability, lack of concentration, and related reactions. The practical significance of the effects of sleep disruption has grown in recent years with the proliferation of routes that cross international time zones and the growth of all-night operations such as the giant, worldwide parcel and mail carrier, Federal Express, and the many similar services.

Sleep deprivation.   There are some parallels between the effects of sleep deprivation on performance and those of the other environmental stressors described earlier. In general, sleep deprivation leads to poorer performance on relatively simple vigilance and reaction-time tasks. The impairment shows up only after a long period of working at the task and leads to a general slowing of responses rather than an increase in the number of errors made. In terms of the Yerkes-Dodson law (see Figure 6.2), it appears that sleeplessness reduces the state of arousal or activation, causing arousal to drop below the optimum level and thus reducing performance.

Support for this idea comes from the finding that, whereas noise and sleeplessness impair performance when they occur separately, noise seems to cancel the effects of sleeplessness (or vice versa) when they occur together. In everyday experience, people who must accomplish some task when tired increase the level of background noise (e.g., turn on a car radio). There is still some cost involved in overcoming the effects of tiredness. Subjects can maintain their levels of performance, but only by exerting greater muscle tension.[24] In the long run this is likely to lead to greater tiredness as well as muscular fatigue.

In terms of the focus of attention, sleeplessness seems to have an effect that is different from the other environmental stressors. Instead of focusing attention on the central or highest priority aspect of a task, sleep-deprived subjects show a tendency to observe all aspects of a task equally—in other words, to be less selective. This might lead to a corresponding reduction in performance of the main task. However, in practical terms this impairment can be overshadowed in the short term if motivation is sufficiently high.

In fact, in one experiment military helicopter pilots with only four hours of sleep per night and 14 hours of flying per day in a simulator maintained an extremely high level of performance over a five-day period.[25] Their performances were up to IFR standards of accuracy even on the fourth day of sleep deprivation. The long-term or cumulative effects of such disruption remain of particular interest, however. As with the term "stress," there is much confusion and disagreement concerning the term "fatigue." At least two separate aspects can be distinguished.

The first, continuous operation for lengthy periods, is now common in commercial aviation with nonstop intercontinental flights of 12 to 15 hours. The second refers to the feelings of tiredness arising from disruption of sleep and regular work periods that commonly arise from crossing several time zones during one flight or from scheduling irregular work periods. Of course, once the extended work period begins to exceed 8 to 10 hours, the two forms of fatigue will often be compounded. Extended east-west segments will involve both sources of fatigue, whereas extended north-south flights may not involve any time-zone crossings.

Most evidence suggests that it is the effects of sleep disruption and irregular scheduling, rather than extended work periods, per se, that are of greater significance in aircrew performance. Nevertheless, all regulatory bodies lay down maximum periods of duty and maximum permissible flying hours within set periods. This practice was established by the Convention on International Civil Aviation in Chicago in 1944. The limits set for professional pilots vary from 80 hours per calendar month in Japan to a maximum of 120 hours in Canada. In the United States, the limit is 100 hours per month, not to exceed 1,000 hours in a calendar year.

Circadian rhythms. Because it appears that disruption to sleep patterns is the key component of fatigue, it is important to look first at the general nature of cyclical bodily processes of which sleep patterns are only one. Several rhythmical bodily processes are regulated by internal biological clocks. The fact that most animals maintain a regular pattern of sleep and wakefulness is the most obvious of these and is referred to as a circadian rhythm. The term "circadian" simply means "about a day." Humans confined in places without external cues of night and day still maintain a regular cycle of physiological rhythms of about 24 hours.

One of the simplest cycles to measure is the variation in body temperature. For most people this rises to its highest point from 8 P.M. to 9 P.M. and falls to its lowest between 4 A.M. and 5 A.M. Some individual differences can be observed, including a phase shift between the cycles of introverts and extraverts.[26] These changes in body temperature are correlated with changes in performance as measured by relatively simple tasks of vigilance and reaction time. In one series of experiments, performance on most of these tasks improved steadily throughout the day, reaching a peak at 9 P.M., coincident with the usual peak of body temperature.

Studies of shift workers show that their cycles of temperature changes can gradually adapt to the shift-work pattern as long as the change to a late shift is maintained as a stable change.[27] Unfortunately, the typical irregular scheduling of a pilot's routine prevents this from

---

BOEING 747 INCIDENT AT NAIROBI, 1974

British Airways Flight 29 from London to Johannesburg was approaching Nairobi and was cleared to descend to 7,500 feet. This was incorrectly read back by the copilot as 5,000 feet, which was not corrected by the trainee controller. The crew was preoccupied with the high workload during the necessarily rapid descent from FL100, and the error was not detected. As Nairobi is 5,327 feet above sea level, setting the altitude select to 5,000 feet was particularly critical. It is estimated that the aircraft descended to 70 feet above ground level before pulling up. By the time of the incident, the crew members had been on duty for nine hours during what was otherwise their normal sleep period. Moreover, at the time of the incident (0500 hours) their biochemical, physiological, and psychological functions would have been at their lowest point on the normal circadian cycle.[28]

happening. For the shift workers, changes in performance followed the changes in body temperature pattern, showing that there is a true relationship between the circadian pattern of body temperature and performance.

While the Nairobi incident highlights a number of considerations relevant to workload (Chapter 7) and crew monitoring procedures (Chapter 8), it also pinpoints the operational significance of circadian rhythms in human performance. These effects are most readily discernible on relatively simple or routine tasks rather than on complex decision-making skills. In fact, although intuitively and subjectively evident, the effects on cognitive skills of any of the factors discussed in this chapter are largely undemonstrated.

It is on the performance of simple vigilance or reaction-time tasks that performance has been shown to vary with the time of day, with peak performance normally occurring between midday and 9 p.m. and minimum performance between 3 a.m. and 6 a.m. The difference between maximum and minimum can be substantial, representing a variation of up to 30 percent of the overall average performance. Evidence for the effect of circadian variation in a flight task comes from experiments in which West German fighter pilots flew standard instrument missions in an F104G simulator at intervals of three hours over a two-day period.[29] The variation in overall performance is shown in Figure 6.3.

In a second study, the same flight simulator tasks were performed by pilots who were transported on long-distance flights between the United States and Europe. Such travel causes the individual's natural circadian rhythms to be desynchronized with the new day-night cycle. Performance on the flight simulator task was still desynchronized up to the fifth day in the new location. Although it takes almost the same amount of time to readjust to the new cycle regardless of the direction of travel, the effects on performance are larger when subjects are traveling eastward rather than westward and the differences become more pronounced as more time zones are crossed.[30]

Crew scheduling.   In the case of travel between the United States and Europe, for example, both military and commercial westward flights are typically scheduled to arrive in the United States in the evening, allowing for an immediate night's sleep. In the eastward direction, subjects typically have a morning arrival followed by a wait of 12 hours or more before sleeping, thus adding to the overall fatigue of traveling. Of operational significance, however, is the finding that the time taken for the circadian rhythms to resynchronize is not much affected by the period of wakefulness before the next sleep, so long as a normal-length sleep period has been obtained before the duty period.

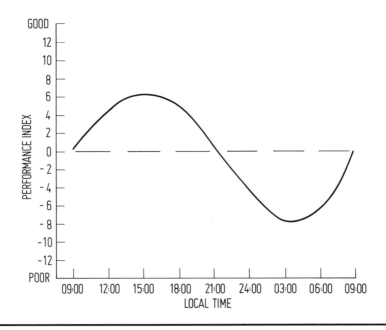

Fig. 6.3 Performance deviations from desired range, speed, and altitude for pilots in an F-104G simulator. To increase the task demands a simulated 200-mile-per-hour wind varying continuously around 360 degrees was employed. This performance curve closely follows the circadian body temperature curve. Adapted from K. E. Klein et al. (1970). *Aerospace Medicine, 41,* 126.

Even when allowance has been made for normal sleep periods in crew scheduling, there is no guarantee that crews will be able to obtain normal sleep, particularly if this falls during the local waking hours. There are also widespread individual differences in ability to readjust to these time-zone changes. Approximately 20 percent of people experience unusual difficulty in adjusting to jet lag or in adapting to irregular shift-work schedules. The time taken to adapt fully to westbound travel has been found to range from less than 2 days for some individuals to 6 days for others and between 3 and 11 days for eastbound travelers. There is some evidence that the difficulty of adapting to time-zone changes increases with age, particularly beyond the age of 40.[31]

It would, of course, be highly desirable to be able to predict exactly the time needed for the body's circadian rhythms to resynchronize as an aid in the management of crew scheduling. A number of formulas have been proposed with this in mind. Unfortunately, when applied to the same data, these formulas produce somewhat discrepant results in a number of cases.[32] The factors that are included in attempting to predict appropriate rest-time requirements are (1) number of time zones crossed, (2) flight duration, (3) departure time, (4) arrival time, (5) direction of travel, (6) multiple night flights, (7) multiple transits, and (8) sleep taken during the day.

To gain a better understanding of some of these factors, a large-scale international study was undertaken to provide operationally useful guidance on the issue of layover sleep for aircrews flying transmeridian routes.[33] Volunteer crew members from four different airlines (British Airways, Pan American, Lufthansa, and Japan Air Lines) were monitored before and after line trips between San Francisco and London, Frankfurt, or Tokyo. Each crew member was monitored for two nights in a laboratory near home base prior to the flight and during the layover period at the end of the flight.

Several techniques were used. The primary method was to monitor brain activity by electroencephalographic recordings (EEG). This is a commonly used method of assessing sleep and involves detecting small changes in cortical activity recorded from electrodes placed on the scalp. Some crew members also provided measures of body temperature, heart rate, and urinary catecholamines. All subjects completed questionnaire judgments of the amount and quality of sleep. The findings are broadly consistent with the general findings outlined above. The authors offer the following conclusions for operational guidance:

- Crews were generally able to get adequate sleep during layovers. There were significant individual differences and significant age differences with a decrease in sleep quality in crew members over 50 years of age.
- Sleep patterns were more disturbed following eastward flights than westward flights. The authors recommend that crews should not sleep immediately after arrival but keep awake until the local sleep time.
- Although crew members on westward schedules generally experienced good quality sleep after arrival, they also experienced drowsiness on the following afternoons. The authors recommend the practice of taking a nap before the following departure.

In general, it is advantageous for crews to remain on the home-based pattern. However, if transmeridian flying prevents this, the recommendations above may provide some useful guidance. In addition, rest time on return to base should be sufficient to allow for circadian resynchronization. West German regulations, for example, require a rest period calculated by multiplying by eight the largest time-zone difference while on duty. A trip covering eight time zones would therefore require 64 hours of rest on return.

Sleep patterns.   Much is known about sleep and the effects of sleep disruption on performance. Curiously, there is no generally accepted answer to the question of why we sleep at all. All mammals sleep, but the time spent sleeping is highly variable across species. A human's average of 7 to 8 hours of sleep a night is about the middle of the range between the relatively insomnious donkey (average 3.1 hours) and the extremely somnolent opossum (average 19.4 hours). It has been known since the 1950s that sleep occurs in different stages during the night.[34] There are approximately 30 changes of sleep state between the five easily recognized stages during one night's sleep.

The most often studied of these stages is the one associated with dream recall during which our eyes move, our muscles twitch, and our characteristic brain electrical activity changes. Known as REM (rapid eye movement) sleep, this can be distinguished from the other sleep stages by examination of the EEG recording. Sleep disruption can therefore involve two separate factors. First, a loss of the total amount of sleep, and second, a loss of a particular phase of the sleeping cycle. Both of these are relevant to the question of how performance is affected.

In contrast to a regular sleeping pattern, the sleep of a pilot on prolonged east-west operations is shown in Figure 6.4. Whereas the normal sleep pattern is closely clustered around the period of six to eight hours, the pattern for the sleep-disturbed pilot shows a number of short naps as well as a small number of extremely lengthy periods of sleep. The greatest operational concern is, of course, the case in which these short "naps" occur while in the cockpit. Some cases have been reported in which entire crews on transatlantic trips have apparently been asleep simultaneously for as long as 20 minutes.

In one study, heart rate and EEG recordings were obtained at intervals throughout a flight from Buenos Aires to London. Two of the crew members were found to exhibit characteristic sleep patterns of brain electrical activity during the early morning hours of 0400–0600.[35] This was 0100–0300 Buenos Aires time. However, high urinary noradrenaline levels observed during the flight, and for the following two days, indicate high levels of autonomic activity during at least some phases of long-duration flights. Nevertheless, the warm, dimly lit cockpit provides the ideal situation on long night flights to induce sleep. The drowsiness comes on at increasing frequency and is more and more difficult to overcome, even by vigorous exercise.

The existence of "microsleep" patterns is not necessarily related to lack of preflight sleep and is not easy to predict. It can affect all of the flight crew at the same stage of flight. The problem of such very low levels of activation or even brief periods of sleep has prompted investigation into warning devices that would relay back to the pilot

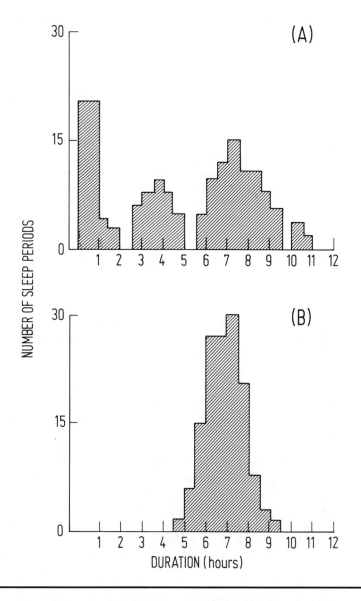

Fig. 6.4 Different sleep patterns for a pilot engaged in long-haul east-west operations (A) and a pilot flying short-haul operations (B). In (A) there are numerous sleep periods of less than two hours each and a few sleep periods of more than ten hours. The sleep pattern in (B) shows less disturbance with an average of 7.6 hours and a much smaller range (4.5 to 9.5 hours). From *Aviation Medicine: Physiology and Human Factors*, edited by G. Dhenin. Copyright 1978 by Tri-Med Books. Adapted by permission.

signs of incipient drowsiness. Although this would be quite feasible in theory, there would be considerable difficulty in finding a means of detecting drowsiness and transmitting a warning acceptable to the pilot.

One limited but interesting study of the performance effects of fatigue was carried out by the Civil Aviation Authority in England.[36] A single pilot aged 58 was monitored throughout a series of 16 flights over an 18-month period. Each flight involved the same visual, instrument, and single-engine maneuvers in an HS748 turboprop. The main interest was in the difference between flights made after 30 hours of sleep deprivation and flights made after several similar flights had already been flown. Both of these circumstances have been considered to cause fatigue. Because of the small number of flights involved and the reliance on a single subject, it is not possible to make any definitive statement regarding the difference between these two sources of fatigue.

However, the observations of the researchers suggest that the two conditions are characteristically different. In the case of sleep deprivation, the change in flying performance seemed to involve a tendency to make a rare but gross error. Performance on the repetitive flights, on the other hand, seemed to be characterized more by boredom and complacency, "a lack of motivation towards fine accuracy on the instruments." Other evidence from studies of airline pilots flying short-haul routes suggests that the higher workload of such operations, as reflected in elevated heart rate levels on takeoff and landing, carries over and is reflected in higher stress-hormone levels as measured each night.[37]

Although long-haul operations involve some sleep loss (estimated to be one to two hours per day en route), this loss has little direct effect on performance. Most disturbance to flying performance is caused by the time-zone changes and the time needed to readapt the body's circadian rhythms. The most pronounced effects are likely to occur when the fatigue of long duty hours coincides with the lowest point of the circadian cycle. Such a combination was exhibited in the British Airways Nairobi incident outlined earlier. In laboratory tests, the performance decrement observed under these conditions has been as large as 35 percent.

ALCOHOL, BLOOD SUGAR, AND CARBON MONOXIDE

Probably the most widespread stress management aid in Western society is the consumption of alcohol. Alcohol brings about immediate mood changes and even in very small quantities can severely affect performance in tasks such as driving or flying. The effects, of course, do vary with quantity!

JOURNEY SCOTCHED

> *One summer afternoon at Provo, Utah, a Grumman American Tiger hove into view flying erratically and aimed itself at a piece of pavement. Two aircraft in the pattern were forced into go-arounds by this maneuver. Lined up on final, the Tiger was aimed not at a runway but at a taxiway. The plane touched down, bounced several times, and was held down by the pilot; it ground-looped and finally came to rest off the taxiway in the brush. The pilot, a 56-year-old male dressed in blue gym shorts and a white polka-dotted shirt, was still in the airplane when the arresting officer arrived. The officer noticed the pilot was sticking a one-quarter-full bottle of Johnny Walker Black Label into his flight bag. (Another empty bottle of the same Scotch whisky would be found in the bag.) The pilot needed help in exiting the aircraft and walking to the patrol car. A blood test showed a blood-alcohol level of 0.23 percent, at least twice the maximal limit for driving. When asked where he thought he was, the pilot responded, "Wyoming," which the officers thought remarkable, because they all had Provo, Utah, written on their arm patches.[38]*

Tragically, alcohol is involved in at least 10 percent of the fatal general aviation accidents in the United States.[39] The National Transportation Safety Board's figures for 1975 through 1981 show that 10.1 percent of the toxicological tests on pilots killed in general aviation accidents were positive. Even more alarming, alcohol involvement was discovered in 6.4 percent of pilots killed in commuter airline crashes. These figures represent a decrease since the late 1960s when nearly 20 percent of pilots in fatal general aviation accidents were found to have some alcohol present in their blood. Available statistics do not describe the complete picture because there is no testing of pilots who survive their accidents.

A survey of 835 pilots revealed that, while only 4 percent reported flying after drinking, a sizeable number failed to recognize the time required for alcohol to metabolize.[40] They thought it was acceptable to fly less than eight hours after consuming several drinks, when in fact even slight remnants degrade performance. In one experiment, 16 experienced pilots flew at night with up to 0.12 percent blood-alcohol.[41] At the highest level, half the flights required the intervention of the safety pilot. At the lower levels the pilots generally managed to keep the aircraft on the glideslope, but "they did so at the expense of the secondary tasks necessary to safe flight."

A DARK AND STORMY NIGHT

> *The pilot of a Piper PA31 was returning to the company base at Walney Island, Cumbria, England. He made a normal approach in heavy rain and strong wind to runway 30 but descended below the runway threshold and crashed into the sea channel surrounding the island. The only mechanical defect found in the wreckage was a crack in the cabin heater that may have been responsible for the high carboxyhemoglobin level in the pilot's bloodstream. The possibility that this contributed to the pilot's misjudgment of the approach cannot be discarded.*[42]

Another substance with toxic effects is carbon monoxide. This has been estimated to account for 0.5 percent of general aviation fatalities in the United States. Carbon monoxide may enter the bloodstream as a result of faulty exhaust systems and cabin heaters or through smoking. The Walney Island pilot's heavy smoking may also have contributed to the high levels of carbon monoxide in his blood. Carbon monoxide replaces oxygen in the hemoglobin, thereby causing the tissues to receive less oxygen than normal from the red blood cells.

The effects of small amounts of carbon monoxide on the ability to perform a range of tasks have been experimentally demonstrated.[43] The effects are essentially the same as those caused by the hypoxia experienced at high altitudes. All of the performance indices referred to in this chapter, such as vigilance and reaction time as well as visual sensitivity, deteriorate with exposure to carbon monoxide. The reduced visual sensitivity with oxygen deprivation is demonstrated by the apparent brightening of altitude chamber lights on returning to a normal oxygen level. At least one U.S. helicopter company now requires its pilots to be nonsmokers.[44]

One effect of hypoxia is to produce an initial increase in blood-glucose levels followed a few hours later by a sharp decline. The condition of an abnormally low level of blood glucose is known as hypoglycemia. A study at United Airlines showed that a quarter of the pilots aged 40 and over exhibited a reactive hypoglycemia following a glucose tolerance test.[45] Two to three hours following the administration of glucose, such as would be obtained by eating a chocolate bar, these pilots exhibited a reactive hypoglycemia in which their blood-sugar levels fell far below normal.

LOW ON FOOD

> *The British student pilot of a Cessna 152 was returning from Sunderland in northeastern England on the final leg of his PPL qualifying crosscountry flight. In deteriorating weather an hour after sunset, the aircraft struck the ground on a hillside at a height of 600 feet. The pilot survived the impact with serious injuries. The only food he had taken that day was a light breakfast nine hours earlier.*[46]

Increasing interest is being shown in matters of diet. It has been suggested that pilot performance can be affected by both the timing and type of food intake prior to travel. In the Sunderland accident, for example, the pilot's low blood-sugar level was considered a factor that might have affected his judgment. The brain and central nervous system rely heavily on glucose as a source of energy. When the body is engaged in heavy exercise, additional glucose is obtained from the liver's store of glycogen. Even after completing a marathon, athletes have been found to have the same blood-glucose levels they started with.

Extreme cases of hypoglycemia may be accompanied by a variety of physiological symptoms and eventual unconsciousness. It has been widely assumed that lower than normal levels of blood sugar can have a noticeably adverse effect on the ability to perform tasks of the kind involved in flying or driving. Laboratory experiments have, however, failed to show any significant effects of variation in blood-glucose levels on performance at a variety of tasks. The implication of blood-glucose levels in accident analysis must, therefore, be regarded as speculative at present.

The problem of discerning the underlying causes of an accident is clearly one of the major concerns of a human factors approach to flightdeck performance. We will discuss various potential contributors to accidents in the following chapters.

LIFE STRESS

The major transition points in people's lives, occurring in the wake of marriage, divorce, death of a family member, or a major change in career, inevitably involve stress and strain. Health statistics show a greater frequency and severity of illness in widowed or divorced people than in married people of the same age. Following a bereavement or divorce, the death rate for males increases by 40 percent during the following six months. Although the psychological effects are difficult to measure directly, there is substantial evidence from indices of health and illness to suggest that exposure to a number of these stressful life events is likely to increase a person's susceptibility to illness.[47]

Subjects in such research typically fill out questionnaires to indicate whether they have experienced various life changes and to report their health records. Some of the items from the most commonly used scale are shown in Table 6.1. The higher the number of "life change units," the greater the degree of stress. A strong association has been found between the number of these changes and reported illnesses. It is not clear, however, whether positive and negative changes should be weighted equally; it seems more likely that unpleasant events would lead to greater stress and illness.[48]

Table 6.1. Some Items from the Schedule of Recent Experiences

Life event	Life change units
Death of spouse	100
Divorce	73
Jail term	63
Marriage	50
Retirement	45
Sex difficulties	39
Business readjustment	39
Death of close friend	37
Son or daughter leaving home	29
Change in living conditions	25
Trouble with boss	23
Change in sleeping habits	16
Vacation	13
Christmas	12

Source: Adapted from Holmes and Rahe (1967).

There is relatively little research that bears directly on the relationship between stressful life events and performance as a pilot or crew member; the evidence offered is mainly anecdotal. For example, investigators for the U.S. Navy have compared the backgrounds of naval aviators who had played a contributory role in major mishaps with other aviators who had similarly been involved in mishaps but were judged not to have been at fault.[49] Flight surgeons administered a questionnaire to other squadron personnel and family members concerning the aviators' capacities for good judgment, marital problems, financial difficulties, interpersonal difficulties, and recent career decisions.

In view of the fact that in most cases the respondents were aware of the individual's accident involvement and whether or not he had been judged at fault, it is not surprising that those who were judged at fault were more likely to be regarded as "not professional in flying" and "incapable of quickly assessing potential trouble." More credible was the finding that the accident-responsible aviators were more likely to have had recent financial problems, made a major career decision, or become engaged to be married.

In a study involving British military aircrews, there was a significant association between worries about wives, bereavements, and love-life events and the overall squadron accident rates.[50] There is no direct evidence that these activities produce stress that in turn leads to accident proneness. It is quite possible that relatively incompetent or less dedicated pilots may be more likely to undertake nonflying activities that lead to financial problems, frequent career changes, and marriages![51] Attempts to demonstrate strong links between these life experiences and subsequent ill health have been both widespread and relatively unsuccessful.

In addition to the difficulty of trying to disentangle the order in which these links might operate, it is clear that individuals have widely different methods of coping with such events. It would therefore be inappropriate to suggest that pilots who experience a larger than average number of life changes should be considered "risks." However, it is possible that the short-term distraction of coping with such events can have unfortunate results. For example, in one study a majority of people accused of shoplifting claimed to be distracted or preoccupied with thoughts of external events.[52] Half of these individuals had recently been involved in several negative life-change events.

COMMUTER CRASH

Henson Airlines Flight 1517 crashed during an instrument approach to Shenandoah Valley Airport, Virginia, on 23 September 1985. The twin-engined Beech 99 had departed from Baltimore-Washington Airport with 12 passengers on board. The National Transportation Safety Board determined that "the probable cause of this accident was a navigational error by the flightcrew resulting from their use of the incorrect navigational facility and their failure to adequately monitor the flight instruments. Factors which contributed to the flightcrew's errors were:. . . intracockpit communications difficulties associated with high ambient noise levels in the airplane;. . . the pilots limited experience in their positions in the Beech 99; and stress-inducing events in the lives of the pilots."[53]

In one discussion of stress and accidents, it was suggested that life-change stress may be the most significant of all the stressors in terms of accident causation.[54] It is difficult to establish such a connection after an accident has occurred because the main source of information on life-change stress is likely to be the pilot or copilot involved in the accident. Nevertheless, in the Henson Beech 99 crash, there was circumstantial evidence that pointed to the existence of a number of stressful life events for both crew members.

The captain had just become engaged to be married and had a job interview with a major airline scheduled for the day after the crash. The first officer was unable to live with her husband in Florida because of her job with the airline. Financial difficulties caused her to postpone further visits to a doctor to check on lumps discovered in her breasts on a previous visit. Her mother had died at age 47 of breast cancer. The NTSB felt able to conclude that these significant life events may have intruded on the pilots' attention and distracted them from properly monitoring the navigational instruments.

Although this suggestion merits careful attention, it must be pointed out that no experimental demonstrations of such an intrusion have yet been reported. There are reports in the ASRS (see Chapter 4) of distraction caused by worry about external circumstances, but the true extent of the problem may be underreported. Furthermore, there is an evident tendency to explain one event in terms of other events that are most closely related in time or place. Traditional accident investigation reports do not commonly highlight the role of less immediate background factors, giving precedence to events occurring in the accident sequence.

A clear link has been established between exposure to stressful life events and the development of depressive symptomatology.[55] The experience of a recent loss of a valued person (for example, death of a partner) is particularly likely to lead to depression. A number of impairments in human performance have been associated with depressive states.[56] It has been suggested that depressives exert less effort at a task, resulting in poorer overall performance. More empirical evidence on the role of life stresses in performance errors would be of great value.

One more commonly recognized component of life stress that may have an adverse effect on a pilot's health has been referred to as supervisory stress.[57] This refers to the extensive organizational control that companies and regulatory bodies exercise over professional pilots, including the 6-month medical and proficiency checks, which, if failed, would automatically result in loss of livelihood. One commonly observed response is "checkitis" that may cause even relatively senior pilots to seek premature retirement rather than continue being tested.[58] Sympathetic handling on the part of the training captain can reduce the severity of checkitis.

In addition, it has been suggested that one of the factors that predicts potential coronary disease is the degree of supervisory stress. Potential for coronary disease was measured by taking the ratio of total serum cholesterol level to high-density lipoprotein cholesterol. Four factors that predicted this ratio were the height/weight index, number of cigarettes smoked, dietary fat, and the level of microsupervision. This is described as "one's supervisor spending too much time on details and requiring unneeded paperwork for the job."[59] This state of affairs is familiar to many professional pilots!

It should be stated that there is no inevitability about the relationship between these life-stress factors and illness. The same is true for well-known causes of illness, such as smoking; a proportion of individuals will remain healthy despite the assault endured by their lungs and heart. Pilots are undoubtedly in a better position to resist the effects of stress by being selected for initial good health. Of course this does not confer immunity from these effects, and the traditional image of a self-reliant and healthy pilot may actually inhibit the seeking of appropriate help and advice with stress management.

FURTHER READING

There is an extremely large psychological literature on stress and anxiety. A simple introduction is presented by C. Spielberger in *Understanding Stress and Anxiety* (New York: Harper & Row, 1979). A more advanced collection of readings has been compiled by V. Hamilton and D. Warburton in *Human Stress and Cognition* (New York: Wiley, 1979). A large-scale study of stress in pilots has been reported by S. Sloan and C. Cooper in *Pilots under Stress* (London: Routledge & Kegan Paul, 1986). The topic of circadian rhythms and aviation is reviewed by K. E. Klein and H. M. Wegmann in *Significance of Circadian Rhythms in Aerospace Operations* (Neuilly-sur-Seine: North Atlantic Treaty Organization; AGARDograph 247, 1980).

The System Approach

[7] Accidents, Human Abilities, and Pilot Errors

THE USUAL verdict was pilot error. I mean, if the rotor blades came off in flight, the pilot was posthumously charged with failure to preflight the ship properly. If you tumbled down the side of a mountain while trying to land on a pinnacle under fire, it was pilot error. There was usually no other conclusion.

ROBERT MASON, *Chickenhawk*

INTRODUCTION

From the earliest pioneering exploits of the Wright brothers in the United States and Richard Pearse in New Zealand to the dramatic feats of the high-altitude rocket-plane test pilots portrayed in Tom Wolfe's *The Right Stuff,* flying has always had a strong public association with risk. Despite the occasional glorification of such risk, the history of aviation represents a steady progress toward making aircraft safer to fly and ensuring that the systems of legislation, training, and air traffic control are as effective as possible in producing competent, safety-conscious pilots.

Major airline crashes receive extensive attention from the media. Such highly publicized events provide vivid and easily remembered examples of the potential dangers of aviation. Our perception of risks can be misled by the availability of these events. The number of lives lost in airline accidents is a tiny fraction of the lives claimed by less-well-publicized transportation modes. Table 7.1 illustrates this point with statistics provided by the National Transportation Safety Board (NTSB) for 1986.

Table 7.1.   Fatalities Associated with Major Modes of Transportation in
              the United States for 1986

Transportation mode	Number of fatalities
HIGHWAY	
Passenger cars, pickup trucks, vans	32,032
Large trucks	919
Motorcycles	4,531
Pedestrians	6,719
RAILROAD	476
MARINE	1,229
AVIATION	
Airlines	4
Commuter, air taxi	68
General aviation	958

Source: Adapted from Chai-Huang (1987).

A total of 15,432 passengers were killed on scheduled air services throughout the world (excluding the USSR) during the 20 years between 1965 and 1984. The yearly average of 771 fatalities represents less than 2 percent of the number killed each year in automobile accidents in the United States alone. To put it another way, in an average year the same number of people are killed on U.S. roads in five days as are killed in a year of worldwide scheduled airline operations. Even the worst year on record for the airlines (1985, with 2,129 fatalities) would equal only a 14-day road traffic toll in the United States. And in Brazil the road fatality rate is five times worse.

Things have changed since the interwar years when there was a rather relaxed attitude toward such things as drinking and flying: "It was reckoned that as every pilot would probably sooner or later find himself flying after a party, he might as well learn to do it properly."[1] Today's approach is more sober in every respect with flight safety as the paramount goal. The general trend in commercial aviation over the past 20 years has been one of increasing safety. Figure 7.1 shows the steady downward trend in accident rates during the period between 1965 and 1985.

The trend shown in Figure 7.1 is based on data supplied by the International Civil Aviation Organization (ICAO) for worldwide scheduled aviation. In practice, these statistics exclude the Soviet Union but reflect the accident record of the remainder of the world's carriers. Major airline operations have become extraordinarily safe with a worldwide fatal accident rate in 1984 of 0.1 per 100,000 hours flown. As can be seen from Figure 7.1, this rate is almost one-third that of just 20 years ago. Airlines in the United States have an even better record with an average fatal accident rate between 1975 and 1983 of 0.057 per 100,000 hours flown.

The rate is considerably higher for commercial operators engaged in commuter or air-taxi operations. The statistics supplied by the

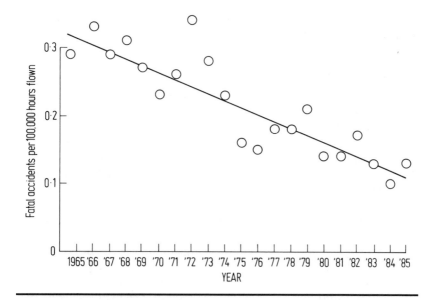

Fig. 7.1 Fatal accident rates for aircraft on world scheduled services between 1965 and 1985. These statistics, from an *ICAO Bulletin* of June 1986 published by the International Civil Aviation Organization, show the overall linear reduction in the fatal accident rate over the 20-year period. Although the number of fatal accidents was not much greater in 1985 than in 1984, the safest year on record, the number of passengers killed was substantially higher in 1985.

NTSB show that the scheduled commuter airlines had a fatal accident rate over the same period of 0.808 per 100,000 hours flown. This rate is more than 14 times higher than that achieved by the major U.S. airlines. The rate of 1.11 fatal accidents per 100,000 hours flown by the nonscheduled commuter carriers is 19 times as great. The very different nature of these three classes of operation makes the problem of finding a suitable unit of comparison quite difficult.

Commuter operators fly shorter distances with a much higher number of takeoffs and landings per 100,000 hours than the major airline operators. When fatal accidents per 100,000 departures are compared, the scheduled commuter airlines had a rate only 1.2 times higher than the major airlines for 1983. A recent review of air transport safety records puts the worldwide airline accident rate for the 1970s at between two and four accidents per million departures.[2] This is still at least three or four times lower than the rate for commuter and air-taxi operators.

Flying done by private pilots for business and pleasure as well as corporate operations flown by professional pilots are referred to as general aviation (GA). The fatal accident rate reported by the NTSB for general aviation in 1983 was 2.87 per 100,000 hours flown, almost 50 times higher than the comparable rate for airline operations. Of course, there are many differences in training, equipment, and operating environment that favor the professional two-pilot operation over the single-pilot operation that is most typical of general aviation. One simple difference is in exposure to the most hazardous parts of flight.

Figure 7.2 charts the relationship between phases of flight and accident occurrence for one year of corporate flying accidents in the United States.[3] The most overrepresented phase of flight in these accident statistics is the final descent, which represents only 2 percent of total flight time but produces 27 percent of the accidents. It is followed by the landing, representing 1 percent of typical flight time but including 20 percent of the accidents. The takeoff is almost as hazardous with 1 percent of exposure and 13 percent of the accidents. Overall, 60 percent of these accidents occur during the 4 percent of flight time spent in maneuvering near the ground. Commuter operations and general aviation flying involve a disproportionate number of takeoffs and landings and hence a greater exposure to risk.

It has been argued that the increase in airline flying since deregulation in the United States has stretched air traffic control and FAA

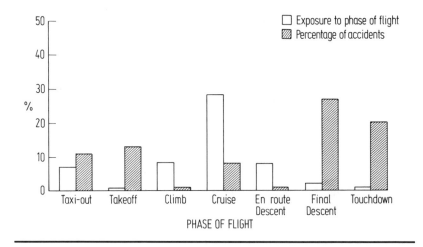

Fig. 7.2 An illustration of the relationship between some phases of flight and the percentage of accidents that occur during those phases for corporate flying. It can be seen, for example, that the takeoff phase represents only 1 percent of typical flight time but that 13 percent of all accidents occur during this segment. In contrast, 28 percent of a typical flight is spent cruising, but only 8 percent of accidents occur during this phase. Adapted from *Cause and Circumstance* by A. Trammell.

inspection resources to the limit. The latter may result in inadequate supervision over the smaller carriers in particular. Table 7.2 compares the risk per hour of different forms of transport using standard life-expectancy statistics based on U.K. data. The overall risk of just being alive is estimated at 0.1 per million hours until the age of 35 or 40, and then it rises gradually to around 5 per million hours at age 70 and 20 per million hours at age 80.[4] The author of these estimates concludes with the comforting thought (at least for the under-55s) that "flying as a passenger is no more risky than being 55 years old."

Table 7.2. Comparative Risks of Different Modes of Transportation

Transportation mode	Deaths per million hours
Bus	0.03
Rail	0.05
Private car	0.06
Airline flying	1.00
Motorcycling	9.00
Canoeing	10.00
Private flying	27.00
Mountaineering	27.00
Motorcycle racing	35.00

Source: Adapted from Stratton (1974).

In the very earliest years of aviation, when aircraft design and construction were still largely experimental arts, there were many mechanical failures involving engines and airframes. Over the years, engines became more reliable, and with the development of the jet engine, it is more than likely that most young pilots will be able to complete their flying careers without ever experiencing a power plant failure. The design of aircraft structures has made similar strides, particularly with the impetus imparted by military requirements.

Although disturbing cases of structural problems have plagued the introduction of new airliners from time to time (the Lockheed Electra, de Havilland Comet, and Douglas DC-10 are three notable examples), airframe construction has become a thoroughly tried and tested process. This is so much the case that manufacturers of light aircraft in particular have tended to stick with proven formulations for such long periods that there have been few significant improvements in performance in light training and touring aircraft in the past 30 years or so!

There are numerous innovative designs and construction techniques involving composite materials that promise great improvements in performance and efficiency for the future. The state of the art of aircraft construction and manufacture is such that aircraft very rarely fail in flight for mechanical reasons. When they have, United States courts have awarded such high punitive damages that the three major American manufacturers of light aircraft were forced to close down almost their entire production of single-engine aircraft during the 1980s because of the burden of product liability insurance.

ACCIDENT CLASSIFICATION

It is difficult to provide precise estimates of the underlying causes of aircraft accidents. Accidents to civil aircraft are normally investigated by an agency of the country in which the accident occurs, and usually a report is also prepared by the country in which the aircraft was registered if this is different. Military accidents are generally not open to widespread scrutiny. There is considerable consistency, however, when it comes to classifying the underlying causes of accidents into the three broad categories of mechanical factors, weather, and pilot error.

An investigation of records at the U.S. Army Agency for Aviation Safety, for example, suggested that human error was the causal factor underlying 84 percent of accidents to army aircraft since 1969.[5] Other estimates of the proportion of aircraft accidents that are attributable principally to pilot error tend to be consistently in the range of 70 to 80 percent. Despite the complexity and sophistication of aircraft, percentages are slightly lower than those generally accepted for all accidents involving industrial or consumer products caused by human error.[6]

To some extent this reflects the high level of mechanical reliability that has been achieved by aircraft designers. With the numbers of mechanical and in-flight structural failures minimized, the accident statistics naturally reflect a greater proportion of failures attributable to the manner in which the equipment was operated. This follows the rule that one prominent accident investigator has called the "law of exception," namely, "If we have ruled out everything except the pilot, the cause must be pilot factor."[7]

There is a clear relationship between the mechanical and aerodynamic characteristics of particular aircraft and their likelihood of involvement in the accident record. *Aviation Consumer* publishes a record of the relative accident rates of different aircraft in each of five categories ranging from two-seaters to corporate jets. The order of difference between the best and worst examples in each class increases with each movement up the scale.

For example, the worst single-engine, two-seater has an accident rate about four times that of the best in that class (the Cessna 150), whereas the worst corporate jet has an accident rate ten times that of the safest. Even higher ratios are reflected in statistics published by the NTSB for accident rates for different models flown by the scheduled airline carriers. For 1982, the accident rate of the worst model cited (Lockheed Electra) was nearly 40 times higher than for the best models (Douglas DC-9 and Boeing 727).[8]

Because the implications of mechanical failure can be disastrous for the designers and manufacturers of an aircraft (the case of the Douglas DC-10 is a particularly good—or bad—example) resulting in sales losses, job losses, and massive legal suits, there has undeniably been some pressure to apportion responsibility for an accident to individual human error. This can be particularly convenient when the crew is no longer able to answer back. Furthermore, it is frequently the case that the full blame is assigned to the pilot in command—the captain—even though the performance of other crew members may have been questionable.

Undoubtedly the development of increasing levels of automation on the flight deck arises from the same desire to reduce the possibility of human error in flying as far as possible. However, as we saw in Chapter 4, the introduction of automation raises many further questions as to what the best role of the human operator should be in a complex system. As we argued at the outset, the finding of human error in an aircraft accident must be regarded as a circumstantial description of a state of affairs rather than a causal explanation.

DESIGNED FOR DISASTER

> At 87 seconds after takeoff, with a 32-degree left bank and rolling left, Captain Kukar exclaimed, "Arey yar, my instrument!"
> Two seconds later, with the bank now 47 degrees, First Officer Virmani replied, "My . . . mine's also (toppled?—not clearly intelligible)," and Captain Kukar simultaneously said, "Check your instrument."
> At 95 seconds, First Officer Virmani repeated more clearly, "Mine has also toppled."
> One second later, just 5 seconds before impact, Flight Engineer Fario interjected, "No, but, go by this, Captain."
> At 99, Captain Kukar, "Just check the instrument. Yar!"
> At 101, First Officer Virmani, "Check what?" (Sound of impact.)[10]
> The flight data recorder gave no indication of any mechanical or electrical failure.

It is necessary to know what the pilot was trying to do at the time as well as how the rest of the system was functioning. This job has been made easier than it once was with the development and widespread use of the cockpit voice recorder (CVR), which is essentially a continuous tape loop that maintains a record of the last 30 minutes of communication in the cockpit, and the flight data recorder (FDR), which provides a record of vital systems information including the power settings, instrument readings, and pilot control inputs.

Both are designed to withstand severe impact forces and heat. The CVR can often throw dramatic light on what was happening prior to the moment of impact. A paperback book consisting solely of excerpts from CVR recordings makes compelling reading.[9] The final seconds of the Air India Boeing 747 crash discussed in Chapter 4 are set out above. Such conversations are not always so interpretable, and even in this case data from the FDR are needed to establish the correct interpretation, namely that the pilot had a horizon control reversal on the flight director indicator.

In the case of Air New Zealand Flight 901 that impacted Mount Erebus in Antarctica, the conversation on the CVR was subject to dramatically different interpretations from the official inspector of air accidents[11] and the royal commission subsequently set up to investigate the crash in more detail.[12] These differences arose because the quality of the recording made some words indistinct. Should the investigators have arrived at a preliminary hypothesis as to the cause of the accident, it would be easy for ambiguous words or phrases to be given an interpretation consistent with their hypothesis. The same would hold true for the commissioner's interpretation. The effects of expectation on perception have been discussed in Chapter 1.

No such information is available in the case of fatal accidents in light aircraft or even much larger aircraft engaged in commuter or air-taxi operations. In these cases, conclusions have to be drawn solely on the basis of wreckage examination and any other information that can be gleaned by interviewing eyewitnesses and acquaintances of the deceased. Just about every human failing imaginable can be located among their reports, from showing off with low-level aerobatics, to flying while drunk, to attempting a takeoff with concrete tiedown weights still attached! Perhaps one of the most improbable examples involved a Piper Cherokee and nude sunbathers.

Leaving such unique incidents aside, a variety of human error causes can be found in the pages of accident investigation reports produced by the NTSB in the United States or the CAA in the United Kingdom. Table 7.3 illustrates some typical examples of cited human errors contained in these reports.

A growing awareness of the significance of going beyond the pilot

PILOTLESS CHEROKEE CRASHES INTO NUDIST PARLOR

Nude sunbathers were forced to dress in a hurry when an unoccupied Piper Cherokee 140 crashed into a building near an airport in Massachusetts. The pilot-owner told police that he was positioning the propeller when the engine started and the plane began to move. The airplane traveled some 3,000 feet, becoming airborne briefly, before striking the building that housed the sun-tanning parlor.[13]

error label to a more adequate understanding of the causes of aircraft accidents has resulted in assigning human factors specialists to civil as well as military accident investigation teams in both the United States and the United Kingdom.[14] The basic orientation of these specialists is to put an aircraft accident or incident into an overall context in which pilots and controllers were attempting to achieve some goal—such as landing in adverse weather.

From a detailed knowledge of the equipment and the task and information needed to acomplish it, the human factors specialist is able to investigate the behavior of the pilots and controllers to discover why they failed to complete their tasks. Behavioral data are available not only from the CVR and FDR but also from interviews with crew members and controllers and other eyewitnesses. Furthermore, the study of human perception in flight, especially the operation of the visual and vestibular systems, has provided a better understanding of some pilot-error accidents, such as those attributable to perceptual illusions. Most of the examples in Table 7.3, however, involve processes other than illusory effects.

Table 7.3. Sample Human Error Findings from Recent Accident Reports

Cited cause	Report
Flight crew's lack of altitude awareness	NTSB-AAR-75-9
Failed to monitor descent rate and altitude	NTSB-AAR-78-13
Complete lack of awareness of airspeed, vertical speed, and aircraft performance	NTSB-AAR-79-2
Misunderstanding between pilots and controllers regarding each other's responsibilities	NTSB-AAR-75-116
The captain's actions and his judgment in initiating a go-around	NTSB-AAR-77-1
Misinterpretation of the external visual situation	DOT-AIB-12-77

COGNITIVE LIMITATIONS: ATTENTION AND WORKLOAD

A major advance has been to apply knowledge and understanding of human memory, information processing, and decision making to an analysis of accidents. Our understanding of human cognitive processes has developed in parallel with the rapid advances in computers. Psychologists have come to think of the brain as the "hardware" of the system and the strategies, plans, and actions of the individual as the result of particular programs or "software." Similar thinking has led to major computing developments in such fields as pattern recognition, voice recognition and production, and language translation.

As a metaphor for human behavior, the computer, in turn, directs attention to the higher-level processes because the mundane, computational details are assumed to be carried out automatically once the appropriate program is running. From this point of view, the hardware limitations of the system are of less concern than the way in which the software operates. This has coincided with a developing interest in these higher-level processes as sources of human error in accidents. For example, attention is now focused on social psychological factors that affect the decision making of crew members. We will deal with this topic in detail in the next chapter.

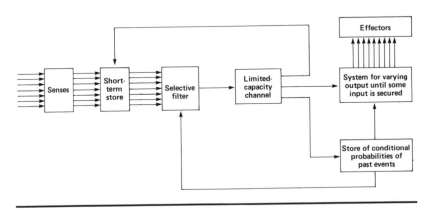

Fig. 7.3 The limited-channel-capacity model of human information processing proposed in the 1960s. A variety of information is acquired and briefly stored by our sensory systems. However, because only a portion of this information can be attended to without delay, it seemed reasonable to propose some kind of central "bottleneck" through which only a limited amount of incoming information can pass at any one time. Models based on more recent research (for example, Fig. 7.4) appear rather different, but the key ideas of selecting from available input and of a limit to the ability to perform concurrent processing are still applicable.

Much of the human factors literature on pilot error has been based on an earlier view of cognitive processes derived from a different metaphor. This was the limited-channel-capacity view, outlined in Figure 7.3, which saw the main limitations on human performance as stemming from inherent limitations in human abilities to process and handle information. The limited-channel-capacity metaphor (derived from telephone and radio engineering) expressed the view of humans as information processors. The key feature of this approach was the assumption of a single central processor through which all information had to pass. In this view, humans were essentially a kind of enigmatic transducer of information.

Investigation of the limitations imposed on the flow of information as a result of having to pass through a central bottleneck had the considerable advantage of permitting precise calculations of information flow through the system. The limited-channel-capacity model shown in Figure 7.3 seemed particularly appropriate to understanding pilot performance, because flying an aircraft requires the pilot to process information from multiple sources concurrently while making rapid choices among alternative courses of action. We will examine factors limiting each of these processes in the following sections.

THE UNPROFESSIONAL APPROACH

> *On 8 May 1978, National Airlines Flight 193, a Boeing 727, crashed into Escambia Bay while on a surveillance-radar approach to Pensacola Regional Airport. The NTSB determined that the probable cause of this accident was the crew's unprofessionally conducted nonprecision instrument approach in which the pilots failed to monitor the descent rate and altitude. Contributing to the accident was the radar controller's failure to provide advance notice of the start-descent point, which accelerated the pace of the crew's cockpit activities after the passage of the final approach fix.*[15]

Processing limitations and attention. The NTSB findings described above include as a probable cause of the accident a lack of attention by the pilot to vital information concerning the aircraft's altitude, speed, and descent rate. The full NTSB report of the Pensacola crash describes in some detail the state of affairs in the cockpit during the last five minutes of the flight. To begin, there was confusion as to the nature of the available instrument approaches at Pensacola. Then the flight controller positioned the aircraft on a final approach course too early.

This "created a situation that would make it impossible for the Captain to configure his aircraft in the manner specified in the flight manual." There then followed a series of mistakes including failure to extend the gear and flaps appropriately and failure to heed a warning from the ground proximity warning system, which was turned off by the flight engineer seconds before impact. Again, from the report, these "increased the Captain's workload . . . and contributed to producing the major causal area of the accident—a lack of altitude awareness."[16]

It has long been accepted that there are limits on the number of activities one can handle concurrently. For example, driving a car and holding a conversation can normally be handled without difficulty. On the other hand, doing mental arithmetic and holding a conversation at the same time is virtually impossible. It might appear that there is some overall limit on the amount of information we are able to deal with at any given moment, but in fact the amount varies with the nature of the activities involved and the extent to which they draw on time-shared common processes.

Nevertheless, it is reasonable to ask whether there is some limit on the information flow set by the inherent characteristics of the brain and nervous system. Early studies of human information processing have shown that the time taken to respond to one of several signals is a linear function of the information contained in the stimuli. This is defined as follows: when a response has to be made to one of two equally probable stimuli, one bit of information is transmitted; if there are four possible stimuli, two bits of information are transmitted; eight equally probable alternatives represent three bits; and so on.

Reaction time increases by a constant amount with each bit of stimulus information. It has been hypothesized that this relationship can be used to determine the upper limit of human information processing capacity in bits per second. However, it seems that the upper limit of processing capacity is actually set by the number of discriminations that can be made per second. One study of subjects' responses to a simple task, discriminating which of two lights was illuminated, showed that the upper limit was reached at 2.5 discriminations per second.[17]

It has also been shown that humans can more easily process two 6-bit discriminations than three 4-bit or four 3-bit discriminations.[18] One explanation of this complexity advantage is that, whereas much processing can take place in parallel, discriminating category alternatives appears to be sequential and single-channel in character. There is therefore an advantage in requiring pilots to make a small number of complex decisions rather than a large number of simpler decisions. This is, of course, the reason why simple flight control functions have largely been automated.

In some circumstances, the task of manually flying a complex landing approach, such as the old harbor approach into Hong Kong, may put the operator very close to the absolute limits of performance.

> The 100-ton jet had to be swung and tightly manoeuvred for eight miles through the narrow sea-channel, constricted at one point to less than half-a-mile wide. Despite the Captain's warning, some passengers momentarily thought the Captain had taken leave of his senses as they peered transfixedly out of the windows—upwards at apartment building balconies. The pilot had to try not to cut the corner to the runway, yet avoid closing in too near the rising apartment buildings.[19]

Only crew members who had memorized the positions and colors of the lead-in lights down the harbor, the compass headings, and the climb and descent rates could fly this approach safely. By memorizing whole procedures or blocks of actions, the pilot can effectively deal with more information. This is similar to the way in which working memory can be increased by chunking material into meaningful units. In this way, although working memory is limited to about seven items, each item can actually contain a great deal of information. We can easily remember 50 digits when these are chunked into five 10-digit telephone numbers, for example.

Workload. Faced with handling several sources of information concurrently, the pilot must decide on priorities. Flight training emphasizes the importance of flying the aircraft first, with navigation and communication as secondary responsibilities. It is suggested through the limited-capacity notion that, as workload increases, performance on the main or primary task may be maintained at the expense of performance on the secondary tasks. In the previously described Pensacola accident, the primary task of flying the aircraft was relegated to a secondary task as the crew struggled to keep up with the procedural activities required to prepare the aircraft for landing.

In studies of human ability to carry out two tasks simultaneously, such as an auditory judgment and a manual tracking task, accurate performance on one can only be maintained under high workload at the expense of worse performance on the other. As stated at the outset, it is possible to perform certain nonconflicting tasks concurrently without decrement to either, and workload studies have shown that this can indeed be the case. This suggests that the simple notion of the human as a limited-capacity processor is incomplete and not entirely accurate.

However, the notion of a trade-off in performing tasks concurrently has formed the basis of most attempts to measure cockpit workload. It would be helpful to have objective measures of workload to assess the effects of introducing new system features, such as direct air-ground data transfer (Chapter 5), automating a function in an existing system (Chapter 4), or reducing the crew from three to two. Workload is difficult to define precisely but rather easy to recognize when it becomes uncomfortably high! This suggests that it is essentially cognitive in character, although various behavioral and physiological measures have been assumed to reflect changes in workload.

The measures used tend to fall in four categories. First, checklist or questionnaire measures of pilots' opinions have been obtained. Second, physiological measures have been used, such as pulse rate, respiration rate, and pupil diameter. The third and fourth categories are derived from the distinction between so-called spare capacity, or residual attention, and attention devoted to the primary task. Thus, measures of mental arithmetic, time estimation, and other secondary tasks have been introduced in parallel with direct measures of aircraft response to assess performance on the primary task. The sensitivity and intrusiveness of measures in each of these categories have been investigated in several studies.[20]

In one series, subjects were qualified pilots with flight experience ranging from 60 hours to 2,700 hours. The studies were carried out in a three-axis moving-base simulator. In one of the experiments, subjects flew three flights during which they were required to monitor their instruments for abnormal indications. The monitoring of the fuel gauges, ammeter, oil temperature and pressure, and an ice warning light were selected to be representative of flight-related perceptual workload. The number of abnormal indications was varied by the experimenter to create conditions of low, medium, and high workload.

The following measures were used:

- Rating scale measures including the Cooper-Harper aircraft-handling rating scale (originally developed to allow test pilots to rate the handling qualities of test aircraft). The rating scales were completed during rest breaks between successive runs.
- Physiological measures including respiration rate and heart rate.
- Primary task measures, such as the number of control inputs and deviations in heading and altitude.
- Secondary task performances such as estimating 10-second time intervals. These were designed to measure spare capacity as described above. Subjects were specifically asked to concentrate on the primary task of flying the simulator accurately.

The results illustrate the difficulty of arriving at a single, unitary measure of workload. The rating scale measures were most sensitive to variations in imposed workload. Furthermore, as they were completed at the end of each flight, they did not intrude on or affect the primary task. It seems that in certain respects pilots do know what they're talking about! The spare capacity measure was able to differentiate between high and low loads but did not discriminate clearly between low-medium and medium-high levels. The primary task measures and the physiological measures were only slightly sensitive to the workload manipulation.

The importance of obtaining several measures of workload is illustrated in a study of NASA test pilots flying a C-141 on high-altitude flights.[21] Subjective ratings and heart-rate measures were obtained. Although the heart-rate and opinion measures were highly correlated, only the heart-rate measure discriminated between the pilot flying and the nonflying pilot, with significantly higher levels for the pilot in command. Both the heart-rate and the opinion measures varied significantly among the different phases of the flight.

Each of the four categories of workload measures has its advantages and disadvantages. Primary task measures may be the most useful in differentiating between levels of load that result in significant performance degradation. At less extreme levels, however, the pilot may maintain performance through increased effort, for which subjective ratings may be most sensitive.[22] Secondary tasks should preserve the priority of the primary task and the compatibility of the competing demands on peripheral sensory and motor channels as well as central resources. Physiological measures seem to reflect the activation level (see Chapter 6), another important component of the notion of workload.

Subjective measures of workload collected at frequent intervals during a simulated flight can show the effects of a momentary change in some activity—for example, in monitoring the proposed cockpit display of traffic information (see Chapter 4).[23] In evaluating the impact of new technology in the cockpit, it would be possible for the overall subjective workload to remain unchanged despite significant differences in mission capabilities and primary performance levels. Because of the complex nature of workload, most investigators will continue to use a battery of measures rather than rely on any single approach.

Time-sharing. The ability to alternate between different sources of information is clearly required in piloting and in air traffic control. In the early stages of training, virtually all of the student's attention will be directed toward the primary task of manipulating the aircraft controls to achieve the desired path through the air. As skill and confidence increase, the student has more time to scan the instruments and keep a proper external lookout. The fact that the student's attention will be fully occupied by the primary task in the early stages of training suggests that extensive elaborations by the instructor and in-flight lectures on aerodynamics will be of little value.

This is consistent with the notion of an overall limit on ability to handle information that emerged from experiments in the 1960s showing that, if a subject were exposed simultaneously to two messages, only one could be attended to.[24] However, it was also found that some characteristics of the other message could be reported, for example, whether the speaker had been male or female. This finding implied some kind of filtering mechanism that is limited in its overall capacity to transfer incoming sensory information into memory and led to the limited-channel-capacity model shown in Figure 7.3.

It is possible, however, to overcome this limitation by developing more efficient ways of attending to the different tasks. For example, a group of U.S. Marine aviators were taught a specific technique to reduce the risk of midair collisions.[25] The training scheme concentrated on improving the pilots' abilities to acquire all the necessary information from the flight instruments before refocusing attention outside the cockpit. Pilots who were exposed to this training were much better at detecting external targets than the untrained pilots. These results are impressive in view of the fact that there was a period of several months between the early stages of the training and the final data collection.

Expert performance of tasks carried out concurrently appears to become both effortless and accurate compared to novice performance. Two different factors may account for this change. First, there is improvement in the performance of each separate task. At the outset, processing is slow, effortful, and largely sequential. With practice, performance becomes faster with elements processed in parallel. These two styles of processing are referred to as controlled and automatic, respectively. Provided there are consistent elements in the task, such as following exactly the same sequence of actions in response to an engine fire warning, extensive practice will lead to more automatic processing.[26]

Second, multiple-task performance may lead to the development of time-sharing skills. Time-sharing is related to the idea of spare capacity available from the performance of the primary activity. It is a hypothesized psychological ability to process multiple inputs in parallel. Individuals differ in their abilities to deal with the demands in flying or air traffic control to perform several tasks concurrently. Both the ability to switch efficiently from one task to another and an ability to process inputs concurrently may be involved.

Evidence that there may be a separate time-sharing ability that is over and above the individual abilities required to carry out the primary and secondary tasks has come from several experiments. In one, nonpilot subjects were tested on a battery of measures used in aircrew selection.[27] These consisted of such items as reacting to various warning signals, monitoring a row of meters, performing mental arithmetic, and tracking. The tasks were first performed one at a time and then concurrently. The conclusion was that performance on these tasks was affected by a higher-order process that was labeled time-sharing ability.

The importance of this ability for predicting flight-training performance was investigated in another experiment.[28] Subjects were given two tasks, a manual-tracking task and a digit-processing task that were performed separately and also concurrently. The majority of subjects were student pilots, and the remainder were flight instructors. A measure was obtained of the proportion of single-task performance retained under the dual-task condition. Some doubt has been expressed as to the appropriateness of this measure, and the following results should be treated cautiously.[29]

Instructors were better than their students at the tracking task, but the reverse was true of the digit task. As in the previous study, when the tasks were performed together there was an element of performance accounted for by individual differences in ability to shift attention between tasks. Comparing the instructors with the students showed that the instructors were able to retain more of their single-task performance when doing the tasks concurrently, and this was attributed to their superior ability to time-share between the tasks.

The student pilots were rated for their "flying potential" after ten hours of dual instruction. There were no differences between the high-rated and low-rated subjects on their single-task performances. However, several dual-task measures discriminated between the two groups. Other studies have failed to support the notion of a generalized time-sharing ability.[30] Nevertheless, with certain combinations of tasks at least, it is evident that individuals differ in their ability to process inputs in parallel.[31]

Furthermore, the ability of pilots to perform multiple tasks has been shown to be related to the processing demands imposed by the individual tasks.[32] In this context, the demands of a task such as monitoring the horizontal situation indicator (HSI) can be thought of as visual and spatial, whereas listening to an air traffic control clearance is essentially aural and verbal. Since spatial and verbal processing can be shown to operate in quite different ways and even to take place in separate parts of the brain, it follows that there will be less conflict between tasks that are not competing for the same resources. A schematic diagram of this multiple-resource view of attention is shown in Figure 7.4.

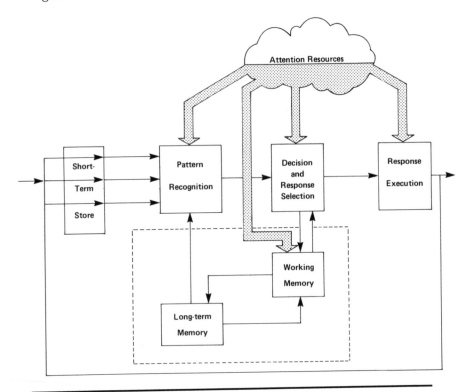

Fig. 7.4 Wickens' multiple-resource model of human information processing. This model suggests that the limits of information processing are more flexible and that attentional resources can be switched from one area to another. This notion is consistent with experimental evidence showing that some tasks can be carried out together quite easily, whereas others that compete for the same kinds of resources cannot. From *Engineering Psychology and Human Performance* by C. D. Wickens. Copyright 1984 by Scott, Foresman and Company. Reprinted by permission.

It is much easier to carry out two tasks such as those described above than two that compete for the same resources—for example, monitoring a checklist and copying a departure clearance. The most important practical application of this principle is in the design of cockpit systems, including instrument displays. Two current examples are the design of voice-activated control systems and auditory displays. These are less likely to interfere with the primarily visual-spatial task of flying than other control systems and displays that compete for the same resources. This represents an exciting extension of the principles of control-display compatibility discussed in Chapter 4.

JUDGMENT AND DECISION MAKING

Decisional skills have always been elusive topics in flying. Decision making is a major component of what was variously referred to in Chapter 3 as situational awareness, airmanship, and good flying judgment. It has been common to pay relatively little explicit attention to this topic in pilot training and to assume that it is naturally developed through experience and exposure to a variety of situations. There is no doubt that many aspects of a pilot's skills improve with practice and experience. However, the possibility that situational awareness, judgment, and decision-making skills can be improved through structured training is a topic of considerable research interest.

Some forms of judgment are quite explicit and easily observable. The calculation of takeoff and landing distances, weight and balance, and reference speeds are made according to prescribed formulas. Decisions to continue or break off a precision instrument approach are made, appropriately enough, at the legal decision height. Even here, the simplicity of the rules (for example, "abandon the approach if the runway is not in sight") can be insufficient to prevent momentary indecision in the case of broken cloud conditions in which glimpses of approach lighting may have been obtained intermittently before reaching the decision height.

NORTHWEST AIRLINES BOEING 727 ACCIDENT

> On 1 December 1974, Northwest Airlines Flight 6321, a Boeing 727-251, crashed about 3.2 nautical miles west of Thiells, New York. The accident occurred about 12 minutes after the flight had departed John F. Kennedy International Airport, New York. The airspeed and the altitude values recorded on the FDR were consistent with the aircraft's predicted climb performance until it reached 16,000 feet (the altitude at which icing was encountered). The airspeed of the aircraft when the stick shaker was first activated was calculated to be 165 knots compared to the 412 knots recorded by the FDR. The pitch attitude would have been about 30-degrees nose-up. The aircraft was destroyed, killing the three crew members on board.[33]

Less easy to deal with are responses to events that require quick detection and diagnosis followed by a choice among alternatives and appropriate action. Opportunities for error can arise at each of these four stages. Good cockpit design and appropriate warning devices can do much to eliminate failure at the detection stage. As we noted earlier, modern transport aircraft have an enormous variety of warning systems in addition to airborne radar and surveillance by air traffic control. None of these provides much help, however, if the problem is incorrectly diagnosed.

The erroneous airspeed and Mach warnings in the Northwest Airlines Boeing 727 accident were the result of a blockage in the pitot heads caused by icing. The crew had not activated the pitot-head heaters. The crew incorrectly diagnosed the stall warnings as Mach buffet and proceeded to pull the plane's nose up, resulting in a stall and spin. In many cases, situational awareness at the diagnosis stage is virtually synonymous with better training and thorough knowledge. As this example shows, it is not only low-time private pilots who find themselves in situations for which they appear to lack the necessary understanding.

Faced with deteriorating weather ahead, a VFR pilot may have to make a rapid choice among continuing, diverting, or returning to the departure point. Each alternative will have different costs in terms of time, money, inconvenience, danger, and possibly social pressures, and each involves probabilistic information. There may, for example, be a possibility of flying over the clouds for a brief period and then safely descending. This likelihood must be estimated rapidly from whatever information is available. It is clear that there are numerous sources of error in arriving at such estimates.[34] A few of these are:

- An event may appear more likely if it can easily be brought to mind. The frequency of vivid events (e.g., engine failure) may be overestimated, whereas less vivid events (e.g., faulty fuel gauges) may be underestimated.
- People have problems combining probabilistic information. A series of likely events will be judged more probable than any one of the component events in violation of basic probability rules.
- People exhibit unjustifiable confidence in their assessments. As information is acquired, confidence increases even though the information may be unreliable or irrelevant.
- Hindsight can make judgments look better than was actually the case.
- The way a problem is framed or presented can change people's responses.
- When faced with an inevitable loss, people tend to gamble on a

risky alternative. This may be part of the reason for pushing on into deteriorating weather rather than accepting the inevitable costs of turning back.

Mistakes and slips. Finally, a quickly detected, correctly diagnosed engine fire, followed by an appropriate decision to shut down the affected engine, can be nullified by a slip in performing the required action—shutting down the good engine. Once again, proper cockpit design can help by improving the discriminability and placement of engine and propeller controls. Whereas the problems at the detection, diagnosis, and decision stages involve formulating the correct plan of action, the problem at the final stage is to carry out the intended plan. Errors in formulating an appropriate plan will be referred to as mistakes. Those that occur in the execution of a plan will be referred to as slips.

The kinds of errors that occur at these two stages are likely to be quite different in nature.[35] Although experience and familiarity can improve the formulation of appropriate plans, these same factors can actually increase the likelihood of slips of action in carrying out the plans. Everyday experience provides examples of slips that commonly occur when carrying out routine, habitual actions, such as dressing, making tea, or driving to a friend's house. We may omit an action from the sequence (forget to put the tea in the pot) or carry out an action from another sequence (arrive at a friend's house and take out one's own front door key to open the door).

Slips are suggestive of an automatic mode of behavior in which conscious attention is diverted elsewhere. The planned sequence, once initiated, is left to operate under its own momentum. Slips are encouraged by lack of standardization. For example, a pilot recently landed a Piper PA28R with the undercarriage retracted.[36] The slip of forgetting to extend the gear was compounded by the fact that the gear-up warning horn on the Piper was the same as the stall warning horn on Cessna aircraft that the pilot regularly flew. The sound of the horn failed to alert the pilot even though it occurred well in advance of the landing flare.

Several schemes for classifying errors have been proposed by different authors. They differ in their degree of specificity and generality across different domains. A simple example used by some aviation psychologists breaks the overall pilot error category into four subcategories: improper technique, overconfidence, insufficient care, and other causes.[37] Although it may be important to distinguish errors due to insufficient skill from those due to carelessness, and overconfidence may be a symptom of poor judgment, such schemes are too general to provide a comprehensive analysis of the causes of human error in any specific case.

An engineer and a psychologist, working together, have produced an error-classification scheme that permits a more detailed analysis of human error.[38] This scheme assumes that the pilot is motivated to accomplish a particular task or achieve a specific goal. The scheme sets out six general categories of behavior needed to arrive at the goal. Within each of these general categories there are from four to nine more specific categories that define the particular characteristics of erroneous decisions or actions. Instead of focusing exclusively on human actions, this scheme is system oriented. A general outline is shown in Table 7.4.

Table 7.4. Outline of a Human Error Classification Scheme

Stage	Opportunities for error (examples)
Observation of system	Misinterpretation of correct readings
	Observation of inappropriate variables
	Failure to observe any variables
Choice of hypothesis	Choice of plausible but unlikely hypothesis
	Choice of irrelevant hypothesis
	Hypothesis inconsistent with observations
Testing of hypothesis	Reached wrong conclusion
	Hypothesis not tested
	Rejected correct conclusion
Choice of goal	Insufficiently specified
	Counterproductive
	Not chosen
Choice of procedure	Would achieve incorrect goal
	Would not fully achieve goal
	Procedure not chosen
Execution of procedure	Required step omitted
	Unnecessary step added
	Steps executed in wrong order
	Unrelated step executed

Source: Adapted from Rouse and Rouse (1983).

The categories "choice of procedure" and "execution of procedure," for example, clearly reflect the distinction between mistakes and slips discussed above. Opportunities for error arise at any stage of the cycle of detection, diagnosis, decision, and execution that reflects the basic activity of the pilot or controller of any complex dynamic system. A detailed error classification scheme such as this is particularly useful for comparing new with existing technology in terms of the kinds and frequencies of errors that may be associated with each.

The scheme just described has already been used to compare the effects of presenting information to the pilot in computerized form and conventional hardcopy form.[39] Such comparisons will need to be made more frequently as the development of CRT cockpit displays proceeds at an accelerated rate. Such classification systems are precisely speci-fied in the manner of a computer program. This has enabled the devel-opment of intelligent computer-based cockpit systems that can moni-tor the pilot's behavior in executing a procedure. The kind of automated checklist system described in Chapter 4 uses a scheme similar to the one shown in Table 7.4.

Can judgment be taught? Decision-making skill, or good judg-ment, one of the three areas of skill that needs to be acquired as part of pilot training (see Chapter 3), has become the subject of explicit atten-tion; it can no longer be assumed that instructors who provide good role models automatically instill similar characteristics in their stu-dents. A study of the NTSB accident files from 1970 to 1974 showed that a majority of the 25,878 nonfatal accidents could be attributed to perceptual-motor activities, such as failing to maintain flying speed.[40] In contrast, the majority (51.6 percent) of the 5,700 fatal accidents during this period were attributable to the decisional activities cate-gory.

It is clear from these statistics, as well as more anecdotal sources, that poor judgment is a major cause of error in general aviation and takes its toll in commercial aviation as well.[41] This may range from

---

AIR FLORIDA FLIGHT 90

> *On 13 January 1982, Air Florida Flight 90, a Boeing 737, was scheduled to Fort Lauderdale, Florida, from Washington National Airport, Washington, DC. There were 74 passengers—including three infants—and five crew members on board. The flight's scheduled departure time was delayed about 1 hour and 45 min-utes because of a moderate to heavy snowfall that necessitated the temporary closing of the airport. Following takeoff from Run-way 36, which was made with snow and ice adhering to the wings and fuselage, the aircraft crashed into the barrier wall of the northbound span of the 14th Street bridge. Four passengers and one crew member survived the crash. The NTSB determined that the probable cause of this accident was the flight crew's failure to use engine anti-ice during ground operation and takeoff, the decision to take off with snow and ice on the airfoil surfaces of the aircraft, and the captain's failure to reject the takeoff during the early stage when his attention was called to anomalous engine-instrument readings.[42]*

---

inadequate preflight planning, to miscalculation of aircraft capabilities, to indulgence in a variety of unsafe practices, such as the continu-
ation of a VFR flight into deteriorating weather conditions. Though far
less frequent, the major airline catastrophes almost always involve
bad judgment calls by pilots or air traffic controllers, or both.

The case of Air Florida Flight 90 is frequently cited as a classic
example of poor judgment and decision making. Although the indications needed to make a sound decision to abandon the takeoff were
clearly available, the crew made numerous individual errors of judgment and performed ineffectively as a team. We will discuss this case
in more detail in the final chapter. Research has begun to throw light
on the nature of pilot decision making, and there are indications that it
may be possible to incorporate explicit instruction in good judgment in
basic flying training programs.

In the first of a series of experiments, the investigators used pencil-
and-paper techniques to study the decision processes of instrument-
rated pilots faced with a need to divert from the planned route.[43] Following a description of a route to fly, together with the necessary
performance figures and a list of equipment on board, a scenario was
developed involving the symptoms of some problem such as an al-
ternator failure. The problem was cast as a choice among 16 possible
alternate airports. Each airport was described in terms of four characteristics: distance from current position, type of approach aids,
weather, and ATC facilities.

The experiment showed systematic differences in pilots' judgments of these problems as a function of type of training (for example
civil versus military) and type of flying normally done (military or airline versus other types). This points to a significant effect of type of
training on judgment over and above that of total flight experience.
For example, there was a much greater value given to the availability
of air traffic control services by civilian-trained pilots than by military
pilots.

In a subsequent study, a computer with a touch-sensitive screen
was used to investigate pilots' diagnostic and decision skills in scenarios involving various equipment malfunctions.[44] Perhaps the most
surprising finding was the relatively low level of basic knowledge of
aircaft systems, weather, and IFR operations shown by the 42 pilots
whose average flight experience was 1,654 hours. Level of knowledge
of systems and operations largely determined performance on these
diagnostic problems. Note that several of the errors of judgment made
by the Air Florida crew reflected a low level of knowledge of the aerodynamic effects of icing on wings and the potentially dangerous effects
of using jetblast to deice an aircraft.

There seems to be some consistency in the way individual pilots tackle problems that reflects a basic orientation to flying judgment. This seems to be the fundamental assumption that underlies judgment training in at least one pilot training program. Originally developed at Embry-Riddle Aeronautical University, this approach to teaching judgment assumes that poor judgment can arise from five basic orientations.[45] These five patterns have not been linked to actual instances of poor judgment but represent the opinions of a variety of experts. A brief description of these five orientations is presented in Table 7.5.

Table 7.5. Five Patterns of Poor Judgment

Type	Example
Antiauthority	"Don't tell me what to do."
Impulsivity	"Do something—quickly!"
Invulnerability	"It won't happen to me!"
Macho	"I can do it."
External control	"What's the use?"

Source: Adapted from Berlin et al. (1982).

Each of the five categories seems to describe a different pilot stereotype. It would be fairly easy for most pilots to recall a particular character that fits each category. On the assumption that poor judgment must surely follow if a pilot displays any one of these orientations, a set of student and instructor material was designed to heighten awareness of the hypothesized causes of poor judgment through numerous examples of flight situations. The original materials were tested on pilot trainees at Embry-Riddle. Most of the 81 subjects were young, male, full-time aviation students.

Three groups were compared. One group received the judgment training followed by a specially conducted observation flight in which the students were assessed in 20 judgment situations. The two control groups received either the same flight test or the same written judgment tests as the experimental subjects, who showed better performance on all sections of the written test than the subjects who had not had the judgment training. Furthermore, subjects who had been given the judgment training performed significantly better on the observation flight.

The apparent success of this exercise led to further revisions of the judgment-training material and attempts to demonstrate its effectiveness with more typical groups of student pilots and to assess its effectiveness over longer periods of time. This subsequent research took place at Canadian flying schools in collaboration with the Canadian Air Transportation Administration. Although student and instructor reaction to the judgment training approach has been quite positive, it has proved difficult to demonstrate any measurable effect on performance in the routine flight situation.[46]

Subjects in the Canadian study averaged 34 years of age compared to 19 years in the original study. On an abbreviated observation flight test requiring 12 decisions, pilots who had received the judgment training performed no better than a control group. Unfortunately, disagreement between the observers rating pilot performance could bring into question the validity of the testing procedure. A similar picture has emerged from a study conducted at five flying schools in Australia.[47] The small number of subjects tested (only eight pilots received the judgment training) precluded finding statistically reliable differences in performance.

It appears that, despite the initial promise, the approach to judgment training described above may not yield the kind of improvements that were initially expected. Part of this problem may be attributed to the difficulties of testing and evaluating pilot performance in the decision-making area. A more fundamental problem may be that, in the rush to develop a judgment-training program, the actual bases of faulty pilot decision making have not been adequately researched. The area of decision making and judgment has thus far proved to be a difficult one for psychological study.

In particular, it is notoriously difficult to define how such judgments should be made. In most cases involving the judgments of experts, such as clinicians, stockbrokers, and graduate admissions officers, it has been found that they use certain simplifying strategies that experience has led them to believe will be effective. Virtually nothing is known about how experts make decisions in flying. The analyses of decision making in complex simulated flight scenarios would appear to be a logical, safe, and manageable approach that could be conducted in conjunction with line-oriented flight training for experienced crews and readily adapted to ab initio training.

The focus in this chapter has been primarily on the individual pilot and the errors that arise from individual judgment. In commercial aviation, the more common arrangement is for multicrew operation in which more than one crew member is required on the flight deck. There will therefore be some division of responsibilities and monitoring of each crew member by the others. In the next chapter, we will turn our attention from the analysis of individual error to the social setting of crew performance and the consequences of breakdowns in communication, cooperation, and coordination.

FURTHER READING

A very readable and nontechnical account of performance errors is presented by J. T. Reason and K. Mycielska in *Absent-Minded: The Psychology of Mental Lapses and Everyday Errors* (Englewood Cliffs, NJ: Prentice-Hall, 1982). A useful collection of articles has been edited by R. Hurst and L. R. Hurst, *Pilot Error: The Human Factors: Second Edition* (London: Granada, 1982). Most of the articles in this volume have been previously published in the human factors journals, and several are referred to in the notes to this chapter.

[8] Social Psychology
in the Cockpit

*A PILOT who turns back and lands because he considers it
dangerous to go on is likely to receive praise and advance-
ment in his profession nowadays, but that was by no means
the mental atmosphere in 1930. In those days, a pilot was
expected to be brave and resolute, a daredevil who was not
afraid to take risks.*

NEVILLE SHUTE, *Slide Rule*

INTRODUCTION

In earlier chapters we have examined factors related to the sensory capacities of the pilot, pilot training, the design and layout of
controls and displays, and the abilities of the pilot to cope with high
workload and to exercise good judgment and decision-making skills.
All of these factors relate primarily to the individual without regard to
social factors outside the individual. Although we are generally aware
that relationships with other people are a source of satisfaction and
well-being in life, we are often insensitive to the pronounced influence
that other people's behavior can have on our own attitudes and judgments.

This does not imply that we are boorishly insensitive to other people but rather illustrates the subtle way in which our behavior can be
affected without our direct awareness. The changed climate of opinion
described in the quotation from Neville Shute is an example of a profound change in the kinds of behavior that are now regarded as appro-

priate and desirable by pilots simply as a result of a change in the attitudes and beliefs of their peers. A moment's consideration of fashions and trends in clothing and popular music will demonstrate the important role that reference to other people plays in establishing what is "normal" and bringing about conformity.

Social psychologists are concerned with studying the kinds of influence that other people have on our attitudes, values, and behavior. The results of such studies have recently been applied to understanding the performance of professional flight crews. Clearly, the influence of other people's behavior will be most apparent in situations where several individuals are required to function together as a crew. However, social factors can also exert influences on smaller groups, such as two- and three-pilot flight crews.

SOCIAL COMPARISON AND DIFFUSION OF RESPONSIBILITY

We discover and assess our abilities, attitudes, and judgments in comparison with those of other people. From an early age our athletic and intellectual abilities are explicitly graded in comparison to the corresponding abilities of others of a similar age. As time goes on we acquire most of our knowledge of our standings on various personal characteristics by comparison with others. Whether we regard ourselves as masculine or feminine, aggressive or passive, outgoing or retiring depends on comparison with those with whom we associate as well as information from society at large through the influence of the mass media.

There is an enormous psychological benefit from knowing that one's views are not held in isolation, and this is evidenced by our tendencies to associate more often with others who are similar to ourselves. Thus informal friendship groups tend to provide support for our views and beliefs. Formal groups and organizations often seek to enforce compliance by their members with particular attitudes or behavioral styles. Expulsion and deprivation of livelihood are the ultimate threats that military, legal, medical, and other organizations can wield in the power game.

More subtle is the influence of explicitly prescribed and proscribed behavior and attitudes. Groups such as doctors or pilots whose members undergo lengthy training and work under relatively stressful conditions tend to develop a greater sense of cohesiveness than other groups. Social comparison with other members of the same occupational group is a powerful influence that, in the case of pilots, can affect attitudes and judgments not only in flying but in matters quite outside the sphere of aviation. The direct influence of social comparison can be seen clearly in an incident involving Eastern Flight 66.

EASTERN 727 CRASH AT NEW YORK, JUNE 1975

> *Eastern Flight 66 encountered a severe wind shear at about 500 feet above the ground while conducting an ILS approach to Runway 22L. The shear was caused by a thunderstorm that was straddling the ILS course. It is uncertain when the captain made his final decision to continue the approach. However, because pilots commonly rely on the degree of success achieved by pilots of preceding flights when they are confronted with common hazards, it is likely that he continued the approach pending receipt of information on the progress of the two flights immediately ahead of him. By the time the second flight had landed without reported difficulty, the captain of Eastern Flight 66 was apparently committed to the approach.*[1]

When the preceding aircraft are of the same type or operated by the same company, the pressure on following pilots to accomplish the same task is multiplied. This pressure contains two distinct elements: the information that a successful approach can be made and that other pilots have just done so. This effect is not confined solely to the approach and landing phase of flight but may operate at the takeoff stage also. It is clear from the CVR recordings from Air Florida Flight 90, which crashed on takeoff from Washington National (see Chapter 7), that the crew's decision to attempt a takeoff without further deicing was influenced by the success of preceding aircraft.

In addition to providing information and acting as a source for comparison, other people can influence our behavior in another way. This has been demonstrated in experiments on the factors that inhibit people from helping others in an emergency.[2] If there is some degree of ambiguity present, for example, when a person has collapsed on the street (possibly after suffering a heart attack or through drunkenness), the likelihood of anyone helping such a victim varies according to the number of other people present. Help is most likely if there is only one bystander and considerably less likely if there is a crowd.

This surprising finding can be caused by a variety of social influences. Once again, social comparison is important in assessing whether other people regard the situation as a serious one. Another factor that operates at this point is that any responsibility for action is shared by all the bystanders present. The greater the number of by-standers, the greater this diffusion of responsibility. This notion of shared or diffused responsibility has clearly played a part in accidents of aircraft under positive radar control involving collision with the ground or other aircraft.

CONTROLLED-FLIGHT-INTO-TERRAIN

> *A Lear 24B left Palm Springs on an instrument departure for Los Angeles. Following the correct readback of the departure clearance, there was a delay of 20 minutes before takeoff. After takeoff the crew received an instruction to maintain 9,000 feet, which they interpreted as requiring them to fly the runway heading at this altitude. The aircraft subsequently struck a hillside in a sector where the minimum safe altitude was 13,000 feet. The investigation report concentrated on the breakdown in communication that occurred between the pilot and the controller. The report also noted that since the advent of radar control there has been a shift from the pilot to the controller of detailed knowledge of the terrain over which the aircraft is flying. At the time of the accident, the crew members believed they were under radar control when in fact no coverage of the area was provided.*[3]

The crew in the case of the Palm Springs Learjet clearly assumed that the controller was exercising responsibility for keeping the aircraft clear of nearby mountainous terrain. The dangerous effects of such diffusion of responsibility have been noted in discussions of mid-air collisions in radar control areas.[4] The responsibility of VFR pilots to see and avoid other traffic does not fully take into account the difficulties involved in locating traffic in the vicinity, which can be increased by equipment factors such as windscreen design. (In the Palm Springs case, it was chart design that contributed to the accident, as explained in Chapter 5.)

The development of intelligent automated decision-making aids for the flight deck will diffuse more pilot responsibility. The human factors problems created by systems in which commands are executed through sidestick controllers over which the human has to retain command authority were discussed briefly in Chapter 4. The introduction of fly-by-wire control systems in airliners, such as the Airbus A320, has already created new problems of apportioning authority whereby conflicting control inputs are received from the pilot's and copilot's controllers.

The wishful claim from the manufacturer of the Airbus that "the more intelligent pilot wins, not the strongest," seems to offer a reversal of the usual Darwinian notions of survival![5] In the A320, inputs from the sidestick controllers are interpreted by the flight management guidance computer. The software determines how the aircraft will react to these inputs. The software incorporates flight control laws that prevent the aircraft from stalling or overspeeding no matter what the pilots' inputs. Similar fly-by-wire systems are included in the Airbus A330 and A340.

CREW COORDINATION

Whereas the success of early commercial flight operations depended heavily on the skill and knowledge of the individual pilot, it has long been accepted that flying highly sophisticated airliners over long distances requires the coordinated action of two or more crew members. At the very least, the existence of more than one crew member in the cockpit provides a certain measure of redundancy in the same way that control, electrical, and power systems are doubled, tripled, or even quadrupled. In the case of complete failure of a vital system, the backup component can be used to provide uninterrupted control.

This principle does not apply so well to the sudden failure of one of the human components of the system, as revealed by two studies. In one experiment, 36 Boeing 727 crews flying a simulator were exposed to a situation involving the incapacitation of one crew member.[6] The crew member would appear conscious but cease performing tasks for which he was responsible. Half of the crews were briefed that one crew member would become incapacitated sometime during the flight, and half received no prior warning. Twenty-five percent of the latter crashed the simulator. Of the remainder, the time taken to detect and react to the situation ranged between 30 seconds and 4 minutes with an average of 1.5 minutes.

In comparison, another group of 50 crews was exposed to incidents involving instrument or system failures. With the exception of one rather obscure failure, the time taken to detect and diagnose these failures ranged from 0.5 seconds to 40 seconds, averaging 10 seconds. The explanation for this difference between response to failures involving aircraft systems and other crew members can be found in the prevailing attitude toward individual performance. In the words of the study report, "Training and checking as required by federal regulation has in years past placed emphasis on individual performance with minimum assistance from other crew members."[7]

The investigators go on to point out that greater attention has been placed on practicing skills involved in much rarer incidents, such as ditching, than in the relatively more frequent case of crew incapacitation. This is somewhat surprising given the importance that is now attached to the efficient operation of airline crew members as integrated crews. Most airline operations manuals now lay some emphasis on crew coordination procedures. All crew members are required to monitor and cross-check the actions of the other crew members.

Despite the widespread adoption of the integrated crew concept, there continue to be airline transport accidents in which failure of crew coordination plays a major role. A Boeing report estimates that 70 percent of major accidents are crew caused.[8] Of these, approximately two-thirds appear to represent failures of crew monitoring and coordination. The following report of a landing accident involving an Allegheny Airlines BAC 1–11 at Rochester, New York, in 1978 provides a classic example.

BAC 1–11 OVERRUN

> A BAC 1–11 overran the end of Runway 28 at Rochester after a precision approach and landing in visual flight conditions. The landing aircraft passed over the runway threshold at 184 knots (61 knots above reference speed) and landed nose wheel first at a point about 2,540 feet down the 5,500 foot runway. The probable cause of the accident was the captain's complete lack of awareness of airspeed, vertical speed, and aircraft performance throughout the approach. Contributing to the accident was the first officer's failure to provide required callouts that might have alerted the captain to the airspeed and sink-rate deviations. The captain was obviously not fully cognizant of the excessive deviations from stabilized parameters because of a breakdown in crew coordination and inadequate monitoring of cockpit instruments by him and his first officer.[9]

On average six or seven accidents each year involve some failure of pilots to function effectively as an integrated crew.[10] Furthermore, a minority of airlines (16 percent) who have made no attempt to modify the fundamental hierarchical role structure on the flight deck account for more than 80 percent of these accidents. There has been a clear recognition by most airlines of the necessity to create a working environment in which all crew members are encouraged to draw attention to deviations from the intended flight path or the existence of abnormal instrument indications or any potentially hazardous situation external to the cockpit, such as intruding traffic or ice on the wings.

All this was made quite clear in the Allegheny flight operations manual that was quoted at length in the NTSB's accident report. The board could find no convincing reason for such an extraordinarily inept performance other than the breakdown of the crew coordination procedures. The report concludes by reiterating a strong statement on copilot assertiveness made in connection with a previous accident involving the same company.

> The concept of command authority and its inviolate nature, except in the case of incapacitation, has become a tenet without exception. This had resulted in second-in-command pilots reacting diffidently in circumstances where they should perhaps be more affirmative. Rather than submitting passively to this concept, second-in-command pilots should be encouraged under certain circumstances to assume a duty and responsibility to affirmatively advise the pilot-in-command that the flight is being conducted in a careless or dangerous manner. Such affirmative advice could very well result in the pilot-in-command's reassessing his procedures.

Perhaps the most tragic case involving what is now commonly referred to as a lack of copilot assertiveness was the world's worst aviation disaster in May 1977, when a KLM 747 collided with a Pan American 747 on the runway at Los Rodeos airport on Tenerife of the Canary Islands. The following brief outline of the pertinent points of the accident was based on the report prepared by the U.S. Air Line Pilots Association.

TENERIFE COLLISION

> A Pan Am 747 and a KLM 747 were preparing to depart Tenerife in conditions of low clouds and rapidly changing visibility. KLM Flight 4805 had taxied to the end of Runway 30 by backtracking, followed on the same runway by the Pan Am aircraft, which had been cleared to backtrack to the third exit and was to leave the runway by that exit. On reaching the end of Runway 30 the KLM aircraft executed a 180-degree turn to line up for takeoff. The captain had already increased the throttle settings as the departure clearance was being received and acknowledged by the copilot with the words, "we are now at takeoff." The tower's reply of "standby for takeoff" was obliterated by a simultaneous transmission from the Pan Am flight deck reporting that they were still on the runway.

The end of the Pan Am transmission was heard in the KLM cockpit and led to a brief discussion indicating that the KLM crew was unsure whether the Pan Am aircraft had, in fact, made the turnoff. Despite this, the captain proceeded with the takeoff unchallenged by the other crew members. The impact took place 13 seconds later despite a desperate attempt to fly the KLM off prematurely. A factor that may have been important in the crew interaction on the KLM flight deck was the great disparity in standing and experience between the KLM copilot and captain. The copilot was only recently checked out on 747s by the company's senior pilot, who was serving as the captain on this flight. As the senior pilot and KLM's chief flying instructor, the captain was one of the most authoritive in the company.

It seems his crew did not query as resolutely as they might have his unwarranted conviction that they were cleared for takeoff.[11]

Incidents of the kind described in the two previous examples have highlighted the need to consider crew performance as a variable over and above individual performance. As recent articles have emphasized, flightdeck management involves a small, highly task-oriented group that must coordinate its actions to achieve the goal of delivering the aircraft safely to its destination. Many separate actions are needed to do this, even in routine circumstances. By one calculation, a short-haul IFR flight of 45 minutes in a Boeing 747 would require 97 normal operating procedures.[12] Of these, at least 21 can be considered to involve crew coordination, including (1) checklist items, (2) callouts (e.g., speeds during takeoff), (3) configuration changes (e.g., extending or retracting flaps), and (4) transfers (one pilot taking over the flight controls from the other).

One study by NASA involved 18 simulated flights by Boeing 747 crews from Washington, DC to London.[13] Cockpit voice recordings were made, and compliance with the procedures and errors were scored. Errors in some categories were quite high. For example, of 50 possible command-announcement-challenge sequences, only 5 were fully completed. Of 170 callout procedures (e.g., altitude callouts), there were 40 errors. Rather less frequent but more dramatic in effect were the three recorded instances in which incomplete transfers of control occurred, leaving "doubt as to which pilot was actually controlling flight parameters."

Nearly half the errors noted involved more than one crew member, which "suggests that human redundancy by itself does not eradicate personnel error."[14] The high error rates strongly suggested that a closer inspection of communication procedures in the cockpit would be helpful in developing an understanding of crew coordination, so a further analysis of the cockpit voice recordings was undertaken.[15] Several aspects of interpersonal communication were found to be related to errors made in crew performance.

The closest relationship with the overall number of errors made was found for the communication category "Acknowledgments" ($r = -0.68$); low error scores were associated with a high number of acknowledgments. Obviously, the acknowledgment by one crew member that a piece of information has been received is important in ensuring that information transfer takes place. It also reinforces the sender and therefore increases the likelihood of further communication from that crew member. Furthermore, the negative correlation between acknowledgments and overall errors suggests that a harmonious flightdeck atmosphere is less likely to produce errors than a tense, strained one.

The negative correlation between the number of commands and the number of errors ($r = -0.64$) reflects the basic role structure of the cockpit. The number of errors tended to be lower when a greater number of commands was issued. It is evidently important that the captain clearly delegate authority for flightdeck tasks by issuing appropriate commands. However, there is a relatively thin line between efficient delegation and autocratic leadership. Further reference to this distinction will be made later.

These relationships may seem surprisingly high for variables that are normally considered outside the scope of the individual task of simply flying an airplane. In line with the argument developed in this chapter, however, they lend confirmation to the view that factors related to crew coordination and communication are critical to understanding crew performance. The experimentally derived data on these issues are scarce, and many important issues remain unexplored—the possible effects of automation and intelligent decision aids on crew coordination, for example.

An interesting study on crew coordination and fatigue was designed to investigate the effects of flying a three-day short-haul cycle involving approximately 18 takeoffs and landings.[16] Crews flew a complicated simulator scenario including poor weather, a missed approach, and hydraulic failure, among other events. The subsequent performance of crews who had completed the three-day cycle was compared to that of crews who had been off duty for two or three days. Somewhat surprisingly, the performance of the rested crews was inferior to that of the fatigued crews. The resolution of this paradox lay in the fact that those crews who had flown together had worked out better communication practices.

Although this study provides further data on the effects of crew communication on performance, it would be unwarranted to conclude that fatigue effects can be entirely overcome by improved crew coordination. First, the fatigued crews in this experiment were probably not nearly as fatigued as crews who work intensive short-haul cycles typically claim.[17] Second, the scenario flown was a highly challenging one that may have been unusually sensitive to differences in crew coordination. Finally, the pilots most likely to complain about fatigue are those engaged in single- rather than multipilot operations.

The techniques of linguistic analysis have recently been used to throw further light on communication patterns in the cockpit.[18] In the first stage of one study, two aviation accident transcripts were carefully examined. A number of hypotheses were developed concerning the relationship between the structure of cockpit communication and successful flight operations. These hypotheses were tested on data obtained from six further transcripts. One of the examples used in the first stage was the crash of United Airlines Flight 173 in Portland, Oregon, in 1978.

OUT OF FUEL OVER PORTLAND

> About 1815 on 28 December 1978, United Airlines Flight 173 crashed into a populated wooded area of suburban Portland, Oregon, during an approach to Portland International Airport. The aircraft had delayed southeast of the airport at a low altitude for about one hour while the flight crew coped with a landing gear malfunction warning. The NTSB determined that the probable cause of the accident was the failure of the captain to monitor properly the aircraft's fuel state and to respond to the crew members' advisories regarding fuel state. This resulted in fuel exhaustion to all engines. His inattention resulted from preoccupation with a possible landing gear malfunction and preparations for an emergency landing. Contributing to the accident was the failure of the other two flight crew members either to comprehend fully the criticality of the fuel state or to communicate their concern to the captain successfully.[19]

In common with the Air Florida crash (Chapter 7) and the Tenerife disaster, the United accident in Portland can be partly attributed to the failure of subordinate crew members to communicate critical information to the captain. The accident report noted that the first officer made several comments about the aircraft's fuel state but "the comments were not given in a positive or direct tone." One variable used in linguistic analysis is mitigation. Various devices can be used in speech to mitigate the effect of a direct request or proposition. Mitigation is used to soften the effect and to avoid giving offense.

A mitigated instruction might be phrased as a question or hedged with qualifications, such as "would" or "could." In this study, it was found that the speech of subordinate crew members was much more likely to be mitigated than the speech of the captains. It was also found that topics introduced in mitigated speech were less likely to be followed-up by other crew members and less likely to be ratified by the captain. Both of these effects relate directly to the situation in which a subordinate crew member makes a correct suggestion that is ignored. This was the case in all three examples cited above. The value of training in unmitigated speech is strongly suggested by these results.

Selection.   The view that the right stuff has little relevance on the computerized flight deck of the 1980s and 1990s has already been advanced in preceding chapters. On present evidence, there is a case to be made for modifying the selection of highly goal-oriented individuals by adding an emphasis on effective interpersonal orientation. There would be no need to regard this as deemphasizing the traditional areas of technical skill required for aircrew selection, because an effective goal orientation and an effective interpersonal orientation are not mutually exclusive. In the short term, however, modification of existing individual behavior is probably a more realistic goal.

Legislation.   The first step in attempting to change group behavior is regulation. To reduce accidents the FAA legislated that cockpit conversation in terminal areas be restricted solely to the business at hand rather than discussions of the stock market, real estate, and marital problems that were showing up on the CVRs. Regulation can only be effective, however, when informal social norms also support the change. The lack of compliance with drug laws provides a good example of legislative prohibitions that are being overridden by prevailing social norms. Altering social norms in the cockpit is one aim of cockpit resource management (CRM) training.

Training.   Several CRM programs have been developed. These include the Command Leadership Resource Management program adopted by United Airlines and the Line-oriented Flight Training (LOFT) program developed by Northwest Airlines in the mid-1970s, both with the cooperation of the FAA and NASA. Several training organizations in the United States and Europe market CRM training programs. United Airlines and KLM are leaders in this field, and versions of their programs have been adopted by major airlines such as Pan Am, Japan Air Lines, Korean Air Lines, Qantas, and several others.[20]

LOFT was designed to supplement existing simulator training, with its traditional emphasis on individual skill development, through training in a realistic operational environment. LOFT sessions are designed to be as authentic as possible from a normal preflight briefing with full trip paperwork to realistic external communications.[21] Crews "fly" a full trip in the normal time. Much of the value of LOFT is realized in the debriefing in which attention is directed to crew coordination and communication. It is apparent that the attitude of the aircrew toward the exercise will be largely determined by the success of the LOFT instructor in promoting a positive but critical self-examination of performance.

The aim of such programs is to heighten individual awareness of the social-psychological factors that operate in a group situation as well as to strengthen the appropriate normative pressures in favor of using all the available resources on the flight deck rather than individual virtuosity and bravado. In terms of their approach, such training schemes fall well within the range of behavior modification programs commonly used by clinical and management psychologists. Making crew members aware of the factors that can influence their behavior as members of a small, goal-oriented team through lecture or demonstration is an important first step.

The impact of such demonstrations can be increased markedly by videotaping crew performance in carrying out simulated flights and then replaying the videotape to the crew members. Taking such an external perspective on one's own actions can be brutally illuminating and can reveal methods of interacting of which the individual was not aware. For example, a captain's failure to acknowledge comments from other crew members can be revealed through this kind of exercise. The resulting shift in perspective helps to overcome a tendency in a group context to underplay the causal role of one's own behavior relative to the roles played by the other participants.

The linguistic analysis of communication patterns discussed earlier is relevant to training in crew member assertiveness. In vivid contrast, the Australian Airlines' Aircrew Team Management Program involves practice at general problem solving in which teamwork is crucial.[22] Unlike the LOFT program, which stresses operational realism, this type of training focuses on modifying individual behavior in the problem-solving and decision-making skills that are thought to underlie successful group performance. The three-day ATM course includes one day in classroom exercises, a simulator session based on ATM principles, and finally a LOFT exercise. Some of the key elements in the Australian Airlines program are shown in Table 8.1.

Table 8.1. Key Elements in the Australian Airlines Aircrew Team Management Program

Objective	Examples
Understanding yourself and others	Understanding the strengths and contributions of others
	Identifying one's own strengths and weaknesses
	Self-development
Communication skills	How to express oneself simply and effectively in the cockpit
	Learning how to listen
	How to contribute information effectively with tact
	How to explain what you are doing
	Managing conflict situations
Teamwork management skills	How to work as a team
	How to organize information
	Developing a supportive environment
	How to delegate and divide workload effectively
	Managing priorities
	Team decision making
	Managing morale and motivation
	Encouraging feedback for improvement

Note: All of these issues were introduced through role playing, case study, behavioral exercises, video presentations, and group discussions.
Source: Adapted from Margerison, McCann, and Davies (Undated).

The differences between the North American and Australian approaches probably reflect cultural differences. Lack of assertiveness, for example, may be less of a problem in a highly egalitarian society such as Australia. The interesting question of how cultural differences in attitudes toward subordinates and the sharing of information are reflected in the cockpit has barely been touched. In one study, investigators surveyed crew members from six different airlines based in Europe, North America, the Pacific, and Asia.[23] Once again there were numerous examples of poor cockpit communication leading to unsatisfactory operational practices, with some evidence that these were culturally dependent.

In any case, it is easy to believe that cultural differences in attitudes towards superiors played a part in the crash of a Japan Air Lines DC-8 at Anchorage, Alaska, in 1977.

The captain of the JAL cargo flight was a 23,000-hour, 53-year-old American pilot. The copilot was a 31-year-old Japanese with 1,603 flying hours, and the Japanese flight engineer, aged 35, had fewer than 5,000 hours. The blood-alcohol level found in the captain was such as to have produced "mental confusion, dizziness, impaired balance, muscular incoordination, staggering gait, and slurred speech." With characteristic understatement, the report notes: "The other crew

---

BEEF AND ALCOHOL

> *On 13 January 1977, a Japan Air Lines DC-8-62F crashed shortly*
> *after takeoff from Anchorage International Airport. All on board*
> *were killed, including the cargo of live beef cattle. The National*
> *Transportation Safety Board determined that the probable cause*
> *of the accident was a stall that resulted from the pilot's control*
> *inputs aggravated by airframe icing while the pilot was under the*
> *influence of alcohol. Contributing to the cause of this accident was*
> *the failure of the other flight crew members to prevent the captain*
> *from attempting the flight.*[24]

---

members must have been aware of this condition." It is tempting to
conclude that cultural differences may have added a further barrier to
the mobilization of concern which the other crew members must have
felt at the captain's condition.

Task restructuring.   Crew coordination is probably the area where
the greatest changes have taken place. Intracrew monitoring and the
integrated crew concept have become the norm in airline and multipilot transport operations. The old-fashioned and somewhat derogatory
view of the second pilot reflected in sayings such as, "My copilot sits
18 inches from the centerline and moves the center of gravity 3 inches
forward," has been largely replaced by a standard operating view in
which the copilot has a principal part to play. To quote further from the
NTSB's view of the Allegheny incident,

> The second-in-command is an integral part of the operational
> control system in flight, a fail-safe factor, and as such has a share of
> the duty and responsibility to assure that the flight is operated
> safely. Therefore, the second-in-command should not passively
> condone an operation of the aircraft which in his opinion is danger-
> ous, or which might compromise safety. He should affirmatively
> advise the captain whenever in his judgment safety of the flight is
> in jeopardy.[25]

VIEWS FROM THE FLIGHT DECK

Because pilots' attitudes have often been held to blame for failure
to capitalize fully on technological development (for example, the case
of the ground proximity warning system), it would be useful to know

what views are held in the cockpit regarding crew coordination and cockpit resource management training. A recent survey of 254 Boeing 737 crew members has shown a fair consensus on the questions of coordination and communication. However, the survey also reveals pilots of the old school of thought who do not feel favorably disposed toward the integrated crew concept.[26]

Interestingly, the major difference between captains and first officers appeared with a question concerning the use of negative comments toward other crew members. Only 15 percent of the captains felt strongly that these should be avoided, compared to nearly half of the first officers. On another key question, 90 percent of first officers felt strongly that they should be encouraged to question procedures, whereas only 75 percent of the captains felt equally strongly. Fourteen percent of the captains felt that "First Officers should not question the decisions or actions of the Captain except when they threaten the safety of the flight."

Another survey reveals the extent of crew coordination problems in airline operations.[27] At least 40 percent of the 250 airline pilots surveyed reported some experience with flightdeck coordination problems. A similar percentage of first officers reported at least one failure to advise the captain of some doubt concerning the operation of the aircraft. The major causes of this problem, as reported by the first officers, are such characteristics of particular captains as "an arrogant and abrasive manner, strong, intransigent attitudes, and a domineering style of work interaction."

This is reflected in the fact that virtually every first officer in the survey stated that there were pilots with whom they preferred not to work. There is no doubt that offensive behavior was considered to be characteristic of certain pilots and not simply the result of difficulties in operating particular kinds of equipment under certain conditions. Interpersonal conflict appears to have played some part in the crash of a British European Airways Trident in 1972.

CRASH OF BEA TRIDENT AT STAINES

> The aircraft was climbing out of London Heathrow bound for Brussels. Ninety seconds after takeoff, at the point where the flaps should have been retracted, the slat lever was selected up, causing the aircraft to approach a stall as the slats started to move. The aircraft entered a deep stall with insufficient height for recovery. The principal cause of the accident was the retraction of the leading-edge slats 60 knots below proper speed, precipitating the stall.[28]

Evidence relating to this accident is largely circumstantial but points to a failure of the crew monitoring system in a crew composed of a first officer with about 250 hours of flight time and an irascible captain who had been involved in a violent argument with another colleague just prior to departure. It is possible that this played a role in precipitating the accident as postmortem inquiry revealed evidence of heart disease in the captain and raised the hypothesis that he experienced a debilitating attack at the critical moment during the climb-out.

The normal crew monitoring procedures should have ensured that a mistaken movement toward the slat lever in place of the flap lever would have been detected and corrected in time. This opens the possibility that the order to retract the slats was given directly and was not challenged by the crew. What is known about the characteristic interpersonal style of this captain leaves this as a plausible possibility. This is particularly so in the light of many subsequent reports of a crew member's failure to challenge a captain's hazardous command that have come to light through the confidential incident reporting schemes in use in several parts of the world.

Now that cockpit resource management programs have become widespread (although still not required by regulation), attention has been directed toward evaluating the effectiveness of such training. As we have seen, there is some variation in the approach taken to cockpit resource management training by different airlines, so there can be no simple answers to questions regarding its effectiveness. Because large-scale evaluation research is both difficult and costly, it might be preferable in the short term to attempt to identify specific components of these programs that may have some clear-cut effect.

For example, it appears that good cockpit management styles can be recognized by check pilots in a reliable manner.[29] It also appears that pilots who are rated effective in cockpit management are likely to possess the following attitudes:

• a recognition that their personal decision-making abilities would be degraded in an emergency situation
• willingness to have crew members question decisions
• favorableness to open discussion of personal stress or problems and the creation of a harmonious atmosphere on the flight deck

In contrast, poor cockpit managers are likely to deny personal limitations and resent the active involvement of other crew members in emergencies. It can be predicted with some confidence that a major focus of concern for aviation psychologists will be the refinement and objective evaluation of cockpit resource management training.

FURTHER READING

Good summaries of recent work in social psychology are presented by L. Berkowitz in *A Survey of Social Psychology*, 3rd ed. (New York: Holt, Rinehart & Winston, 1986) and by B. Raven and J. Rubin in *Social Psychology*, 2nd ed. (New York: Wiley, 1983). The application of a social psychological perspective to aircrew performance is of extremely recent origin, and there are few readings in this area in the public domain. The analysis of flightdeck communication patterns is discussed in detail by J. A. Goguen and C. Linde in *Linguistic Methodology for the Analysis of Aviation Accidents* (Washington, DC: National Aeronautics and Space Administration, 1983).

Conclusion

[9] Perfect Failures

IT WAS SO OBVIOUS—so painfully obvious—but most of those engaged in commercial aviation couldn't see it, or wouldn't. Human beings engaged in a human enterprise are subject to human failures. Pilots and controllers and maintenance people err and cause accidents because they are human, and we imperfect humans are all prone to make such mistakes. Discovering that a human error—pilot error or otherwise—has occurred is merely the starting point. To have any hope of preventing such an error from causing such an accident again and again, the reason the error was made in the first place must be discovered, and the underlying cause of that human failure must be revealed and addressed in future operations.

J. J. NANCE, Blind Trust

INTRODUCTION

Many of the reasons that underlie human failures in aviation have been explored in the preceding chapters. Time and again, these failures have been shown to occur as a result of (1) the apparently normal functioning of our perceptual systems, (2) the design of aircraft cockpit systems, (3) the stress and fatigue imposed by working conditions, (4) the numerous possibilities for mistakes in diagnosis and decision making and slips in execution in a complex dynamic environment, and (5) the social influences that impinge on every individual whether alone or acting as part of a crew.

Although our examination of these reasons for error has benefited

229

substantially from the results of relatively recent research, the basic problems have been recognized and called out by aviation psychologists since the 1950s.[1] We are now witnessing a belated recognition by others of the importance of human factors in modern technological systems. This slowly developing awareness is manifesting itself in books and journals, in the makeup of accident investigation boards, in the airline training programs, in the regulations of civil aviation departments, and in the advanced design and simulation activities of aircraft companies.

Psychological research in aviation is still in its comparative youth, but it is abundantly clear that predictions of human behavior can be made with reasonable accuracy. This is far from asserting that the sum total of human experience in all its richness and complexity is adequately understood. It is not. The study of behavior under controlled and objectively measured conditions is capable, however, of demonstrating clear links between circumstances and actions. It is axiomatic, however, that no two subjects ever behave identically. Human character is reflected in the variability of responses obtained from different pilots in the same situation.

Despite this wide range of individual variability, significant group differences in performance under different conditions have been demonstrated in all the experiments reported in this book. In some cases, with the use of appropriate statistical techniques, these individual differences can be used to improve on the accuracy of predictions made on the basis of the experimental differences alone. This provides the scientific basis to the claim that human behavior can be predicted if something is known about the circumstances in which it occurs and about the characteristics and training of the individual being tested.

The existence of such variability in human behavior provides a clue to the difference in predictability between the physical sciences and the human sciences. The overall difference between two individuals is much greater than the overall difference between two samples of physical material. The predictability observed in the human sciences is, with a few notable exceptions, at a statistical or average level rather than at a uniquely individual level. A failure to appreciate this difference explains the difficulty that the engineering and physical sciences sometimes have in accepting evidence from the behavioral sciences on the question of accident causation and analysis.

Despite the difficulty of predicting human behavior, it can be shown that failure is considerably more likely given particular circumstances; however, not every individual will necessarily fail. A proportion of highly stressed, overloaded pilots would manage to operate a poorly designed system for some period without error, but the proportion who could operate a well-designed system safely under the same conditions is much higher. The evidence presented in this book overwhelmingly suggests that this evident fact be taken into account as early as possible in planning and designing the technological systems of tomorrow's aircraft.

A full account of the reasons for human error also needs to be considered in the aftermath of any accident. The numerous examples that we have drawn on in preceding chapters have each been selected to illuminate one or another particular reason for human error, yet it is widely recognized in accident investigation that there will be multiple causes of any given accident. To some extent, the number of causes considered will be determined by how far back in the accident chain the investigator is prepared to search. Yet even the immediate circumstances normally examined in the investigator's report are generally sufficient to bear out this assertion.

To illustrate this point we will conclude with a brief examination of two examples of perfect failures in flightdeck performance, one a modern classic.

EVERYBODY CONTRIBUTED IN A SMALL WAY

> On 27 November 1983, an Avianca Boeing 747 from Paris was descending at night to land at Madrid. Flight 11 was cleared to descend to FL 190, then for an approach to Runway 33, with an instruction to contact the tower. The crew was busy with the descent and later the landing checklist while descending through 7,500 feet at 1,900 feet per minute and through 4,100 feet at 273 feet per minute. With flaps and gear extended, the 747 hit the ground near the outer marker with an airspeed of 139 knots and a descent rate of 1,015 feet per minute. All the crew and 158 passengers died; 11 passengers survived, all seriously injured. The firefighting vehicles took 52 minutes to reach the site and another hour to extinguish the burning wreckage.[2]

The Avianca crew members were experienced (the 57-year-old captain had more than 20,000 hours of flying experience), were legally qualified for their jobs, and were operating in calm, stable weather. The thoroughly tried and tested Boeing 747 was airworthy, mechanically sound, and correctly fueled and loaded. Flight 11 collided with three low hills 12 kilometers southeast of the airport as the captain made his 26th approach to Madrid that year. The record of the last 30 minutes of the flight reveals a sequence of individually undramatic errors by the crew and controllers that culminated in the impact. In summary, it clearly provides illustrations of six factors that repeatedly contribute to aviation incidents and accidents:

1. Lack of response to warning systems
2. Overreliance on automated systems
3. Chart reading errors
4. Communication errors
5. Diffusion of responsibility
6. Crew monitoring failures

Some of the details relating to each of these points are the following:

Lack of response to ground proximity warning. Fourteen seconds before impact the GPWS delivered its warning as it was designed to do. Neither of the pilots responded with any urgency or apparent alarm. The captain reduced the aircraft's rate of descent slightly, just moments before impact. Although the crew members were clearly aware of the warning, they evidently interpreted it as a false alarm and failed to take the necessary actions.

Overreliance on automated systems. Even while navigating within the terminal control area, an attempt was made to insert new coordinates into the inertial navigation system instead of obtaining a direct position fix using the VOR/DME facilities. This resulted in the inference that the position was closer to the start of the ILS than it really was. The apparent difficulty that the first officer had in entering the erroneous new coordinates may have provided an additional distraction.

Chart reading errors. The most crucial error involved the co-pilot's misreading of the ILS approach chart for Runway 33 at Madrid, which indicates that the outer marker should be crossed at an altitude of 3,282 feet. The copilot transposed the first two digits and read this figure as 2,382 feet. The aircraft was allowed to descend well below the correct altitude as a result of this error.

Communication errors. Communications between air traffic control and the crew and among the ground controllers failed to exchange information that was available. The crew made no position reports during the approach, and no position information was exchanged by the ground controllers. The fact that the aircraft had not intercepted the ILS glideslope therefore did not become apparent to the ground controllers. There was nothing transmitted from the controllers that might have affected the crew's belief that the airplane was on a normal approach path to the VOR.

Diffusion of responsibility. The crew members knew that the flight was under radar surveillance and may have assumed that they would be alerted to any large deviation from the desired course or vertical profile. The approach controller was not, in fact, monitoring the radar screen, so such an assumption would not have been well founded.

Crew monitoring. The crew was not functioning as a well-coordinated team. This is evidenced by the failure of anyone to cross-check the copilot's misreading of the approach chart. The fact that the aircraft was permitted to descend below the minimum safe altitude was not queried by any crew member. The transcript also reveals a lack of teamwork during the execution of the descent checklist procedure that included confirming items out of sequence and extending the landing gear before the correct flap setting was achieved.

Each one of these factors has been discussed in preceding chapters (4, 5, and 8) and its contribution to a variety of accidents established. Each of these failures continues to be repeated with some regularity (as evidenced by the incidents documented in the anonymous reporting schemes) but fortunately leads to accidents, rather than incidents, in only a small proportion of such cases. The fate of Avianca Flight 11 demonstrates particularly clearly how a concatenation of such errors can greatly increase the overall probability of disaster.

The effect of an accumulation of predisposing factors is illustrated even more dramatically in the crash of Air Florida Flight 90 described in Chapter 7. The lessons that can be drawn from this disaster deserve widespread recognition from all those involved in aviation.

PLUMBING THE LOWER LIMITS OF COMPETENCY

Air Florida Flight 90 failed to become fully airborne largely because of an accumulation of snow and ice on the leading edge of the wings of the Boeing 737. Weather conditions at Washington National Airport were extremely poor at the time with a very low overcast, poor visibility in snow showers, and below-freezing temperatures. Although all aircraft are adversely affected by the presence of ice on their wings, the demise of Flight 90 was the result of a combination of factors that have been identified separately as increasing the probability of ultimate human failure. They have all been discussed previously (Chapters 3, 7, and 8) and include:

- Inadequate training
- Poor judgment and decision making
- Diffusion of responsibility
- Peer pressure
- Copilot unassertiveness

Inadequate training. Air Florida had no formal program of training in operating techniques for the kind of wintry conditions faced by the crew of Flight 90. The fact that Air Florida had few routes extending into the northern United States meant that its crews developed little direct experience in operating under conditions of snow and ice. The safety board could discover only eight previous occasions in which the captain had operated a jet aircraft in conditions conducive to icing since his upgrading to captain, and only two occasions when the copilot had operated in such conditions as copilot of a 737.

In addition, the report said, "The board believes that the captain of Flight 90 missed the seasoning experience normally gained as a first officer as a result of the rapid expansion of Air Florida, Inc., from 1977 through 1981, wherein pilots were upgrading faster than the industry norm to meet the increasing demands of growing schedules."[3] Both crew members were remarkably inexperienced by airline standards. The 34-year-old captain had less than 2 years of turbojet experience against the 14 years normally required to upgrade to the captain's seat on the major carriers.

Although all the information needed to operate the aircraft safely in the existing conditions was contained in the aircraft's operating manual, neither crew member appeared to have a sound knowledge of this information. Contrary to these procedures, the crew attempted to move the aircraft away from the gate by starting the engines and applying reverse thrust. This procedure would be likely to blow melted ice and snow over the leading edges of the wings where it might subsequently refreeze. The NTSB report observed that "the flightcrew's actions in using reverse thrust contrary to advice and guidance provided indicates a lack of professional judgment consistent with their total performance."[4]

Poor judgment and decision making. One of the key errors made by the crew was to fail to switch on the engine anti-ice system.

This error resulted in false instrument readings of the power being delivered by the engines. In setting the throttles to offset the faulty power readings, the crew deprived the takeoff of 25 percent of the potential power output of the engines. The reduced power in combination with the accumulation of ice on the wings meant that the 737, while able to reach its takeoff speed, was unable to sustain flight.

It was determined from the CVR that during the takeoff checklist callout the anti-ice was called "off." Given the crew's lack of experience with winter operations, this would have been the familiar response to this item. Although the iced pitot probes were sending false information to the engine pressure ratio (EPR) gauge (the primary means of setting the engine's power output), there would have been anomalous readings on at least three other gauges to suggest that the engines were not delivering their proper power output.

The first officer realized that there was something wrong during the takeoff roll, and in fact expressed this concern four times. The captain, who had sole responsibility for rejecting the takeoff, did not respond to any of these expressions of unease. Although the first officer's scan of the engine instruments led him to believe that the engines were not delivering their normal power, this concern was not effectively mobilized into action that would have saved the lives of those on board, including his own.

Diffusion of responsibility.   From the earliest days of flight training, the pilot in command is expected to assume total responsibility for the safety of flight. This begins with the gathering of all pertinent information, flight planning, and an external inspection of the aircraft before the flight. This last item would be of particular importance in conditions in which snow or ice might be adhering to the aircraft. Neither of the Flight 90 crew members left the cockpit to inspect the condition of the aircraft following the deicing operations.

The crew was concerned about the continued snowfall, and the captain asked the Air Florida station manager for his opinion on the amount of snow on the wings. Although the crew was required by law to ensure that there was no ice or snow adhering to the wings before takeoff, both pilots remained in their warm cockpit, surrounded by the familiar technology. "They had no idea whether their airplane was free of ice or snow. They simply trusted the ground crewmen to make sure nothing was wrong."[5]

Peer pressure.   Because Washington National Airport had been closed for more than an hour by the terrible weather conditions, there was a large backlog of aircraft waiting to depart when the airport reopened. There was a 25-minute delay following the completion of the deicing before Flight 90 was finally pushed back from the gate, followed by a further 25-minute delay in a queue of 16 aircraft taxiing to the runway. During the delay, the crew continued to discuss the presence of ice and snow on the runway and on the aircraft. Moderate to heavy snowfall continued throughout the 50-minute delay before takeoff.

The crew taxied the aircraft closer than normal to the preceding DC-9 in the mistaken belief that its jet blast would assist in melting the ice that was by this stage adhering to the wings and fuselage of the 737. The Safety Board believed that the pressure to remain in the taxi line rather than return to the ramp for a further deice was increased by the successful departures of the aircraft ahead of Flight 90. The conversation in the cockpit revealed considerable unease about the buildup of snow and ice, and it seems likely that without this element of peer pressure, the crew might have returned for further deicing.

Copilot unassertiveness.   Air Florida did not provide any specific training in copilot assertiveness. Unlike major carriers, such as United or Northwest and many others, there is no evidence that Air Florida provided any training at all in cockpit management procedures or human relations. Despite its undeniable value, the FAA only suggests rather than requires that airlines conduct such training. Flight 90 provides a particularly graphic example of the need for assertiveness at appropriate moments. Although the copilot clearly realized that something was seriously wrong, he failed to get his message through to the captain.

Information indicating an abnormal power condition was detected and correctly diagnosed by the first officer, who attempted to draw the captain's attention to the situation. The safety board commented, "while he clearly expressed his view that something was not right during the takeoff roll, his comments were not assertive."[6] The dilemma facing the copilot of Flight 90 was one that has confronted any individual faced with an unresponsive authority. The powerful forces that inhibit people from acting according to the dictates of their own consciences have been explored in a particularly dramatic series of psychological experiments.

THE DILEMMA OF AUTHORITY

The difficulties faced by individuals attempting to assert themselves in the face of authority were investigated at Yale University in the early 1960s.[7] In these experiments, subjects of all ages and from all walks of life were recruited to participate in a study of learning. They were given lists of words to read to a second person. The second person was in reality an accomplice, or confederate, of the experimenter. The subject was instructed to deliver an electric shock to the learner if the learner failed to respond correctly to any of the words on the list.

In front of the subject was an impressive-looking shock generator with a scale reading from 15 volts to 450 volts and the label "DANGER: SEVERE SHOCK." To convince subjects of the reality of this setup, they were given a mild sample electric shock. In addition, the confederate responded in fairly dramatic ways to increasing levels of shock. At 120 volts, the victim started shouting at the subject, complained vociferously about the pain, and demanded to be let out of the experiment. After 300 volts, nothing further was heard from the victim. It should be emphasized that, apart from the sample shock, no actual shocks were used.

The whole experiment was a theatrically arranged procedure designed to place the real subject in a situation of conflict. The conflict was presumed to be between the instructions of the experimenter to continue the experiment and the subject's own conscience, which would normally prevent the infliction of harm on another human. From a description of the setup alone, it is hard to imagine anyone remaining in the experiment and continuing to deliver the 450-volt electric shocks to an apparently inert victim.

Contrary to our own introspections that we would certainly not do so, 65 percent of the subjects tested in fact proceeded right through the scale. It can be emphatically stated that this was not because subjects saw through the experiment. It is clear from film of the experiment that subjects were desperately unsure of how to behave in a situation that required them to carry out an immoral act under the instructions of a person in a position of trust and authority. Although this experimental situation is far removed from the flight deck, the personal conflict can be compared to that experienced by the first officer of Air Florida Flight 90.

Despite severe doubts, he was unable to bring himself to save his own life and that of the passengers on board. The electric shock experiment shows that this was anything but an unusual response. In these staged situations, hundreds of ordinary people, including nurses, school teachers, housewives, salesmen, engineers, and laborers, inflicted what would have been lethal shocks on another person. The degree of trust in ostensibly benevolent authority and the difficulty of standing up to such authority are so great that most of us choose to ignore our personal doubts and continue to behave in the manner demanded.

The flightdeck situation combines the two aspects of responding to an authority and trusting in a more experienced figure, in each case the captain. Explanations of behavior in the electric shock experiment have centered on the element of obedience to authority, the inability to override the commands of a trusted figure, as Adolf Hitler became in Nazi Germany. For the first officer of Flight 90, this can also be seen as a question of the costs and benefits involved, as must also have been the case with the German populace.

The likely costs of overriding the captain's failure to abort the takeoff would have included, at worst, the possibility of causing the 737 to slide off the end of the runway, balking the approach of the airliner landing behind them, or, at best, a significant rupturing of the normal relationships in the cockpit. As other investigators have pointed out, this last consideration weighs heavily with aircrew members who wish neither to jeopardize their relationships with their senior partners nor to gain a reputation in their company as difficult customers.[8] Causing embarrassment or humiliation to another, particularly one in authority, is one of the most difficult disruptions to repair.

It seems likely that subjects in the shock experiment found it almost impossible to inflict this embarrassment even on a total stranger with whom they would have no further contact or continuing relationship. "The act of disobedience requires a mobilization of inner resources . . . into a domain of action. But the psychic cost is considerable."[9] In the flightdeck situation, the problems are of course further compounded by the speed with which events are moving and the uncertainty of the information on which the doubts may be based (e.g., is the aircraft accelerating normally?).

Mobilizing resources.   If the points just made are substantially correct, then it follows that attention must be paid to the problem of mobilizing appropriate doubts into effective action. The main costs that prevent this are social, and therefore these costs must be reduced to make timely intervention more likely. This is one of the aims of the cockpit resource management programs. These are still unevenly spread throughout the industry, and their effectiveness must largely depend on management attitudes.

If the threshold for demurring is to be lowered, it follows that airline management must create the conditions in which appropriately developed dissent can be safely expressed as a positively regarded, fully professional action. The last thing anyone needs, of course, is to have cockpits full of airborne mutineers ready to override the captain's authority. At the same time, the existence of overly autocratic captains supported by unreceptive management attitudes should not be allowed to prevent positive improvements to the management of command decisions.[10]

The discussion of demurring and mobilizing resources in the face of trusted authority emphasizes a point made repeatedly throughout this book. This is that the rare occurrences of accidents do not result from the operation of unusual or idiosyncratic processes; they occur mostly as the result of fairly well-understood perceptual, cognitive, and social forces that can be seen in our everyday behavior. If each accident can be regarded not as a unique event but as the result of these psychological processes, then it can contribute—beyond the mere attribution of error—to the proper understanding of causes.

NORMAL ACCIDENTS

Public hostility to nuclear technology has grown in recent years with the well-publicized accident at the Three Mile Island reactor in Pennsylvania in May 1979 and the more severe accident at Chernobyl in the Soviet Union in April 1986. According to one analyst, these may be regarded as normal, or system, accidents arising out of the inherent complexity and tight coupling of the nuclear reaction process.[11] Obviously the process of nuclear fission is a complex one. The key element of this complexity is the capacity for unexpected interactions among elements of the process.

In the Three Mile Island accident, the multiple concurrent failures induced by interactions among separate subsystems presented an incomprehensible picture to the operators struggling to control the process. The second characteristic of tight coupling is that there is little slack or give in the system. What happens at one point has immediate effects on other points in the system. Inevitably there will be component failures in such a system. Because of the complexity and tight coupling of the system, these failures "become accidents rather than incidents because of the nature of the system itself; they are system accidents, and are inevitable or normal for these systems."[12]

It might have been expected that the designers of complex, tightly coupled systems would pay particular attention to the design of displays and controls, operator training, and other human factors. In fact, the picture of the nuclear industry even since Three Mile Island reveals an astonishing lack of attention to the human factors of design and training.[13] Display panels are sometimes so poorly designed that critical controls and associated instruments are placed on opposite sides of the panel or can be inadvertently covered. In other cases controls are placed appreciable distances from the displays to which they relate. Violations of nearly all the principles of display design discussed in Chapter 4 are commonly found.

In short, the nuclear industry has increased the normal accident potential of the system by failing to minimize the risks created by poor design and inadequate training. Compared to nuclear and other high-risk technologies, a considerable understanding has been gained in the operation of complex airplanes, and the expected number of normal, or system, accidents is at a very low level. Nevertheless, the opportunity for such accidents remains and can be illustrated by the management failures that accompanied the development of the Douglas DC-10.

Problems with the design of a rear cargo door had been suspected as early as 1969.[14] In a pressure test conducted in May 1970, a door blew out and the cabin floor collapsed. Because of the intense competition among the DC-10, Boeing 747, and Lockheed L-1011 for the lucrative wide-body market, a thorough redesign of the door mechanism and floor was not undertaken. The FAA did not even issue a mandatory directive regarding the door. On 3 March 1974, a fully laden DC-10 crashed just outside Paris following an explosive decompression resulting from the loss of the unmodified cargo door.

As might be expected in a complex, tightly coupled system, this component failure had immediate repercussions on a separate subsystem, the hydraulic lines and control cables that passed under the cabin floor. The collapse of the floor meant that the crew had no means of controlling the aircraft, which crashed killing 346. "One obvious conclusion of this review of some DC-10 accidents is that with complex, tightly coupled systems with catastrophic potential, there is precious little room for management error."[15]

Management pressures are discussed by John Nance in an analysis of the effects of the 1978 deregulation act on aviation safety in the United States. "Management is the key. The way the company is run—the way the people are trained and motivated, controlled, and supervised at all levels—has a direct and vital impact on whether or not it can operate airliners safely."[16] Economic pressures may be one source of management failures of the kind revealed in the analysis of a fatal commuter accident.

The crash of Downeast Flight 46, approaching the fogbound Rockland airport in Maine in May 1979, led to an unusually extensive report from the NTSB of the pressures brought to bear by the management of the airline.[17] Among the "inordinate management pressures" were directing pilots to violate the FAA-determined minimum safe altitudes on instrument approaches, to adopt an alternate on the basis of convenience of ground transportation rather than weather considerations, and to exceed weight limits with limited fuel reserves.

The difficulties of self-assertion in the face of authority and the powerful role of peer pressure were the mechanisms by which this unsafe management style came to influence the actions and decisions of the Downeast pilots. Once again, it would be wrong to dismiss this as a unique or idiosyncratic case. The NTSB cited management and supervisory deficiencies as contributory factors in three separate fatal accidents involving commuter airlines in late 1986.[18]

The relationship between management pressures and safety can be seen clearly in other fields, such as maritime transport, the nuclear industry, and even the spaceflight industry. The loss of the space shuttle "Challenger" was largely caused by managerial pressures, from the top of government down, that allowed known technical deficiencies to go unheeded and uncorrected.[19] It is clear that safety must not be traded off against other economic goals but should be shielded from undue production pressures by management.

It has been argued that the likelihood of normal accidents decreases as the operating dynamics of the system become better understood. This may result from extensive operating experience, regulation and control, and research into accident causation. The aviation system has much of the first two of these factors and has begun to appreciate the value of the third. Ultimately, it is in a progression from the unknown and unavoidable to the known and therefore avoidable accident causes that will enable us to meet the goal of a safer and more effective aviation system.

FURTHER READING

A controversial contribution to the aviation safety literature is the documentary book by J. J. Nance titled *Blind Trust* (New York: William Morrow, 1986). It includes a devastating analytical treatment of the effects of government and managerial attitudes on aviation safety. A general discussion of the accident potential of high-risk technologies is presented by C. Perrow in *Normal Accidents* (New York: Basic Books, 1984). A more recent collection of papers edited by E. L. Wiener and D. C. Nagel provides a comprehensive overview of *Human Factors in Aviation* (San Diego: Academic Press, 1988).

Glossary of Aviation Terminology

ADF:	Automatic direction finding loop antenna. A navigation aid that indicates the direction to a nondirectional radio transmitter from which signals are being received
AINS:	Area inertial navigation system. A navigation system based on redundant inertial platforms that continuously updates aircraft position and provides computed course guidance to preset navigation waypoints; often referred to simply as an INS
ASRS:	Aviation Safety Reporting System
ATC:	Air traffic control
CAA:	Civil Aviation Authority. The aviation regulatory authority of the United Kingdom
CAAS:	Computer-assisted approach sequencing
CDTI:	Cockpit display of traffic information
CIRCUIT:	The rectangular flight path around an airport consisting of the takeoff (normally upwind), the crosswind leg, the downwind leg, the base leg (also normally crosswind), and the final approach to a landing (normally upwind), all connected in sequence by turns appropriately compensated for the wind

COMMERCIAL PILOT LICENSE:	The license that enables the holder to act as a pilot on aircraft carrying passengers and/or freight and operating for hire or reward
CRM:	Cockpit resource management
CROSSCOUNTRY:	Any flight to a destination more than 25 miles from the airport of departure
CROSSWIND:	A condition in which the wind blows at an angle to an airplane's direction of flight
CRS:	Criterion referenced (performance) scoring
CRT:	Cathode-ray tube
CVR:	Cockpit voice recorder
DECISION HEIGHT (DH):	The height at which a decision legally must be made either to continue a precision ILS or MLS landing approach with the runway in sight or execute a missed approach
DEICING:	The removal of ice from an aircraft by mechanical, chemical, or thermal means
DME:	Distance measuring equipment. Airborne and ground-based equipment used interactively to measure in nautical miles the distance of an aircraft from a ground station
FAA:	Federal Aviation Administration. The aviation regulatory authority of the United States
FDR:	Flight data recorder
FINAL APPROACH:	The final stage of flight in which an airplane is brought from an initial approach position and altitude to a landing
FL:	Flight level. When altimeters are adjusted to the standard barometric pressure setting (29.92 inches of mercury or 1013.2 hectopascals), vertical distances given in flight levels in hundreds of feet to the nearest 1,000 feet (e.g., 29,000 feet = FL 290)

FLAPS:

Attachments to the wings of an airplane articulated to change the lifting capacity and the wind resistance (drag) of the wings by changing the area and/or curvature of the resulting combined airfoils

FLARE:

To round out a landing approach to touch down smoothly by gradually raising the nose of the aircraft to reduce the rate of descent and airspeed

FLY-BY-WIRE:

The continuous automatic transformation of manual control inputs by computers to provide stabilized coordinated control of the airplane through optimum setting of the flying surfaces

GLASS COCKPIT:

A generic term used in reference to aircraft with flightdeck instruments that display information via electronic means rather than by the traditional electromechanical devices

GLIDEPATH:

(1) The flight path of an airplane in a glide (i.e., with reduced engine thrust); (2) the path used by an aircraft in an approach procedure. Path determined visually or sensed and indicated electronically. Correct glidepath necessary to avoid undershooting or overshooting the runway aimpoint

GLIDESLOPE:

A radio beam transmitted by an instrument landing system that defines a desired glidepath, normally inclined three degrees, and deviations above and below the desired glidepath within limits of ±0.5 degree

GPWS:

Ground proximity warning system. A warning device on the flight deck that is activated when the rate of closure with terrain or departure from the glideslope is outside prescribed limits

HSI:

Horizontal situation indicator. An instrument that provides indications of aircraft heading, position relative to a selected course, and horizontal steering guidance based on various sources of position information depending on the selection of the ILS, VOR, INS, or other navigation mode

HUD: Head-up display. A device that reflects CRT-generated images from an angled transparent surface above the glareshield so that steering guidance and flight display symbology can be viewed concurrently with the real-world forward visual scene

ICR: Interactive conflict resolution. A computer-based decision aid for approach controllers

IFR: Instrument flight rules. The regulations covering flight operations solely by reference to instruments (often but not necessarily in instrument meteorological conditions)

ILS: Instrument landing system. A pilot-interpreted radio navigation aid providing vertical (glideslope) and lateral (localizer) angular displacement (deviation) from a final approach path to an airport runway

INS: See AINS

LOFT: Line-oriented flight training

MDA: Minimum descent altitude. The lowest altitude to which descent is authorized without visual contact with the runway in the execution of a nonprecision instrument approach procedure (one not made by reference to an ILS, MLS, or other electronic precision approach system)

MLS: Microwave landing system. A volumetric position sensing system incorporating time-referenced scanning beams to provide azimuth, elevation, and distance information for precise guidance on multiple and flexible approach paths and timed arrivals at a landing threshold

NASA: National Aeronautics and Space Administration

NDB: Non-directional beacon that emits a continuous radio wave, the directional origin of which can be sensed by an ADF antenna to guide the aircraft to a fixed position

NTSB: National Transportation Safety Board

OVERSHOOTING: Landing past the intended touchdown point on the runway (or executing a missed approach procedure to avoid doing so)

PRIVATE PILOT LICENSE: The license that enables the holder to act as a pilot of an aircraft carrying passengers or cargo but not for hire or reward

RMI: Radio magnetic indicator. An ADF instrument with a compass card driven by a gyro-stabilized compass or a directional gyro. It may also have a needle that responds to a VOR signal. In either case, a needle indicates course to the station

RNAV: Originally ARNAV, denoting any *area navigation* method that allows a pilot to fly any desired route, regardless of the location of radio facilities, usually by entering imaginary waypoints referenced to VOR stations into an RNAV computer or latitude and longitude coordinates into an INS or doppler navigation computer

SLATS: Slotted airfoils in their extended forward position

STICK SHAKER: A warning system whereby the control column shakes to warn the pilot of the imminent approach to a stall

TRICYCLE: A landing gear arrangement in which a wheel is placed well forward under the nose of the airplane and the main wheels are placed aft of the center of gravity

T-VASI SYSTEM:　　　An Australian refinement of the original VASI visual approach slope indicator system (see VASI System)

UHF:　　　Ultra high frequency. A radio spectrum used exclusively by the military

UNDERSHOOTING:　　　To follow an approach path that will lead to a landing short of the intended touchdown point

VASI SYSTEM:　　　Visual approach slope indicator system. A ground-based system incorporating three sets of lights that appear red or white or some combination thereof as the pilot approaches a runway so equipped. It provides vertical descent guidance to a predetermined runway threshold (the point at which the flare is to be initiated)

VFR:　　　Visual flight rules. The regulations governing flight operations when weather conditions are at or above certain minima of visibility and cloud base

VHF:　　　Very high frequency. The radio spectrum used for most aerial communication and aircraft navigation

VISUAL APPROACH:　　　An approach made to a runway by visual reference to the surface

VOR:　　　VHF omnidirectional radio. A radio navigation system that provides indications of the bearing of the aircraft to or from the ground transmitter, from which directions to the left or right of a selected course to or from the facility are derived and displayed

WIND SHEAR:　　　An abrupt change in wind direction and/or velocity, often but not necessarily associated with a change in altitude following takeoff or on a final approach to a landing

Notes

CHAPTER 1

1. Gibson, J. J. (1955). The optical expansion-pattern in aerial locomotion. *American Journal of Psychology, 68,* 480–484. A more extensive treatment of the relationship between perception and action is advanced by J. J. Gibson (1966) in *The senses considered as perceptual systems.* Boston: Houghton Mifflin. A more recent summary of this approach is presented by V. Bruce and P. Green (1985) in *Visual perception: Physiology, psychology and ecology.* New York: Lawrence Erlbaum.

2. Lee, D. N. (1980). The optic flow field: The foundation of vision. *Philosophical Transactions of the Royal Society of London, B290,* 169–179. An application of this perspective to pilot performance is illustrated by D. H. Owen and R. Warren (1982) in Optical variables as measures of performance during simulated flight. *Proceedings of the 26th annual meeting of the Human Factors Society* (pp. 312–315). Santa Monica: Human Factors Society.

3. Werblin, F. (1973, January). Control of sensitivity in the retina. *Scientific American, 228,* 70–79.

4. Carr, R. M. (1967). The effects of color coding indicator displays on dark adaptation. *Human Factors, 9,* 175–179. This study was designed to investigate the operation of sonar equipment under different lighting conditions. The conclusion was that "dark adaptation is primarily dependent on the overall illumination level rather than the red lighting."

5. Helicopter in near miss with large pink pig. (1983, October). *Pilot,* p. 58. There have been several tragic collisions between airliners and light aircraft in recent years. The worst involved a Pacific Southwest Airlines Boeing 727 that collided with a Cessna 172 over San Diego on September 25, 1978, killing 144 people. On 31 August 1986 an Aeromexico DC-9 and a Piper Warrior collided near Los Angeles International Airport, killing at least 75.

6. Roscoe, S. N. (1985). Bigness is in the eye of the beholder. *Human Factors, 27,* 615–636. For a later treatment of this subject see S. N. Roscoe (1989). The zoom-lens hypothesis. In M. Hershenson (Ed.), *The moon illusion.* Hillsdale, NJ: Lawrence Erlbaum Associates.

7. Roscoe, S. N. (1979). When day is done and shadows fall, we miss the airport most of all. *Human Factors, 21,* 721–731.

8. Roscoe, S. N. (1982). Landing airplanes, detecting traffic, and the dark focus. *Aviation, Space, and Environmental Medicine, 53,* 970–976.

9. Mertens, H. W., & Lewis, M. F. (1982). Effect of different runway sizes on pilot performance during simulated night landing approaches. *Aviation, Space, and Environmental Medicine, 53,* 463–471.

10. Vette, G. (1983). *Impact Erebus.* Auckland, New Zealand: Hodder & Stoughton.

11. Visual illusions: Runway width and slope. (1975). *FAA Aviation News, 5* (11), 12–13.

12. Morphew, G. R. (1985). Transcript of open forum session. In G. B. McNaughton (Ed.), *Aircraft Attitude Awareness Workshop Proceedings* (p. 3-8-1). Wright-Patterson Air Force Base, OH: Flight Dynamics Laboratory.

13. Hull, J. C., Gill, R. T., & Roscoe, S. N. (1982). Locus of the stimulus to visual accommodation: Where in the world or where in the eye? *Human Factors, 24,* 311–319. See also Iavecchia, J. H., Iavecchia, H. P., & Roscoe, S. N. (1988). Eye accommodation to head-up virtual images. *Human Factors, 30,* 689–702; and Randle, R. J., Roscoe, S. N., & Petitt, J. (1980). *Effects of magnification and visual accommodation on aimpoint estimation in simulated landings with real and virtual image displays* (Technical Paper NASA-TP-1635). Washington, DC: National Aeronautics and Space Administration; and Norman, J., & Ehrlich, S. (1986). Visual accommodation and virtual image displays: Target detection and recognition. *Human Factors, 28,* 135–151.

14. See last paper cited in note 13.

15. Flying display tragedy. (1984, July). *Pilot,* p. 48.

16. Lee, D. N., Lishman, J. R., & Thomson, J. A. (1982). Regulation of gait in long jumping. *Journal of Experimental Psychology: Human Perception and Performance, 8,* 448–459. David Lee of Edinburgh University in Scotland has carried out studies ranging from an examination of the changes in wing position made by diving gannets just before entering the sea to the control of braking by car drivers. See also Lee, D. N., & Reddish, P. (1981). Plummeting gannets: A paradigm of ecological optics. *Nature, 293* (5830), 293–294.

17. Kruk, R. V., et al. (1983). Flying performance on the advanced simulator for pilot training and laboratory tests of vision. *Human Factors, 25,* 457–466.

18. Lee, D. N. (1976). A theory of visual control of braking based on information about time-to-collision. *Perception, 5,* 437–459.

CHAPTER 2

1. National Transportation Safety Board. (1986). *Aircraft accident report—Henson Airlines Flight 1517, Beech B99, N339HA, Grottoes, Virginia, September 23, 1985* (Report NTSB/AAR-86/07). Springfield, VA: National Technical Information Service. See also National Transportation Safety Board. (1986). *Aircraft accident report—Bar Harbor Airlines Flight 1808, Beech BE-99, N300WP, Auburn–Lewiston Municipal Airport, Auburn, Maine, August 25, 1985* (Report NTSB/AAR-86/06). Springfield, VA: National Technical Information Service.

2. National Transportation Safety Board. (1981). *Aircraft accident report—Cascade Airways Inc., Beechcraft 99A, N390CA, Spokane, Washington, January 20, 1981* (Report NTSB-AAR-81-11). Springfield, VA: National Technical Information Service.

3. Sharp, G. R., & Ernsting, J. (1978). The effects of long duration acceleration. In G. Dhenin (Ed.), *Aviation medicine: Physiology and human factors.* London: Tri-Med Books.

4. Crashed during missed approach in fog. (1983, February). *Pilot*, pp. 46–48.

5. Clark, B., & Graybiel, A. (1949). Linear acceleration and deceleration as factors influencing nonvisual orientation during flight. *Journal of Aviation Medicine, 20,* 92–101.

6. Barlay, S. (1969). *Aircrash detective.* London: Hamish Hamilton.

7. MacCorquodale, K. (1948). Effects of angular acceleration and centrifugal force on nonvisual space orientation during flight. *Journal of Aviation Medicine, 19,* 146–157.

8. Reason, J. T., & Brand, J. D. (1975). *Motion sickness.* London: Academic Press. This book cites several reviews of wartime surveys of airsickness in crews as well as the study of Royal Air Force cadets at Cranfield.

9. Simson, L. R. (1971). Investigation of fatal aircraft accidents; "Physiological incidents." *Aerospace Medicine, 42,* 1002–1006.

10. 178 seconds. (1983, July). *Pilot*, p. 53. Another study of spatial disorientation is discussed by A. J. Benson (1978) in Spatial disorientation—General aspects. In G. Dhenin (Ed.), *Aviation medicine: Physiology and human factors* (pp. 424–425). London: Tri-Med Books. The classic experiment in this area was reported by L. A. Bryan, J. W. Stonecipher, and K. Aron (1954) in 180-degree turn experiment. *University of Illinois Bulletin, 52* (11).

11. National Transportation Safety Board. (1977). *Aircraft accident report—American Airlines Boeing 727-95, N1963, St. Thomas, Virgin Islands, April 27, 1976* (Report NTSB-AAR-77-1). Springfield, VA: National Technical Information Service.

12. Roscoe, S. N. (1980). *Aviation psychology.* Ames: Iowa State University Press. See Chapter 14, p. 168. The point was first made by S. N. Roscoe in 1976 in Appendix 1: Human factors and crew performance in the St. Thomas accident. In *Accident investigation post-hearing submission to the National Transportation Safety Board: Boeing 727 accident, St. Thomas, Virgin Islands, April 27, 1976.* Arlington, TX: Allied Pilots Association.

13. Collins, W. E., Schroeder, D. J., & Hill, R. J. (1973). Some effects of alcohol on vestibular responses. In C. R. Pfaltz (Ed.), *Advances in oto-rhinolaryngology* (Vol. 19, pp. 295–303). Basel, Switzerland: Karger.

14. See book cited in note 8; it presents a detailed discussion of the neural mismatch theory.

15. Benson, A. J. (1978). Spatial disorientation—Common illusions (p. 467). In G. Dhenin (Ed.), *Aviation medicine: Physiology and human factors.* London: Tri-Med Books.

CHAPTER 3

1. Hunt, G. J. F., & Crook, C. (1985). *International trends in professional flight crew development.* Palmerston North, New Zealand: Massey University.

2. Telfer, R. A., & Biggs, J. (1985). *The psychology of flight training.* Cessnock, NSW, Australia: Civil Air Training Academy. This book was subsequently revised and published by the Iowa State University Press in 1988.

3. Williams, A. C., Jr. (1980). Discrimination and manipulation in flight. In S. N. Roscoe, *Aviation psychology.* Ames: Iowa State University Press.

4. See p. 28 of reference cited in note 3.

5. Roscoe, S. N., & Corl, L. (1987). Wondrous original method for basic airmanship testing. In R. S. Jensen (Ed.), *Proceedings of the Fourth International Symposium on Aviation Psychology* (pp. 493–499). Columbus: Ohio State University, Department of Aviation.

6. Hunt, G. J. F., & Crook, C. (1986). *Flight crew–aeroplane curriculum schema: Civil aviation needs assessment project.* Palmerston North, New Zealand: Massey Aviation Institute.

7. Hunt, G. J. F. (1984). NEBEAT—The systems approach updated. *PLET— Programmed Learning and Systems Training, 21,* 53–60.

8. Office of Air Accidents Investigation. (1986). *Aircraft accident—Cessna 152 ZK–EJX, Rabbit Island, Nelson Province, 1 June 1986* (Report 86–047). Wellington, New Zealand: Government Printer.

9. Cattell, R. B., & Kline, P. (1977). *The scientific analysis of personality and motivation.* London: Academic Press. Personality profiles for various occupations are presented on p. 306.

10. Krahenbuhl, G. S., et al. (1981). Instructor pilot teaching behavior and student pilot stress in flight training. *Aviation, Space, and Environmental Medicine, 52,* 594–597.

11. Melton, C. E., et al. (1975). Effect of a general aviation trainer on the stress of flight training. *Aviation, Space, and Environmental Medicine, 46,* 1–5.

12. Kahneman, D., & Tversky, A. (1973). On the psychology of prediction. *Psychological Review, 80,* 237–251.

13. Tricky T-tail. (1984, April/May). *New Zealand Flight Safety,* p. 9.

14. Adams, J. A. (1987). Historical review and appraisal of research on the learning, retention, and transfer of human motor skills. *Psychological Bulletin, 101,* 41–74.

15. Simon, C. W., & Roscoe, S. N. (1984). Application of a multifactor approach to transfer of training research. *Human Factors, 26,* 591–612.

16. Prather, D. C. (1973). Prompted mental practice as a flight simulator. *Journal of Applied Psychology, 57,* 353–355.

17. Adams, J. A. (1961). Some considerations in the design and use of dynamic flight simulators. In H. W. Sinaiko (Ed.), *Selected papers on human factors in the design and use of control systems.* New York: Dover.

18. Wightman, D. C., & Lintern, G. (1985). Part-task training for tracking and manual control. *Human Factors, 27,* 267–283.

19. Wightman, D. C., & Sistrunk, F. (1987). Part-task training strategies in simulated carrier landing final approach training. *Human Factors, 29,* 245–254.

20. Schneider, W. (1985). Training high-performance skills: Fallacies and guidelines. *Human Factors, 27,* 285–300.

21. Koonce, J. M. (1984). A brief history of aviation psychology. *Human Factors, 26,* 499–508.

22. Gopher, D., & Kahneman, D. (1971). Individual differences in attention and the prediction of flight criteria. *Perceptual and Motor Skills, 33,* 1335–1342. A more extensive validation study, involving 2,000 Israeli Air Force flight cadets, is reported by D. Gopher (1982) in A selective attention test as a predictor of success in flight training. *Human Factors, 24,* 173–183.

23. Wickens, C. D. (1984). *Engineering psychology and human performance.* Columbus, OH: Charles E. Merrill.

24. Damos, D. L. (1978). Residual attention as a predictor of pilot performance. *Human Factors, 20,* 435–440.

25. Damos, D. L., & Lintern, G. (1981). A comparison of single- and dual-task measures to predict simulator performance of beginning student pilots. *Ergonomics, 24,* 673–684.

26. Jensen, R. S. (1982). Pilot judgment: Training and evaluation. *Human Factors, 24,* 61–73.

27. Mané, A. (1981). Airmanship: An introduction. In R. S. Jensen (Ed.), *Proceedings of the First Symposium on Aviation Psychology* (pp. 161–165). Columbus: Ohio State University, Department of Aviation.

28. Williams, A. C., Jr., & Flexman, R. E. (1949). Evaluation of the School Link as an aid in primary flight instruction. *University of Illinois Bulletin, 46* (71). See also Flexman, R. E., et al. (1972). Studies in pilot training: The anatomy of transfer. *Aviation Research Monographs, 2* (1).

29. Povenmire, H. K., & Roscoe, S. N. (1971). An evaluation of ground-based flight trainers in routine primary flight training. *Human Factors, 13,* 109–116.

30. Roscoe, S. N., & Williges, B. H. (1980). Measurement of transfer of training. In S. N. Roscoe, *Aviation psychology.* Ames: Iowa State University Press.

31. Povenmire, H. K., & Roscoe, S. N. (1973). Incremental transfer effectiveness of a ground-based general aviation trainer. *Human Factors, 15,* 534–542.

32. Trollip, S. R. (1979). The evaluation of a complex computer-based flight procedures trainer. *Human Factors, 21,* 47–54.

33. Koonce, J. M. (1974). *Effects of ground-based aircraft simulator motion conditions upon prediction of pilot proficiency* (Technical Report ARL–74–5/AFOSR–74–3). Savoy: University of Illinois, Aviation Research Laboratory.

34. Woodruff, R. R., et al. (1976). *Full mission simulation in undergraduate pilot training: An exploratory study* (Technical Report AFHRL–TR–76–84, AD–A039 267). Williams Air Force Base, AZ: Air Force Human Resources Laboratory, Flying Training Division.

35. Waag, W. L. (1981). *Training effectiveness of visual and motion simulation* (Technical Report AFHRL–TR–79–72). Brooks Air Force Base, TX: Air Force Human Resources Laboratory.

36. Westra, D. P. (1982). *Simulator design features for carrier landing: II. In-simulator transfer of training* (Interim Technical Report NAVTRAEQUIPCEN 81–C–0105–1). Orlando: Naval Training Equipment Center. See also Westra, D. P. (1983). *Simulator design features for air-to-ground bombing: I. Performance experiment 1* (Interim Technical Report NAVTRAEQUIPCEN 81–C–0105–4). Orlando: Naval Training Equipment Center.

37. Jacobs, R. S., & Roscoe, S. N. (1975). Simulator cockpit motion and the transfer of initial flight training. *Proceedings of the 19th Annual Meeting of the Human Factors Society.* Santa Monica: Human Factors Society.

38. Payne, T. A., et al. (1954). *Improving landing performance using a contact landing trainer* (Contract N6ori–71, Task Order XVI, TR SPECDEVCEN 71–16–11, AD121200). Port Washington, NY: Office of Naval Research, Special Devices Center.

39. Roscoe, S. N., & Eisele, J. E. (1980). Visual cue requirements in contact flight simulators. In S. N. Roscoe, *Aviation psychology.* Ames: Iowa State University Press.

40. Lintern, G., & Roscoe, S. N. (1980). Visual cue augmentation in contact

flight simulation. In S. N. Roscoe, *Aviation psychology.* Ames: Iowa State University Press.

41. Seminal reports advancing the economical holistic research strategy applied in the VTRS program include the following: Simon, C. W. (1977). *New research paradigm for applied experimental psychology: A system approach* (Technical Report TR CWS-04-77A). Westlake Village, CA: Canyon Research Group, Inc.; Simon, C. W. (1977). *Design, analysis, and interpretation of screening designs for human factors engineering research* (Technical Report TR CWS-04-77B). Westlake Village, CA: Canyon Research Group, Inc.; Simon, C. W. (1979). *Applications of advanced experimental methodologies to AWAVS training research* (Technical Report NAVTRAEQUIPCEN 77-C-0065-1, AD A064-332). Orlando: Naval Training Equipment Center; Simon, C. W. (1981). *Applications of advanced experimental methods to visual technology research simulator studies: Supplemental techniques* (Technical Report NAVTRAEQUIPCEN 78-C-0060-3). Orlando: Naval Training Equipment Center; and Simon, C. W., and Roscoe, S. N. (1984). Application of a multifactor approach to transfer of training research. *Human Factors, 26,* 591–612. (Abbreviated version of same title issued as Technical Report NAVTRAEQUIPCEN 78-C-0060-6, 1981).

CHAPTER 4

1. Professional Affairs Board, British Psychological Society. (1984). Presenting a case for the economic importance of psychology. *Bulletin of the British Psychological Society, 37,* 253–255; Williges, R. C. (1984). The tide of computer technology. *Human Factors, 26,* 109–114.

2. The Optica tragedy. (1986, November). *Pilot,* pp. 56–57.

3. Ellis, G. (1984). *Air crash investigation of general aviation aircraft.* Greybull, WY: Capstan.

4. Fitts, P. M., Jones, R. E., & Milton, J. L. (1950). Eye movements of aircraft pilots during instrument-landing approaches. *Aeronautical Engineering Review, 9,* 24–29.

5. Harris, R. L., Sr., et al. (1982). Visual scanning behavior and pilot workload. *Aviation, Space, and Environmental Medicine, 53,* 1067–1072.

6. Federal Aviation Administration. (1987). *Code of federal regulations, 14CFR.* Washington, DC: Government Printing Office.

7. Fitts, P. M., & Jones, R. E. (1947). *Analysis of factors contributing to 460 "pilot error" experiences in operating aircraft controls* (Report TSEAA-694-12). Wright-Patterson Air Force Base, OH: Aeromedical Laboratory, Air Materiel Command.

8. Courtney, A. J. (1986). Chinese population stereotypes: Color associations. *Human Factors, 28,* 97–100. A more general discussion of the principles of display-control compatability is presented by S. L. Smith (1981) in Exploring compatibility with words and pictures. *Human Factors, 23,* 305–315.

9. Ministry of Transport and Civil Aviation. (1958). *Report on the accident to Viscount Type 802, G–AORC, 28th April 1958, Tarbolton, Ayrshire.* London: Her Majesty's Stationery Office.

10. Hopkin, V. D. (1982). Psychology and aviation. In S. Canter & D. Canter (Eds.), *Psychology in practice.* Chichester, England: Wiley. Includes a description of the design of an alternative to the three-pointer altimeter.

11. Mid-air collision. (1984, July). *Pilot,* p. 49.

12. Gomer, F. E., & Eggleston, R. G. (1978). Perceived magnitudes of distortion, secondary imaging, and rainbowing in aircraft windshields. *Human Factors, 20,* 391-400.

13. Bergmann, J. (1982). Collision over San Diego. *Aviation Accident Investigator, 1*(1), 1-3. The article notes that "As for the 727 windscreen, it's awful, but average for airliners of its age."

14. Roscoe, S. N., & Hull, J. C. (1982). Cockpit visibility and contrail detection. *Human Factors, 24,* 659-672. A less technical account of these experiments was given by S. N. Roscoe (1982) in Cockpit visibility: How window design and scanning habits work against you. *Aviation Accident Investigator, 1*(2), 1-3.

15. National Transportation Safety Board. (1974). *Aircraft accident report—Pan American World Airways, Inc., Boeing 707-321B, N454PA, Pago Pago, American Samoa, January 30, 1974* (Report NTSB-AAR-74-15). Springfield, VA: National Technical Information Service. The original report laid the blame for the accident on the crew, particularly the captain, who was conducting his first instrument approach after a four-month break from flying. This was superceded in 1977 by a second report bearing the same title (NTSB-AAR-77-7) in which more attention was given to the existence and contribution of wind shear.

16. Roscoe, S. N. (1968). Airborne displays for flight and navigation. *Human Factors, 10,* 321-332. A systematic investigation of direction of motion variables in aircraft attitude and steering guidance displays was conducted at the University of Illinois during the early 1970s for the Office of Naval Research and the Air Force Office of Scientific Research. This series of simulator and flight experiments was reported in 1975 in a set of three papers in Vol. 17 of *Human Factors:* Motion relationships in aircraft attitude and guidance displays: A flight experiment (pp. 374-387) by S. N. Roscoe and R. C. Williges; Aircraft simulator motion and the order of merit of flight attitude and steering guidance displays (pp. 388-400) by F. Ince, R. C. Williges, and S. N. Roscoe; and The transition of experienced pilots to a frequency-separated aircraft attitude display (pp. 401-414) by D. B. Beringer, R. C. Williges, and S. N. Roscoe.

17. Roscoe, S. N. (1983). 747 dives into Arabian Sea. *Aviation Accident Investigator, 2*(9), 1-3.

18. Roscoe, S. N., Johnson, S. L., & Williges, R. C. (1980). Display motion relationships. In S. N. Roscoe, *Aviation psychology.* Ames: Iowa State University Press.

19. Roscoe, S. N., & Jensen, R. S. (1981). Computer-animated predictive displays for microwave landing approaches. *IEEE Transactions on Systems, Man, and Cybernetics, SMC-11,* 760-765.

20. See Figure 1 of Loomis, J. P., & Porter, R. F. (1982). The performance of warning systems in avoiding controlled-flight-into-terrain (CFIT) accidents. *Aviation, Space, and Environmental Medicine, 53,* 1085-1090. The regulations requiring the use of a GPWS were introduced in the United States by the FAA in December 1974. A related system, the Minimum Safe Altitude Warning (MSAW), was initially introduced as part of the uprated radar systems in November 1976.

21. Hart, S. G., & Loomis, L. L. (1980). Evaluation of the potential format and content of a cockpit display of traffic information. *Human Factors, 22,* 591-604.

22. Palmer, E. A., et al. (1980). Perception of horizontal aircraft separation on a cockpit display of traffic information. *Human Factors, 22,* 605–620.

23. Smith, J. D., Ellis, S. R., & Lee, E. C. (1984). Perceived threat and avoidance maneuvers in response to cockpit traffic displays. *Human Factors, 26,* 33–48.

24. Ellis, S. R., McGreevy, M. W., & Hitchcock, R. J. (1987). Perspective traffic display format and airline pilot traffic avoidance. *Human Factors, 29,* 371–382.

25. Beringer, D. B. (1978). Collision avoidance response stereotypes in pilots and non-pilots. *Human Factors, 20,* 529–536.

26. Wiener, E. L., & Curry, R. E. (1980). Flight-deck automation: Promises and problems. *Ergonomics, 23,* 995–1011.

27. Boehm-Davis, et al. (1983). Human factors of flight-deck automation: Report on a NASA-industry workshop. *Ergonomics, 26,* 953–961. This report was the result of a NASA-sponsored workshop in which participants from NASA, the FAA, and various airlines met to discuss the issues raised by flight-deck automation.

28. van Eekhout, J. M., & Rouse, W. B. (1981). Human errors in detection, diagnosis, and compensation for failures in the engine control room of a supertanker. *IEEE Transactions on Systems, Man, and Cybernetics. SMC-12,* 813–816.

29. Sheridan, T. B. (1980). Human error in nuclear power plants. *Technology Review, 82,* 23–33.

30. Sheridan, T. B. (1980). Understanding human error and aiding human diagnosis behavior in nuclear power plants. In J. Rasmussen & W. B. Rouse (Eds.), *Human detection and diagnosis of system failures.* New York: Plenum.

31. False alarms. (1984, November). *British Airways Flight Safety Review.*

32. NASA's Aviation Safety Reporting System. (1982, March). Inhibiting lights that glare and horns that blare. *Callback* (No. 34).

33. National Transportation Safety Board. (1975). *Aircraft accident report—Eastern Air Lines, Inc., Douglas DC-9-31, N8984E, Charlotte, North Carolina, September 11, 1974* (Report NTSB-AAR-75-9). Springfield, VA: National Technical Information Service. The quoted paragraph is on p. 15 of the report.

34. Hopkins, H. (1986). Now hear this. *Flight International,* pp. 26–28.

35. Patterson, R. D. (1982). *Guidelines for auditory warning systems in civil aircraft* (Paper 82017). London: Civil Aviation Authority.

36. NASA's Aviation Safety Reporting System. (1986, February). Human factors associated with altitude alert systems. *Callback* (No. 80).

37. National Transportation Safety Board. (1973). *Aircraft accident report—Eastern Airlines L-1011, N310EA, Miami, Florida, December 29, 1972* (Report NTSB-AAR-73-14). Springfield, VA: National Technical Information Service. This accident is widely cited in discussions of the effects of automation on the flight deck. Despite having information from the MSAW (see note 20, above), the controller did not alert the crew to the altitude deviation, nor was he required to do so.

38. National Transportation Safety Board. (1984). *Aircraft accident report—Scandinavian Airlines System Flight 901, McDonnell Douglas DC-10-30, LN-RKB, at John F. Kennedy International Airport, Jamaica, New York, February 28, 1984* (Report NTSB-AAR-84-15). Springfield, VA: National Technical Information Service.

39. Wickens, C. D., & Kessel, C. J. (1981). Failure detection in dynamic systems. In J. Rasmussen & W. B. Rouse (Eds.), *Human detection and diagnosis of system failures.* New York: Plenum.

40. Ephrath, A. R., & Curry, R. E. (1977). Detection by pilots of system failures during instrument landings. *IEEE Transactions on Systems, Man, and Cybernetics, SMC-7,* 841–848.

41. People make poor monitors. (1986, July 26). *Flight International,* p. 1.

42. National Transportation Safety Board. (1986). *Aircraft accident report—China Airlines Boeing 747-SP, N4522V, 300 nautical miles northwest of San Francisco, California, February 19, 1985* (Report NTSB/AAR-86/03). Springfield, VA: National Technical Information Service.

43. Wolfe, T. (1980). *The right stuff.* New York: Bantam.

44. Gerathewohl, S. J. (1976). Optimization of crew effectiveness in future cockpit design: Biomedical implications. *Aviation, Space, and Environmental Medicine, 47,* 1182–1187.

45. Rouse, S. H., Rouse, W. B., & Hammer, J. M. (1982). Design and evaluation of an onboard computer-based information system for aircraft. *IEEE Transactions on Systems, Man, and Cybernetics, SMC-12,* 451–463.

46. Reising, J. M., & Hitchcock, L. (1982). Fitts' principles still applicable: Computer monitoring of fighter aircraft emergencies. *Aviation, Space, and Environmental Medicine, 53,* 1080–1084. Although this approach to warning systems was not actually implemented on the F-18, it is illustrative of future directions in the use of computer-aiding in the cockpit.

CHAPTER 5

1. Kozlowski, L. T., & Bryant, K. J. (1977). Sense of direction, spatial orientation, and cognitive maps. *Journal of Experimental Psychology: Human Perception & Performance, 3,* 510–598.

2. Thorndyke, P. W., & Stasz, C. (1980). Individual differences in procedures for knowledge acquisition from maps. *Cognitive Psychology, 12,* 137–175.

3. National Transportation Safety Board. (1975). *Aircraft accident report—Trans World Airlines, Inc., Boeing 727-231, N54328, Berryville, Virginia, December 1, 1974* (Report NTSB-AAR-75-16). Springfield, VA: National Technical Information Service.

4. Fowler, F. D. (1980). Air traffic control problems: A pilot's view. *Human Factors, 22,* 645–654. The quoted passage is from p. 647.

5. Christ, R. E. (1975). Review and analysis of color coding research for visual displays. *Human Factors, 17,* 542–570. A more recent review is presented by J. Davidoff (1987) titled The role of color in visual displays. In D. J. Oborne (Ed.), *International reviews of ergonomics* (Vol. 1., pp. 21–42). London: Taylor & Francis.

6. Taylor, R. M., & Hopkin, V. D. (1975). Ergonomic principles and map design. *Applied Ergonomics, 6,* 196–204.

7. Bloomfield, J. R. (1979). Visual search with embedded targets: Color and texture differences. *Human Factors, 21,* 317–330. The experimental stimuli were complex, textured forms that may be more representative of map searching tasks than many of the simpler stimuli often used in such studies.

8. Leachtenauer, J. C. (1978). Peripheral acuity and photointerpretation performance. *Human Factors, 20,* 537–551.

9. Welsh, K. W., Vaughan, J. A., & Rasmussen, P. G. (1976). Readability of approach charts as a function of visual acuity, luminance, and printing format. *Aviation, Space, and Environmental Medicine, 47*, 1027–1031. The 12 subjects all wore corrective lenses but were within the standards prescribed for pilot licenses by the FAA. The average age was 52.1 years.

10. Johnson, R. W. (1986). *Shootdown: The verdict on KAL 007*. London: Chatto & Windus.

11. Wiener, E. L. (1985). Beyond the sterile cockpit. *Human Factors, 27*, 75–90.

12. Butterbaugh, L. C., & Rockwell, T. H. (1982). Evaluation of alternative alphanumeric keying logics. *Human Factors, 24*, 521–533.

13. Brett, G. (1985). North Atlantic navigation errors. *IFALPA Monthly News Bulletin, 146*, 2–3.

14. Roscoe, S. N., & Kraus, E. F. (1973). Pilotage error and residual attention: The evaluation of a performance control system in airborne area navigation. *Navigation, 20*, 267–279. This experiment in the early 1970s also involved two different flight control systems, both employing a sidearm stick controller in place of the conventional yoke. It is interesting to note that a sidearm stick control was designed as the primary flight control in the prototype Convair F-106 and was flight tested with good results in 1956. However, the control was returned to its central location in the production airplane, and it was many years later that a sidearm control came into use in commercial aviation with the European Airbus A320.

15. See the accident report cited in note 3.

16. Stager, P., et al. (1980). Bilingual air traffic control in Canada. *Human Factors, 22*, 655–670.

17. NASA's Aviation Safety Reporting System. (1981, October). Listening in. *Callback* (No. 28).

18. Billings, C. E., & Cheaney, E. S. (Eds.). (1981). *Information transfer problems in the aviation system*. (Technical Paper NASA-TP-1875). Moffett Field, CA: National Aeronautics and Space Administration.

19. Kahneman, D., & Tversky, A. (1982). The simulation heuristic. In D. Kahneman, P. Slovic, & A. Tversky (Eds.), *Judgment under uncertainty: Heuristics and biases*. Cambridge: Cambridge University Press.

20. Grayson, R. L., & Billings, C. E. (1981). Information transfer between air traffic control and aircraft: Communication problems in flight operations. In C. E. Billings & E. S. Cheaney (Eds.), *Information transfer problems in the aviation system* (Technical Paper, NASA-TP-1875). Moffett Field, CA: National Aeronautics and Space Administration.

21. Office of Air Accidents Investigation. (1985). *Aircraft incident— HS748–Mount Cook Airlines/F27–Air New Zealand, air transport, south of Rotorua Airdrome, 4 Oct 85* (Reference 85-0-429). Wellington, New Zealand: Author. A brief review of problems with aircraft call signs is presented by NASA's Aviation Safety Reporting System (1987, May) in Addressee errors in ATC communications: The call sign problem. *Callback* (No. 95). The International Federation of Airline Pilots Associations expressed concern at the potential for confusion between similar call signs. See Hopkins, H. (1986, May 3). Pilot power for security and safety. *Flight International*, p. 32–34.

22. Hopkin, V. D. (1980). The measurement of the air traffic controller. *Human Factors, 22*, 547–560.

23. Gershzohn, G. (1980). Air traffic control using a microwave landing system. *Human Factors, 22*, 621–629.

24. Whitfield, D., Ball, R. G., & Ord, G. (1980). Some human factors aspects of computer-aiding concepts for air traffic controllers. *Human Factors, 22,* 569–580.

25. Sperandio, J. C. (1971). Variation of operator's strategies and regulating effects on workload. *Ergonomics, 14,* 571–577.

26. Loftus, G. R., Dark, V. J., & Williams, D. (1979). Short-term memory factors in ground controller/pilot communication. *Human Factors, 21,* 169–181.

27. Weston, R. C., & Hurst, R. (1972). *Zagreb one four—Cleared to collide?* London: Granada.

28. Crump, J. H. (1979). Review of stress in air traffic control: Its measurement and effects. *Aviation, Space, and Environmental Medicine, 50,* 243–248.

29. Cobb, S., & Rose, R. M. (1973). Hypertension, peptic ulcer, and diabetes in air traffic controllers. *Journal of the American Medical Association, 224,* 489–492.

30. Cooper, C. L. (1983). *Stress research: Issues for the eighties.* Chichester, England: Wiley.

CHAPTER 6

1. Salvendy, G. (Ed.). (1987). *Handbook of human factors.* New York: Wiley.

2. Sanders, M. S., & McCormick, E. J. (1987). *Human factors in engineering and design* (6th ed.) New York: McGraw-Hill. The effects of temperature on performance are investigated by R. D. Pepler (1960) in Warmth, glare, and a background of quiet speech: A comparison of their effects on performance. *Ergonomics, 3,* 68–73. This research was carried out by the Applied Psychology Unit at Cambridge, England. The subjects living in the tropics were tested at the Royal Navy Tropical Research Unit in Singapore. See also, Pepler, R. D. (1958). Warmth and performance: An investigation in the tropics. *Ergonomics, 2,* 63–88.

3. Postlethwaite, A. (1986, May 17). Helicopters in the dock. *Flight International,* pp. 22–25.

4. Sharp, G. R. (1978). Vibration. In G. Dhenin (Ed.), *Aviation medicine: Physiology and human factors.* London: Tri-Med Books.

5. Taylor, W., et al. (1965). Study of noise and hearing in jute weaving. *Journal of the Acoustical Society of America, 38,* 113–120.

6. Civil Aviation Authority. (1982). *CAP 371: The avoidance of excessive fatigue in aircrews: Guide to requirements* (2nd ed.). Cheltenham, England: Author. The reduction in maximum flying duty periods for helicoptor pilots was promulgated in an amendment to CAP 371, published in October 1986.

7. Mills, F. J. (1985). The endocrinology of stress. *Aviation, Space, and Environmental Medicine, 56,* 642–650.

8. Troxler, R. G., & Schwertner, H. A. (1985). Cholesterol, stress, lifestyle, and coronary heart disease. *Aviation, Space, and Environmental Medicine, 56,* 660–665.

9. Melton, C. E., et al. (1975). Effect of a general aviation trainer on the stress of flight training. *Aviation, Space, and Environmental Medicine, 46,* 1–5.

10. Roscoe, A. H. (1978). Stress and workload in pilots. *Aviation, Space, and Environmental Medicine, 49,* 630–636. This paper contains data from the Harrier, VC-10, and BAC-1-11 tests, additional results from monsoon penetra-

tion flights in the F4K Phantom, and an unusual case in which one pilot of an HS748 turboprop transport suffered an inflamed appendix while being monitored.

11. Lewis, C. E., et al. (1967). Flight research program: IX. Medical monitoring of carrier pilots in combat—II. *Aerospace Medicine, 38,* 581–592. These data were collected as part of a joint NASA/Navy project on the effect of exposure to nonphysical stress. The study was carried out on board the aircraft carrier *USS Constellation* in the fall of 1966.

12. Wolfe, T. (1980). *The right stuff* (p. 265). New York: Bantam.

13. Broadbent, D. E. (1971). *Decision and stress.* London: Academic Press. A thorough review of early work in this area.

14. Poulton, E. C. (1976). Arousing environmental stresses can improve performance, whatever people say. *Aviation, Space, and Environmental Medicine, 47,* 1193–1204.

15. McKenzie, J. M., & Fiorica, V. (1967). Stress responses of pilots to severe weather flying. *Aerospace Medicine, 38,* 576–580.

16. Krahenbuhl, G. S., et al. (1985). Biogenic amine/metabolite response during in-flight emergencies. *Aviation, Space, and Environmental Medicine, 56,* 576–580.

17. Berkun, M. M., et al. (1962). Experimental studies of psychological stress in man. *Psychological Monographs, 76* (15, Whole No. 534). An overview of these studies is given by M. M. Berkun (1964) in Performance decrement under psychological stress. *Human Factors, 6,* 21–30.

18. Mid-air collision in the circuit. (1983, January). *Pilot,* pp. 48–49.

19. Davis, D. R. (1948). *Pilot error* (Air Ministry Publication A.P. 3139A). London: Her Majesty's Stationery Office.

20. Weltman, G., Smith, J. E., & Egstrom, G. H. (1971). Perceptual narrowing during simulated pressure-chamber exposure. *Human Factors, 13,* 99–107. The phenomenon of perceptual narrowing is reviewed by A. D. Baddeley (1972) in Selective attention and performance in dangerous environments. *British Journal of Psychology, 63,* 537–546.

21. Hornick, R. J., & Lefritz, N. M. (1966). A study and review of human response to prolonged random vibration. *Human Factors, 8,* 481–492.

22. Hockey, G. R. J. (1970). Effect of loud noise on attentional selectivity. *Quarterly Journal of Experimental Psychology, 22,* 28–36. A more general review is presented by R. Hockey (1979) in Stress and the cognitive components of skilled performance. In V. Hamilton & D. M. Warburton (Eds.), *Human stress and cognition.* Chichester, England: Wiley.

23. See p. 632 of paper cited in note 10.

24. See paper cited in note 14.

25. Krueger, G. P., Armstrong, R. N., & Cisco, R. R. (1985). Aviator performance in week-long extended flight operations in a helicopter simulator. *Behavior Research Methods, Instruments, & Computers, 17,* 68–74. A bibliography of performance in sustained or continuous work has been produced by G. P. Krueger, L. Cardenales-Ortiz, & C. Loveless (1985) in *Human performance in continuous/sustained operations, and the demands of extended work/rest schedules: An annotated bibliography.* Washington, DC: Walter Reed Army Institute of Research.

26. Blake, M. J. F., & Corcoran, D. (1972). Introversion-extraversion and circadian rhythms. In W. P. Colquhoun (Ed.), *Aspects of human efficiency.* London: English Universities Press.

27. Colquhoun, W. P. (1971). Circadian variations in mental efficiency. In W. P. Colquhoun (Ed.), *Biological rhythms and human performance*. London: Academic Press.

28. Department of Trade, Accidents Investigation Branch. (1975). *Report on the accident to Boeing 747 G-AWNJ, Nairobi, 3 September, 1974* (Civil Aircraft Accident Report 14/75). London: Her Majesty's Stationery Office.

29. Klein, K. E., et al. (1970). Circadian rhythm of pilot's efficiency and effects of multiple time zone travel. *Aerospace Medicine, 41*, 125–132.

30. Klein, K. E., et al. (1976). Air operations and circadian performance rhythms. *Aviation, Space, and Environmental Medicine, 47*, 221–230.

31. Preston, F. S. (1973). Further sleep problems in airline pilots on worldwide schedules. *Aerospace Medicine, 44*, 775–782.

32. Klein, K. E., & Wegmann, H. M. (1980). *Significance of circadian rhythms in aerospace operations* (AGARDograph 247). Neuilly-sur-Seine: North Atlantic Treaty Organizaiton.

33. Graeber, R. C., et al. (1986). International aircrew sleep and wakefulness after multiple time zone flights: A cooperative study. *Aviation, Space, and Environmental Medicine, 57*(12, Supplement), B3-9. The implications for flight operations are summarized by R. C. Graeber, et al. (1986) in International cooperative study of aircrew layover sleep: Operational summary. *Aviation, Space, and Environmental Medicine, 57*(12, Supplement), B10-13.

34. Simon, C. W., & Emmons, W. H. (1956). EEG, consciousness, and sleep. *Science, 124*, 1066–1069.

35. Caruthers, M., Aerguelles, A. E., & Mosovich, A. (1976). Man in transit: Biochemical and physiological changes during intercontinental flights. *The Lancet, 1*(2), 977–980.

36. Howitt, J. S., et al. (1978). Workload and fatigue—Inflight EEG changes. *Aviation, Space, and Environmental Medicine, 49*, 1197–1202.

37. Ruffell Smith, H. P. (1967). Heart-rate of pilots flying aircraft on scheduled airline routes. *Aerospace Medicine, 38*, 1117–1119. The regular increase of heart rate during takeoff and landing was observed in a study of British European Airways Trident pilots.

38. Journey scotched. (1984, May). *Pilot*, p. 48.

39. National Transportation Safety Board. (1984). *Safety study: Statistical review of alcohol-involved aviation accidents* (Report NTSB/SS–84/03). Springfield, VA: National Technical Information Service.

40. Damkot, D. K., & Osga, G. A. (1978). Survey of pilots' attitudes and opinions about drinking and flying. *Aviation, Space, and Environmental Medicine, 49*, 390–394.

41. Billings, C. E., et al. (1973). Effects of ethyl alcohol on pilot performance. *Aerospace Medicine, 44*, 379–382.

42. Department of Trade, Accidents Investigation Branch. (1977). *Report on the accident to Piper PA31, Walney Island, Cumbria, 26 November, 1976* (Civil Aircraft Accident Report 12/77). London: Her Majesty's Stationery Office.

43. Shepard, R. J. (1982). *The risks of passive smoking*. London: Croom Helm.

44. Goold, I. (1986, 5 July). Hospital helicopters. *Flight International*, pp. 24–27.

45. Harper, C. R., & Kidera, G. J. (1973). Hypoglycemia in airline pilots. *Aerospace Medicine, 44*, 769–771.

46. Student pilot lost at dusk. (1983, June). *Pilot*, p. 53.

47. Holmes, T. H., & Rahe, R. H. (1967). *The schedule of recent experiences.* Seattle: University of Washington, School of Medicine. A more recent application is discussed by G. Andrews (1981) in A prospective study of life events and psychological symptoms. *Psychological Medicine, 11,* 795–801.

48. Cohen, F. (1979). Personality, stress, and the development of physical illness. In G. C. Stone, F. Cohen, & N. E. Adler (Eds.), *Health psychology.* San Francisco: Jossey-Bass.

49. Alkov, R. A., Gaynor, J. A., & Borowsky, M. S. (1985). Pilot error as a symptom of inadequate stress coping. *Aviation, Space, and Environmental Medicine, 56,* 244–247.

50. Aitken, R. C. B. (1969). Prevalence of worry in normal aircrew. *British Journal of Medical Psychology, 42,* 283–286. These data were obtained from 90 Royal Air Force fighter pilots in eight different squadrons.

51. Alkov, R. A., Borowsky, M. S., & Gaynor, J. A. (1982). Stress coping and the U.S. Navy aircrew factor mishap. *Aviation, Space, and Environmental Medicine, 53,* 1112–1115.

52. Reason, J. T., & Lucas, D. (1984). Absent-mindedness in shops: Its incidence, correlates, and consequences. *British Journal of Clinical Psychology, 23,* 121–131.

53. National Transportation Safety Board. (1986). *Aircraft accident report—Henson Airlines Flight 1517, Beech B99, N339HA, Grottoes, Virginia, September 23, 1985* (Report NTSB/AAR–86/07). Springfield, VA: National Technical Information Service.

54. Green, R. (1985). Stress and accidents. *Aviation, Space, and Environmental Medicine, 56,* 638–641.

55. Finlay-Jones, R., & Brown, G. W. (1981). Types of stressful life events and the onset of anxiety and depressive disorders. *Psychological Medicine, 11,* 803–815.

56. Johnson, M. H., & Magaro, P. A. (1987). Effects of mood and severity on memory processes in depression and mania. *Psychological Bulletin, 101,* 28–40.

57. Johnston, N. (1985). Occupational stress and the professional pilot: The role of the pilot advisory group (PAG). *Aviation, Space, and Environmental Medicine, 56,* 633–637.

58. O'Connor, P. J. (1975). Testitis (excessive anxiety about flying checks). *Aviation, Space, and Environmental Medicine, 46,* 1407–1409.

59. Hendrix, W. H. (1985). Factors predictive of stress and coronary heart disease. *Aviation, Space, and Environmental Medicine, 56,* 654–659.

CHAPTER 7

1. Welch, A. (1983). *Happy to fly: An autobiography.* London: John Murray.

2. Wood, E. C. (1983). Two decades of air carrier jet operation. *Flight Safety Digest, 2,* 1–4.

3. Trammell, A. (1980). *Cause and circumstance.* New York: Ziff-Davis.

4. Stratton, A. (1974). Safety and air navigation. *The Journal of Navigation, 27,* 407–449.

5. Ricketson, D. S., Brown, W. R., & Graham, K. N. (1980). 3W approach to the investigation, analysis, and prevention of human-error aircraft accidents. *Aviation, Space, and Environmental Medicine, 51,* 1036–1042.

6. Drury, C. G., & Brill, M. (1983). Human factors in consumer product accident investigation. *Human Factors, 25*, 329–342.

7. Parker, G. B. (1983). Human factors: The next step forward in accident investigation. *ISASI Forum, 16*, 72–77.

8. Safety ratings: The best and the worst. (1985, December 1). *Aviation Consumer.* This analysis is based on data subsequently published in the National Transportation Safety Board's (1986) *Annual review of aircraft accident data: U.S. air carrier operations calendar year 1982* (Report NTSB/ARC-86-01). Springfield, VA: National Technical Information Service.

9. MacPherson, M. (1984). *The black box: Cockpit voice recorder accounts of in-flight accidents.* London: Panther Books.

10. Roscoe, S. N. (1986). Designed for disaster. *Human Factors Society Bulletin, 29*(6), 1–2.

11. Office of Air Accidents Investigation. (1980). *Aircraft accident: Air New Zealand McDonnell-Douglas DC-10-30 ZK-NZP, Ross Island, Antarctica, 28 November 1979* (Report 79-139). Wellington, New Zealand: Government Printer. The report of the New Zealand Chief Inspector of Air Accidents was released seven months after the accident. Comments from the CVR were used to support the conclusion that the probable cause of the accident was the captain's decision to descend "toward an area of poor surface and horizon definition when the crew were not certain of their position."

12. A different interpretation of the CVR tape was arrived at in the course of the Royal Commission's hearing on the accident. New Zealand Royal Commission. (1981). *Report of the Royal Commission to inquire into the crash on Mount Erebus, Antarctica of a DC-10 aircraft operated by Air New Zealand Ltd.* Wellington, New Zealand: Government Printer. The conclusions reached by the commissioner, the Honourable P. T. Mahon, were consistent with our analysis of the perceptual factors that allowed the tragedy to occur. See also Mahon, P. T. (1984). *Verdict on Erebus.* Auckland, New Zealand: William Collins; and Vette, G. (1983). *Impact Erebus.* Auckland, New Zealand: Hodder & Stoughton.

13. Pilotless Cherokee crashes into nudist parlor. (1985, January). *Pilot*, p. 50.

14. Feggetter, A. J. (1982). A method for investigating human factor aspects of aircraft accidents and incidents. *Ergonomics, 25*, 1065–1075.

15. National Transportation Safety Board. (1978). *Aircraft accident report—National Airlines, Inc., Boeing 727-235, N4744NA, Escambia Bay, Pensacola, Florida, May 8, 1978* (Report NTSB-AAR-78-13). Springfield, VA: National Technical Information Service.

16. See p. 28 of report cited in note 15.

17. Debecker, J., & Desmedt, J. E. (1970). Maximum capacity for sequential one-bit auditory decisions. *Journal of Experimental Psychology, 83*, 366–373.

18. Alluisi, E. A., Muller, P. F., Jr., & Fitts, P. M. (1957). An information analysis of verbal and motor responses in a forced-pace serial task. *Journal of Experimental Psychology, 53*, 153–158.

19. Vette, G. (1983). *Impact Erebus.* Auckland, New Zealand: Hodder & Stoughton.

20. Wierwille, W. W., Rahimi, M., & Casali, J. G. (1985). Evaluation of 16 measures of mental workload using a simulated flight task emphasizing mediational activity. *Human Factors, 27*, 489–502.

21. Hart, S. G., & Hauser, J. R. (1987). Inflight application of three pilot

workload measurement techniques. *Aviation, Space, and Environmental Medicine, 58,* 402–410.

22. Rehmann, J. T., Stein, E. S., & Rosenberg, B. L. (1983). Subjective pilot workload assessment. *Human Factors, 25,* 297–307.

23. Kreifeldt, J. G. (1980). Cockpit displayed traffic information and distributed management in air traffic control. *Human Factors, 22,* 671–691.

24. Lindsay, P. H., & Norman, D. A. (1972). *Human information processing.* London: Academic Press.

25. Gabriel, R. F., & Burrows, A. A. (1968). Improving time-sharing performance of pilots through training. *Human Factors, 10,* 33–40.

26. Shiffrin, R. M., & Schneider, W. (1977). Controlled and automatic human information processing: II. Perceptual learning, automatic attending, and general theory. *Psychological Review, 84,* 127–190.

27. Jennings, A. E., & Chiles, W. D. (1977). An investigation of time-sharing ability as a factor in complex performance. *Human Factors, 19,* 535–547.

28. North, R. A., & Gopher, D. (1976). Measures of attention as predictors of flight performance. *Human Factors, 18,* 1–13.

29. Ackerman, P. L., & Wickens, C. D. (1982). Methodology and the use of dual and complex-task paradigms in human factors research. *Proceedings of the 26th Annual Meeting of the Human Factors Society* (pp. 354–358). Santa Monica: Human Factors Society.

30. Ackerman, P. L., Schneider, W., & Wickens, C. D. (1984). Deciding the existence of a time-sharing ability: A combined methodological and theoretical approach. *Human Factors, 26,* 71–82.

31. Braune, R. J., & Wickens, C. D. (1986). Time-sharing revisited: Test of a componential model for the assessment of individual differences. *Ergonomics, 29,* 1399–1414.

32. Wickens, C. D., Vidulich, M. A., & Sandry-Garza, D. L. (1984). Principles of S-C-R compatability with spatial and verbal tasks: The role of display-control location and voice interactive display-control interfacing. *Human Factors, 26,* 533–543.

33. Trammell, A. (1980). *Cause and circumstance* (pp. 205–210). New York: Ziff-Davis.

34. Kahneman, D., Slovic, P., & Tversky, A. (Eds.). (1982). *Judgment under uncertainty: Heuristics and biases.* Cambridge: Cambridge University Press.

35. Norman, D. A. (1981). Categorization of action slips. *Psychological Review, 88,* 1–15.

36. Office of Air Accidents Investigation. (1984). *Aircraft accident brief—Piper PA28R, ZK–EBR, air transport, charter, Kaitaia Aerodrome, 29 June 84* (Reference 84–068). Wellington, New Zealand: Author.

37. Allnut, M. (1982). Human factors: Basic principles. In R. Hurst & L. R. Hurst (Eds.), *Pilot error: The human factors* (2nd ed.). London: Granada.

38. Rouse, W. B., & Rouse, S. H. (1983). Analysis and classification of human error. *IEEE Transactions on Systems, Man, and Cybernetics, SMC-13,* 539–549.

39. Rouse, S. H., Rouse, W. B., & Hammer, J. M. (1982). Design and evaluation of an onboard computer-based information system for aircraft. *IEEE Transactions on Systems, Man, and Cybernetics, SMC-12,* 451–463.

40. Jensen, R. S. (1982). Pilot judgment: Training and evaluation. *Human Factors, 24,* 61–73.

41. Moll, N. (Ed.). (1985). *More I learned about flying from that.* New York:

Secker & Warburg. This is a collection of articles, first published in *Flying* magazine, containing confessions of close calls by pilots of all levels of experience.

42. National Transportation Safety Board. (1982). *Aircraft accident report—Air Florida, Inc., Boeing 737-222, N62AF, collision with 14th Street Bridge, near Washington National Airport, Washington, DC, January 13, 1982* (Report NTSB-AAR-82-8). Springfield, VA: National Technical Information Service.

43. Flathers, G. W., Giffin, W. C., & Rockwell, T. H. (1982). A study of decision-making behavior of aircraft pilots deviating from a planned flight. *Aviation, Space, and Environmental Medicine, 53,* 958–963.

44. Giffin, W. C., & Rockwell, T. H. (1984). Computer-aided testing of pilot response to critical in-flight events. *Human Factors, 26,* 573–581.

45. Berlin, J. I., et al. (1982). *Pilot judgment training and evaluation* (Vol. 1) (Report DOT/FAA/CT-82/56-I). Atlantic City Airport, NJ: Federal Aviation Administration Technical Center. The three volumes of this report contain full details of the instructional materials as well as the results of the evaluation study.

46. Lester, L. F., Diehl, A. E., & Buch, G. (1985). Private pilot judgment training in flight school settings: A demonstration project. In R. S. Jensen (Ed.), *Proceedings of the Third Symposium on Aviation Psychology* (pp. 353–366). Columbus: Ohio State University, Department of Aviation.

47. Telfer, R. A., & Ashman, A. F. (1986). *Pilot judgment training—An Australian validation study.* Newcastle, NSW, Australia: University of Newcastle, Faculty of Education.

CHAPTER 8

1. National Transportation Safety Board. (1976). *Aircraft accident report—Eastern Airlines Boeing 727-225, Kennedy International Airport, June 24, 1975* (Report NTSB-AAR-76-8). Springfield, VA: National Technical Information Service.

2. Latané, B., & Darley, J. (1970). *The unresponsive bystander: Why doesn't he help?* New York: Appleton-Century-Crofts.

3. National Transportation Safety Board. (1977). *Aircraft accident report—Jet Avia, Ltd., Learjet LR24B, N12MK, Palm Springs, California, January 6, 1977* (Report NTSB-AAR-77-8). Springfield, VA: National Technical Information Service.

4. Wiener, E. L. (1980). Midair collisions: The accidents, the systems, and the realpolitik. *Human Factors, 22,* 521–533.

5. Hopkins, H. (1985, July 6). Flying the A320. *Flight International,* p. 27.

6. Harper, C. R., Kidera, G. J., & Cullen, J. F. (1970). Study of simulated airline pilot incapacitations. Phase 1—Obvious and maximal loss of function. *Aerospace Medicine, 41,* 1139–1142. The second study, by the same investigators in the medical department of United Airlines, appeared in 1971 as Study of simulated airline pilot incapacitation: Phase II. Subtle or partial loss of function. *Aerospace Medicine, 42,* 946–948.

7. See p. 947 of second study cited in note 6.

8. Lautman, L. G., & Gallimore, P. L. (1987, June). Control of the crew-caused accident. *FSF Flight Safety Digest,* pp. 1–6.

9. National Transportation Safety Board (1979). *Aircraft accident report—Allegheny Airlines, Inc., BAC 1-11, N1550, Rochester, New York, July 9, 1978*

(Report NTSB–AAR–79–2). Springfield, VA: National Technical Information Service.

10. Foushee, H. C. (1984). Dyads and triads at 35,000 feet: Factors affecting group process and aircrew performance. *American Psychologist, 39,* 885–893.

11. Air Line Pilots Association. (Undated). *Human factors report on the Tenerife accident.* Washington, DC: Author.

12. Schofield, J. E., & Giffin, W. C. (1982). An analysis of aircrew procedural compliance. *Aviation, Space, and Environmental Medicine, 53,* 964–969. This paper presents a reanalysis of data collected in an unpublished study by H. P. Ruffell Smith at the NASA–Ames Research Center in 1979.

13. Ruffell Smith, H. P. (1979). *A simulator study of the interaction of pilot workload with errors, vigilance, and decisions* (Technical Memorandum NASA-TM-78483). Washington, DC: National Aeronautics and Space Administration.

14. See p. 967 of the paper cited in note 12.

15. Foushee, H. C. (1982). The role of communications, socio-psychological, and personality factors in the maintenance of crew coordination. *Aviation, Space, and Environmental Medicine, 53,* 1062–1066.

16. Foushee, H. C. (1986, May). Assessing fatigue. *Airline Pilot,* pp. 18–22.

17. Green, R., & Skinner, R. (1987, October). CHIRP and fatigue. *The Log,* pp. 6–11.

18. Goguen, J. A., & Linde, C. (1983). *Linguistic methodology for the analysis of aviation accidents* (Contractor Report NASA–CR–3741). Washington, DC: National Aeronautics and Space Administration.

19. National Transportation Safety Board. (1979). *Aircraft accident report—United Airlines, Inc., McDonnell-Douglas DC–8–61, N8082U, Portland, Oregon, December 18, 1978* (Report NTSB–AAR–79–7). Springfield, VA: National Technical Information Service.

20. Lauber, J. K., & Foushee, H. C. (1981). *Guidelines for line-oriented flight training* (Vol. 1) (Conference Publication NASA–CP–2184). Moffett Field, CA: National Aeronautics and Space Administration.

21. Babcock, G. L., & Istock, P. H. (1985). Cockpit resource management: The line pilot's view. In R. S. Jensen (Ed.), *Proceedings of the Third Symposium on Aviation Psychology* (pp. 427–430). Columbus: Ohio State University, Department of Aviation.

22. Davies, R., McCann, D. J., & Margerison, C. J. (Undated). *Team management on the flight deck of commercial jet aircraft.* Brisbane: University of Queensland, Management Education Research Unit.

23. Redding, S. G., & Ogilvie, J. G. (1984). Cultural effects on cockpit communications in civilian aircraft. Paper presented to the Conference on Human Factors in Managing Aviation Safety, Zurich, Switzerland, October 1984.

24. National Transportation Safety Board. (1979). *Aircraft accident report—Japan Air Lines Co., Ltd. McDonnell-Douglas DC–8–62F, JA8054, Anchorage, Alaska, January 13, 1977* (Report NTSB–AAR–78–7). Springfield, VA: National Technical Information Service.

25. See p. 26 of accident report cited in note 9.

26. Helmreich, R. L. (1984). Cockpit management attitudes. *Human Factors, 26,* 583–589.

27. Wheale, J. L. (1984). An analysis of crew co-ordination problems in commercial transport aircraft. *International Journal of Aviation Safety, 2,* 83–89.

28. Department of Transport, Accidents Investigation Branch. (1973). *Report on the crash of a British European Airways Trident, G–ARP1, on the 18th June 1972* (Civil Aircraft Accident Report 4/73). London: Her Majesty's Stationery Office.

29. Helmreich, R. L., et al. (1985). Cockpit resource management: Exploring the attitude-performance link. In R. S. Jensen (Ed.), *Proceedings of the Third Symposium on Aviation Psychology* (pp. 445–450). Columbus: Ohio State University, Department of Aviation.

CHAPTER 9

1. McFarland, R. A. (1953). *Human factors in air transportation.* New York: McGraw-Hill.

2. Short cut; misread approach chart. (1986, February). *Pilot,* p. 48. Additional information was obtained from a translation of the original Spanish report by Captain J. Elberse (Informe Technico 1/85 Abridged).

3. National Transportation Safety Board. (1982). *Aircraft accident report—Air Florida, Inc., Boeing 737–222, N62AF, collision with 14th Street Bridge, near Washington National Airport, Washington, DC, January 13, 1982* (Report NTSB-AAR-82-8). Springfield, VA: National Technical Information Service. The report was also published in six sections in *Aviation Week and Space Technology* between 22 September and 22 November 1982.

4. See p. 59 of aircraft accident report cited in note 3.

5. See p. 256 of Nance, J. J. (1986). *Blind trust: How deregulation has jeopardized airline safety and what you can do about it.* New York: Morrow.

6. See p. 68 of aircraft accident report cited in note 3.

7. Milgram, S. (1974). *Obedience to authority.* New York: Harper & Row.

8. Komich, J. N. (1985). An analysis of the dearth of assertiveness by subordinate crewmembers. In R. S. Jensen (Ed.), *Proceedings of the Third Symposium on Aviation Psychology* (pp. 431–436). Columbus: Ohio State University, Department of Aviation.

9. See p. 163 of book cited in note 7.

10. See book cited in note 5 for more on this subject.

11. Perrow, C. (1984). *Normal accidents: Living with high-risk technologies.* New York: Basic Books.

12. See p. 330 of book cited in note 11.

13. Sugarman, R. (1979, November). Nuclear power and the public risk. *IEEE Spectrum,* pp. 59–69.

14. Godson, J. (1975). *The rise and fall of the DC-10.* London: New English Library.

15. See p. 141 of book cited in note 11.

16. See p. 323 of the book cited in note 5.

17. National Transportation Safety Board. (1980). *Aircraft accident report—Downeast Airlines, Inc., DeHavilland DHC-6-200, N68DE, Rockland, Maine, May 30, 1979* (Report NTSB-AAR-80-5). Springfield, VA: National Technical Information Service.

18. NTSB faults commuter safety standards. (1986, October 18). *Flight International,* p. 4. See also Chapter 2, notes 1 and 2.

19. McConnell, M. (1987). *Challenger: A major malfunction.* London: Simon & Schuster.

References

Ackerman, P. L., & Wickens, C. D. (1982). Methodology and the use of dual and complex-task paradigms in human factors research. *Proceedings of the 26th Annual Meeting of the Human Factors Society* (pp. 354–358). Santa Monica: Human Factors Society.

Ackerman, P. L., Schneider, W., & Wickens, C. D. (1984). Deciding the existence of a time-sharing ability: A combined methodological and theoretical approach. *Human Factors, 26,* 71–82.

Adams, J. A. (1961). Some considerations in the design and use of dynamic flight simulators. In H. W. Sinaiko (Ed.), *Selected papers on human factors in the design and use of control systems.* New York: Dover.

Adams, J. A. (1987). Historical review and appraisal of research on the learning, retention, and transfer of human motor skills. *Psychological Bulletin, 101,* 41–74.

Air Line Pilots Association. (Undated). *Human factors report on the Tenerife accident.* Washington, DC: Author.

Aitken, R. C. B. (1969). Prevalence of worry in normal aircrew. *British Journal of Medical Psychology, 42,* 283–286.

Alkov, R. A., Borowsky, M. S., & Gaynor, J. A. (1982). Stress coping and the U. S. Navy aircrew factor mishap. *Aviation, Space, and Environmental Medicine, 53,* 1112–1115.

Alkov, R. A., Gaynor, J. A., & Borowsky, M. S. (1985). Pilot error as a symptom of inadequate stress coping. *Aviation, Space, and Environmental Medicine, 56,* 244–247.

Allnut, M. (1982). Human factors: Basic principles. In R. Hurst & L. R. Hurst (Eds.), *Pilot error: The human factors* (2nd ed.). London: Granada.

Alluisi, E. A., Muller, P. F., Jr., & Fitts, P. M. (1957). An information analysis of verbal and motor responses in a forced-pace serial task. *Journal of Experimental Psychology, 53,* 153–158.

Andrews, G. (1981). A prospective study of life events and psychological symptoms. *Psychological Medicine, 11,* 795–801.

Babcock, G. L., & Istock, P. H. (1985). Cockpit resource management: The line pilot's view. In R. S. Jensen (Ed.), *Proceedings of the Third Symposium on Aviation Psychology* (pp. 427–430). Columbus: Ohio State University, Department of Aviation.

Baddeley, A. D. (1972). Selective attention and performance in dangerous environments. *British Journal of Psychology, 63,* 537–546.

Barlay, S. (1969). *Aircrash detective*. London: Hamish Hamilton.

Benson, A. J. (1978a). Motion sickness. In G. Dhenin (Ed.), *Aviation medicine: Physiology and human factors*. London: Tri-Med Books.

Benson, A. J. (1978b). Spatial disorientation—Common illusions. In G. Dhenin (Ed.), *Aviation medicine: Physiology and human factors*. London: Tri-Med Books.

Benson, A. J. (1978c). Spatial disorientation—General aspects. In G. Dhenin (Ed.), *Aviation medicine: Physiology and human factors*. London: Tri-Med Books.

Bergmann, J. (1982). Collision over San Diego. *Aviation Accident Investigator, 1*(1), 1–3.

Beringer, D. B. (1978). Collision avoidance response stereotypes in pilots and non-pilots. *Human Factors, 20*, 529–536.

Beringer, D. B., Williges, R. C., & Roscoe, S. N. (1975). The transition of experienced pilots to a frequency-separated aircraft attitude display. *Human Factors, 17*, 401–414.

Berkun, M. M. (1964). Performance decrement under psychological stress. *Human Factors, 6*, 21–30.

Berkun, M. M., Bialek, H. M., Kern, R. P., & Yagi, K. (1962). Experimental studies of psychological stress in man. *Psychological Monographs, 76*(15, Whole No. 534).

Berlin, J. I., Gruber, E. V., Holmes, C. W., Jensen, P. K., Lau, J. R., Mills, J. W., & O'Kane, J. M. (1982). *Pilot judgment training and evaluation—Vol. 1* (Report DOT/FAA/CT-82/56-I). Atlantic City Airport, NJ: Federal Aviation Administration Technical Center.

Billings, C. E., & Cheaney, E. S. (Eds.). (1981). *Information transfer problems in the aviation system* (Technical Paper NASA–TP-1875). Moffett Field, CA: National Aeronautics and Space Administration.

Billings, C. E., Wick, R. L., Jr., Gerke, R. J., & Chase, R. C. (1973). Effects of ethyl alcohol on pilot performance. *Aerospace Medicine, 44*, 379–382.

Blake, M. J. F., & Corcoran, D. (1972). Introversion extraversion and circadian rhythms. In W. P. Colquhoun (Ed.), *Aspects of human efficiency*. London: English Universities Press.

Bloomfield, J. R. (1979). Visual search with embedded targets: Color and texture differences. *Human Factors, 21*, 317–330.

Boehm-Davis, D. A., Curry, R. E., Wiener, E. L., & Harrison, R. L. (1983). Human factors of flight-deck automation: Report on a NASA-industry workshop. *Ergonomics, 26*, 953–961.

Braune, R. J., & Wickens, C. D. (1986). Time-sharing revisited: Test of a componential model for the assessment of individual differences. *Ergonomics, 29*, 1399–1414.

Brett, G. (1985). North Atlantic navigation errors. *IFALPA Monthly News Bulletin, 146*, 2–3.

Broadbent, D. E. (1971). *Decision and stress*. London: Academic Press.

Bruce, V., & Green, P. (1985). *Visual perception: Physiology, psychology and ecology*. New York: Lawrence Erlbaum.

Bryan, L. A., Stonecipher, J. W., & Aron, K. (1954). 180-degree turn experiment. *University of Illinois Bulletin, 52*(11).

Butterbaugh, L. C., & Rockwell, T. H. (1982). Evaluation of alternative alphanumeric keying logics. *Human Factors, 24*, 521–533.

Canter, S., & Canter, D. (Eds.). *Psychology in practice.* Chichester, England: Wiley.

Carr, R. M. (1967). The effects of color coding indicator displays on dark adaptation. *Human Factors, 9,* 175–179.

Caruthers, M., Aerguelles, A. E., & Mosovich, A. (1976). Man in transit: Biochemical and physiological changes during intercontinental flights. *The Lancet, 1*(2), 977–980.

Cattell, R. B., & Kline, P. (1977). *The scientific analysis of personality and motivation.* London: Academic Press.

Chai-Huang, S. (1987, June). 1986 U.S. transportation fatalities. *FSF Flight Safety Digest,* pp. 7–9.

Christ, R. E. (1975). Review and analysis of color coding research for visual displays. *Human Factors, 17,* 542–570.

Civil Aviation Authority. (1982). *CAP 371: The avoidance of excessive fatigue in aircrews: Guide to requirements* (2nd ed.). Cheltenham, England: Author.

Clark, B., & Graybiel, A. (1949). Linear acceleration and deceleration as factors influencing nonvisual orientation during flight. *Journal of Aviation Medicine, 20,* 92–101.

Cobb, S., & Rose, R. M. (1973). Hypertension, peptic ulcer, and diabetes in air traffic controllers. *Journal of the American Medical Association, 224,* 489–492.

Cohen, F. (1979). Personality, stress, and the development of physical illness. In G. C. Stone, F. Cohen, & N. E. Adler (Eds.), *Health psychology.* San Francisco: Josey-Bass.

Collins, W. E., Schroeder, D. J., & Hill, R. J. (1973). Some effects of alcohol on vestibular responses. In C. R. Pfaltz (Ed.), *Advances in oto-rhino-laryngology,* (Vol. 19, pp. 295–303). Basel, Switzerland: Karger.

Colquhoun, W. P. (1971). Circadian variations in mental efficiency. In W. P. Colquhoun (Ed.), *Biological rhythms and human performance.* London: Academic Press.

Colquhoun, W. P. (Ed.). (1971). *Biological rhythms and human performance.* London: Academic Press.

Colquhoun, W. P. (Ed.). (1972). *Aspects of human efficiency.* London: English Universities Press.

Cooper, C. L. (1983). *Stress research: Issues for the eighties.* Cichester, England: Wiley.

Courtney, A. J. (1986). Chinese population sterotypes: Color associations. *Human Factors, 28,* 97–100.

Crashed during missed approach in fog. (1983, February). *Pilot,* pp. 46–48.

Crump, J. H. (1979). Review of stress in air traffic control: Its measurement and effects. *Aviation, Space, and Environmental Medicine, 50,* 243–248.

Damkot, D. K., & Osga, G. A. (1978). Survey of pilots' attitudes and opinions about drinking and flying. *Aviation, Space, and Environmental Medicine, 49,* 390–394.

Damos, D. L. (1978). Residual attention as a predictor of pilot performance. *Human Factors, 20,* 435–440.

Damos, D. L. & Lintern, G. (1981). A comparison of single- and dual-task measures to predict simulator performance of beginning student pilots. *Ergonomics, 24,* 673–684.

Danaher, J. W. (1980). Human error in ATC system operations. *Human Factors,* *22,* 535–545.

Davidoff, J. (1987). The role of color in visual displays. In D. J. Oborne (Ed.), *International reviews of ergonomics, 1* (pp. 21–42). London: Taylor & Francis.

Davies, R., McCann, D. J., & Margerison, C. J. (Undated). *Team management on the flight deck of commercial jet aircraft.* Brisbane: University of Queensland, Management Education Research Unit.

Davis, D. R. (1948). *Pilot error* (Air Ministry Publication A.P. 3139A). London: Her Majesty's Stationery Office.

Debecker, J., & Desmedt, J. E. (1970). Maximum capacity for sequential one-bit auditory decisions. *Journal of Experimental Psychology, 83,* 366–373.

Department of Trade, Accidents Investigation Branch. (1975). *Report on the accident to Boeing 747 G–AWNJ, Nairobi, 3 September, 1974* (Civil Aircraft Accident Report 14/75). London: Her Majesty's Stationery Office.

Department of Trade, Accidents Investigation Branch. (1977). *Report on the accident to Piper PA31, Walney Island, Cumbria, 26 November, 1976* (Civil Aircraft Accident Report 12/77). London: Her Majesty's Stationery Office.

Department of Transport, Accidents Investigation Branch. (1973). *Report on the crash of a British European Airways Trident, G–ARPI, on the 18th June 1972* (Civil Aircraft Accident Report 4/73). London: Her Majesty's Stationery Office.

Dhenin, G. (Ed.). (1978). *Aviation medicine: Physiology and human factors.* London: Tri-Med Books.

Drury, C. G., & Brill, M. (1983). Human factors in consumer product accident investigation. *Human Factors, 25,* 329–342.

Ellis, G. (1984). *Air crash investigation of general aviation aircraft.* Greybull, WY: Capstan.

Ellis, S. R., McGreevy, M. W., & Hitchcock, R. J. (1987). Perspective traffic display format and airline pilot traffic avoidance. *Human Factors, 29,* 371–382.

Ephrath, A. R., & Curry, R. E. (1977). Detection by pilots of system failures during instrument landings. *IEEE Transactions on Systems, Man, and Cybernetics, SMC-7,* 841–848.

False alarms. (1984, November). *British Airways Flight Safety Review.*

Federal Aviation Administration. (1987). *Code of federal regulations, 14CFR.* Washington, DC: Government Printing Office.

Feggetter, A. J. (1982). A method for investigating human factor aspects of aircraft accidents and incidents. *Ergonomics, 25,* 1065–1075.

Finlay-Jones, R., & Brown, G. W. (1981). Types of stressful life events and the onset of anxiety and depressive disorders. *Psychological Medicine, 11,* 803–815.

Fitts, P. M., & Jones, R. E. (1947). *Analysis of factors contributing to 460 "pilot error" experiences in operating aircraft controls* (Report TSEAA-694-12). Wright-Patterson Air Force Base, OH: Air Materiel Command, Aeromedical Laboratory.

Fitts, P. M., Jones, R. E., & Milton, J. L. (1950). Eye movements of aircraft pilots during instrument-landing approaches. *Aeronautical Engineering Review, 9,* 24–29.

Flathers, G. W., Giffin, W. C., & Rockwell, T. H. (1982). A study of decision-making behavior of aircraft pilots deviating from a planned flight. *Aviation, Space, and Environmental Medicine, 53,* 958–963.

Flexman, R. E., Roscoe, S. N., Williams, A. C., Jr., & Williges, B. H. (1972). Studies in pilot training: The anatomy of transfer. *Aviation Research Monographs, 2*(1).

Flying display tragedy. (1984, July). *Pilot*, p. 48.

Foushee, H. C. (1982). The role of communications, socio-psychological, and personality factors in the maintenance of crew coordination. *Aviation, Space, and Environmental Medicine, 53*, 1062-1066.

Foushee, H. C. (1984). Dyads and triads at 35,000 feet: Factors affecting group process and aircrew performance. *American Psychologist, 39*, 885-893.

Foushee, H. C. (1986, May). Assessing fatigue. *Airline Pilot*, pp. 18-22.

Fowler, F. D. (1980). Air traffic control problems: A pilot's view. *Human Factors, 22*, 645-654.

Gabriel, R. F., & Burrows, A. A. (1968). Improving time-sharing performance of pilots through training. *Human Factors, 10*, 33-40.

Gerathewohl, S. J. (1976). Optimization of crew effectiveness in future cockpit design: Biomedical implications. *Aviation, Space, and Environmental Medicine, 47*, 1182-1187.

Gershzohn, G. (1980). Air traffic control using a microwave landing system. *Human Factors, 22*, 621-629.

Gibson, J. J. (1950). *The perception of the visual world.* Boston: Houghton Mifflin.

Gibson, J. J. (1955). The optical expansion-pattern in aerial locomotion. *American Journal of Psychology, 68*, 480-484.

Gibson, J. J. (1966). *The senses considered as perceptual systems.* Boston: Houghton Mifflin.

Giffin, W. C., & Rockwell, T. H. (1984). Computer-aided testing of pilot response to critical in-flight events. *Human Factors, 26*, 573-581.

Godson, J. (1975). *The rise and fall of the DC-10.* London: New English Library.

Goguen, J. A., & Linde, C. (1983). *Linguistic methodology for the analysis of aviation accidents* (Contractor Report NASA-CR-3741). Washington, DC: National Aeronautics and Space Administration.

Gomer, F. E., & Eggleston, R. G. (1978). Perceived magnitudes of distortion, secondary imaging, and rainbowing in aircraft windshields. *Human Factors, 20*, 391-400.

Goold, I. (1986, July 5). Hospital helicopters. *Flight International*, pp. 24-27.

Gopher, D. (1982). A selective attention test as a predictor of success in flight training. *Human Factors, 24*, 173-183.

Gopher, D., & Kahneman, D. (1971). Individual differences in attention and the prediction of flight criteria. *Perceptual and Motor Skills, 33*, 1335-1342.

Graeber, R. C., Dement, W. C., Nicholson, A. N., Sasaki, M., & Wegmann, H. M. (1986). International cooperative study of aircrew layover sleep: Operational summary. *Aviation, Space, and Environmental Medicine, 57*(12, Supplement), B10-13.

Graeber, R. C., Lauber, J. K., Connell, L. J., & Gander, P. H. (1986). International aircrew sleep and wakefulness after multiple time zone flights: A cooperative study. *Aviation, Space, and Environmental Medicine, 57*(12, Supplement), B3-9.

Grayson, R. L., & Billings, C. E. (1981). Information transfer between air traffic control and aircraft: Communication problems in flight operations. In C. E. Billings & E. S. Cheaney (Eds.), *Information transfer problems in the aviation system* (Technical Paper NASA-TP-1875). Moffett Field, CA: National Aeronautics and Space Administration.

Green, R. (1985). Stress and accidents. *Aviation, Space, and Environmental Medicine, 56,* 638–641.

Green, R., & Skinner, R. (1987, October). CHIRP and fatigue. *The Log,* pp. 6–11.

Hamilton, V., & Warburton, D. M. (Eds.). (1979). *Human stress and cognition.* Chichester, England: Wiley.

Harper, C. R., & Kidera, G. J. (1973). Hypoglycemia in airline pilots. *Aerospace Medicine, 44,* 769–771.

Harper, C. R., Kidera, G. J., & Cullen, J. F. (1970). Study of simulated airline pilot incapacitations; Phase 1—Obvious and maximal loss of function. *Aerospace Medicine, 41,* 1139–1142.

Harper, C. R., Kidera, G. J., & Cullen, J. F. (1971). Study of simulated airline pilot incapacitations; Phase II. Subtle or partial loss of function. *Aerospace Medicine, 42,* 946–948.

Harris, R. L., Sr., Tole, J. R., Stephens, A. T., & Ephrath, A. R. (1982). Visual scanning behavior and pilot workload. *Aviation, Space, and Environmental Medicine, 53,* 1067–1072.

Hart, S. G., & Hauser, J. R. (1987). Inflight application of three pilot workload measurement techniques. *Aviation, Space, and Environmental Medicine, 58,* 402–410.

Hart, S. G., & Loomis, L. L. (1980). Evaluation of the potential format and content of a cockpit display of traffic information. *Human Factors, 22,* 591–604.

Helicopter in near miss with large pink pig. (1983, October). *Pilot,* p. 58.

Helmreich, R. L. (1984). Cockpit management attitudes. *Human Factors, 26,* 583–589.

Helmreich, R. L., Foushee, H. C., Bevison, R., & Russini, W. (1985). Cockpit resource management: Exploring the attitude–performance link. In R. S. Jensen (Ed.), *Proceedings of the Third Symposium on Aviation Psychology* (pp. 445–450). Columbus: Ohio State University, Department of Aviation.

Hendrix, W. H. (1985). Factors predictive of stress and coronary heart disease. *Aviation, Space, and Environmental Medicine, 56,* 654–659.

Hershenson, M. (1989). *The moon illusion.* Hillsdale, NJ: Lawrence Erlbaum Associates.

Hockey, G. R. J. (1970). Effect of loud noise on attentional selectivity. *Quarterly Journal of Experimental Psychology, 22,* 28–36.

Hockey, R. (1979). Stress and the cognitive components of skilled performance. In V. Hamilton & D. M. Warburton (Eds.), *Human stress and cognition.* Chichester, England: Wiley.

Holmes, T. H., & Rahe, R. H. (1967). *The schedule of recent experiences.* Seattle: University of Washington, School of Medicine.

Hopkin, V. D. (1980). The measurement of the air traffic controller. *Human Factors, 22,* 547–560.

Hopkin, V. D. (1982). Psychology and aviation. In S. Canter & D. Canter (Eds.), *Psychology in practice.* Chichester, England: Wiley.

Hopkins, H. (1985, July 6). Flying the A320. *Flight International,* p. 27.

Hopkins, H. (1986, May 3). Pilot power for security and safety. *Flight International,* pp. 32–34.

Hopkins, H. (1986, August 23). Now hear this. *Flight International,* pp. 26–28.

Hornick, R. J., & Lefritz, N. M. (1966). A study and review of human response to prolonged random vibration. *Human Factors, 8,* 481–492.

Howitt, J. S., Hay, A. E., Shergold, G. R., & Ferres, H. M. (1978). Workload and fatigue—Inflight EEG changes. *Aviation, Space, and Environmental Medicine, 49,* 1197–1202.

Hull, J. C., Gill, R. T., & Roscoe, S. N. (1982). Locus of the stimulus to visual accommodation: Where in the world or where in the eye? *Human Factors, 24,* 311–319.

Hunt, G. J. F. (1984). NEBEAT—The systems approach updated. *PLET—Programmed Learning and Systems Training, 21,* 53–60.

Hunt, G. J. F., & Crook, C. (1985). *International trends in professional flight crew development.* Palmerston North, New Zealand: Massey University.

Hunt, G. J. F., & Crook, C. (1986). *Flight crew–aeroplane curriculum schema: Civil aviation needs assessment project.* Palmerston North, New Zealand: Massey Aviation Institute.

Hurst, R., & Hurst, L. R. (Eds.). (1982). *Pilot error: The human factors* (2nd ed.). London: Granada.

Iavecchia, J. H., Iavecchia, H. P., & Roscoe, S. N. (1988). Eye accommodation to head-up virtual images. *Human Factors, 30,* 689–702.

Ince, F., Williges, R. C., & Roscoe, S. N. (1975). Aircraft simulator motion and the order of merit of flight attitude and steering guidance displays. *Human Factors, 17,* 388–400.

Jacobs, R. S., & Roscoe, S. N. (1975). Simulator cockpit motion and the transfer of initial flight training. *Proceedings of the 19th Annual Meeting of the Human Factors Society.* Santa Monica: Human Factors Society.

Jennings, A. E., & Chiles, W. D. (1977). An investigation of time-sharing ability as a factor in complex performance. *Human Factors, 19,* 535–547.

Jensen, R. S. (1982). Pilot judgment: Training and evaluation. *Human Factors, 24,* 61–73.

Johnson, M. H., & Margaro, P. A. (1987). Effects of mood and severity on memory processes in depression and mania. *Psychological Bulletin, 101,* 28–40.

Johnson, R. W. (1986). *Shootdown: The verdict on KAL 007.* London: Chatto & Windus.

Johnston, N. (1985). Occupational stress and the professional pilot: The role of the pilot advisory group (PAG). *Aviation, Space, and Environmental Medicine, 56,* 633–637.

Journey scotched. (1984, May). *Pilot,* p. 48.

Kahneman, D., Slovic, P., & Tversky, A. (Eds.). (1982). *Judgment under uncertainty: Heuristics and biases.* Cambridge: Cambridge University Press.

Kahneman, D., & Tversky, A. (1973). On the psychology of prediction. *Psychological Review, 80,* 237–251.

Kahneman, D., & Tversky, A. (1982). The simulation heuristic. In D. Kahneman, P. Slovic, & A. Tversky (Eds.), *Judgment under uncertainty: Heuristics and biases.* Cambridge: Cambridge University Press.

Kantowitz, B. H., & Sorkin, R. D. (1983). *Human factors.* New York: Wiley.

Klein, K. E., Bruner, H., Holtmann, H., Rehme, H., Stolze, J., Steinhoff, W. D., & Wegmann, H. M. (1970). Circadian rhythm of pilot's efficiency and effects of multiple time zone travel. *Aerospace Medicine, 41,* 125–132.

Klein, K. E., & Wegmann, H. M. (1980). *Significance of circadian rhythms in aerospace operations.* (AGARDograph 247). Neuilly-sur-Seine: North Atlantic Treaty Organization.

Klein, K. E., Wegmann, H. M., Athanassenas, G., Hotilweck, H., & Kuklinski, P. (1976). Air operations and circadian performance rhythms. *Aviation, Space, and Environmental Medicine, 47,* 221–230.

Komich, J. N. (1985). An analysis of the dearth of assertiveness by subordinate crewmembers. In R. S. Jensen (Ed.), *Proceedings of the Third Symposium on Aviation Psychology* (pp. 431–436). Columbus: Ohio State University, Department of Aviation.

Koonce, J. M. (1974). *Effects of ground-based aircraft simulator motion conditions upon prediction of pilot proficiency* (Technical Report ARL–74–5/AFOSR–74–3). Savoy: University of Illinois, Aviation Research Laboratory.

Koonce, J. M. (1984). A brief history of aviation psychology. *Human Factors, 26,* 499–508.

Kozlowski, L. T., & Bryant, K. J. (1977). Sense of direction, spatial orientation, and cognitive maps. *Journal of Experimental Psychology: Human Perception & Performance, 3,* 510–598.

Krahenbuhl, G. S., Darst, P. W., Marett, J. R., Reuther, L. C., Constable, S. H., Swinford, M. E., & Reid, G. B. (1981). Instructor pilot teaching behavior and student pilot stress in flight training. *Aviation, Space, and Environmental Medicine, 52,* 594–597.

Krahenbuhl, G. S., Harris, J., Malchow, R. D., & Stern, J. R. (1985). Biogenic amine/metabolite response during in-flight emergencies. *Aviation, Space, and Environmental Medicine, 56,* 576–580.

Kreifeldt, J. G. (1980). Cockpit displayed traffic information and distributed management in air traffic control. *Human Factors, 22,* 671–691.

Krueger, G. P., Armstrong, R. N., & Cisco, R. R. (1985). Aviator performance in week-long extended flight operations in a helicopter simulator. *Behavior Research Methods, Instruments, & Computers, 17,* 68–74.

Krueger, G. P., Cardenales-Ortiz, L., & Loveless, C. (1985). *Human performance in continuous/sustained operations, and the demands of extended work/rest schedules: An annotated bibliography.* Washington, DC: Walter Reed Army Institute of Research.

Kruk, R. V., Regan, D., Beverley, K. I., & Longridge, T. M. (1983). Flying performance on the advanced simulator for pilot training and laboratory tests of vision. *Human Factors, 25,* 457–466.

Lanners, E. (1977). *Illusions.* Munich: Bucher Verlag.

Latané, B., & Darley, J. (1970). *The unresponsive bystander: Why doesn't he help?* New York: Appleton-Century-Crofts.

Lauber, J. K., & Foushee, H. C. (1981). *Guidelines for line-oriented flight training* (Vol. 1) (Conference Publication NASA–CP–2184). Moffett Field, CA: National Aeronautics and Space Administration.

Lautman, L. G., & Gallimore, P. L. (1987, June). Control of the crew-caused accident. *FSF Flight Safety Digest,* pp. 1–6.

Leachtenauer, J. C. (1978). Peripheral acuity and photointerpretation performance. *Human Factors, 20,* 537–551.

Lee, D. N. (1976). A theory of visual control of braking based on information about time-to-collision. *Perception, 5,* 437–459.

Lee, D. N. (1980). The optic flow field: The foundation of vision. *Philosophical Transactions of the Royal Society of London, B290,* 169–179.

Lee, D. N., Lishman, J. R., & Thomson, J. A. (1982). Regulation of gait in long jumping. *Journal of Experimental Psychology: Human Perception and Performance, 8,* 448–459.

Lee, D. N., & Reddish, P. (1981). Plummeting gannets: A paradigm of ecological optics. *Nature, 293*(5830), 293–294.

Lester, L. F., Diehl, A. E., & Buch, G. (1985). Private pilot judgment training in flight school settings: A demonstration project. In R. S. Jensen (Ed.), *Proceedings of the Third Symposium on Aviation Psychology* (pp. 353-366). Columbus: Ohio State University, Department of Aviation.

Lewis, C. E., Jones, W. L., Austin, F., & Roman, J. (1967). Flight research program: IX. Medical monitoring of carrier pilots in combat—II. *Aerospace Medicine, 38,* 581-592.

Lindsay, P. H., & Norman, D. A. (1972). *Human information processing.* London: Academic Press.

Lintern, G., & Roscoe, S. N. (1980). Visual cue augmentation in contact flight simulation. In S. N. Roscoe, *Aviation psychology.* Ames: Iowa State University Press.

Loftus, G. R., Dark, V. J., & Williams, D. (1979). Short-term memory factors in ground controller/pilot communication. *Human Factors, 21,* 169-181.

Loomis, J. P., & Porter, R. F. (1982). The performance of warning systems in avoiding controlled-flight-into-terrain (CFIT) accidents. *Aviation, Space, and Environmental Medicine, 53,* 1085-1090.

MacCorquodale, K. (1948). Effects of angular acceleration and centrifugal force on nonvisual space orientation during flight. *Journal of Aviation Medicine, 19,* 146-157.

MacPherson, M. (1984). *The black box: Cockpit voice recorder accounts of inflight accidents.* London: Panther Books.

Mahon, P. (1984). *Verdict on Erebus.* Auckland, New Zealand: William Collins.

Mané, A. (1981). Airmanship: An introduction. In R. S. Jensen (Ed.), *Proceedings of the First Symposium on Aviation Psychology* (pp. 161-165). Columbus: Ohio State University, Department of Aviation.

Margerison, C. J., McCann, D. J., & Davies, R. (Undated). *Human resource management for TAA pilots and flight engineers.* Brisbane, Australia: Queensland University, Management Education Research Unit.

Mason, R. (1984). *Chickenhawk.* New York: Penguin Books.

McConnell, M. (1987). *Challenger: A major malfunction.* London: Simon & Schuster.

McFarland, R. A. (1953). *Human factors in air transportation.* New York: McGraw-Hill.

McKenzie, J. M., & Fiorica, V. (1967). Stress responses of pilots to severe weather flying. *Aerospace Medicine, 38,* 576-580.

Melton, C. E., McKenzie, J. M., Kellin, J. R., Hoffman, S. M., & Saldivar, J. T. (1975). Effect of a general aviation trainer on the stress of flight training. *Aviation, Space, and Environmental Medicine, 46,* 1-5.

Mertens, H. W., & Lewis, M. F. (1982). Effect of different runway sizes on pilot performance during simulated night landing approaches. *Aviation, Space, and Environmental Medicine, 53,* 463-471.

Mid-air collision. (1984, July). *Pilot,* p. 49.

Mid-air collision in the circuit. (1983, January). *Pilot,* pp. 48-49.

Milgram, S. (1974). *Obedience to authority.* New York: Harper & Row.

Mills, F. J. (1985). The endocrinology of stress. *Aviation, Space, and Environmental Medicine, 56,* 642-650.

Ministry of Transport and Civil Aviation. (1958). *Report on the accident to Viscount type 802, G-AORC, 28th April 1958, Tarbolton, Ayrshire.* London: Her Majesty's Stationery Office.

Moll, N. (Ed.). (1985). *More I learned about flying from that.* New York: Secker & Warburg.

Morphew, G. R. (1985). Transcript of open forum session. In G. B. McNaughton

(Ed.), *Aircraft Attitude Awareness Workshop Proceedings* (p. 3-8-1). Wright-Patterson Air Force Base, OH: Flight Dynamics Laboratory.

Nance, J. J. (1986). *Blind trust: How deregulation has jeopardized airline safety and what you can do about it.* New York: Morrow.

NASA's Aviation Safety Reporting System. (1981, October). Listening in. *Callback* (No. 28).

NASA's Aviation Safety Reporting System. (1982, March). Inhibiting lights that glare and horns that blare. *Callback* (No. 34).

NASA's Aviation Safety Reporting System. (1986, February). Human factors associated with altitude alert systems. *Callback* (No. 80).

NASA's Aviation Safety Reporting System. (1987, May). Addressee errors in ATC communications: The call sign problem. *Callback* (No. 95).

National Transportation Safety Board. (1973). *Aircraft accident report—Eastern Airlines L-1011, N310EA, Miami, Florida, December 29, 1972* (Report NTSB-AAR-73-14). Springfield, VA: National Technical Information Service.

National Transportation Safety Board. (1974). *Aircraft accident report—Pan American World Airways, Inc., Boeing 707-321B, N454PA, Pago Pago, American Samoa, January 30, 1974* (Report NTSB-AAR-74-15). Springfield, VA: National Technical Information Service.

National Transportation Safety Board. (1975). *Aircraft accident report—Eastern Air Lines, Inc., Douglas DC-9-31, N8984E, Charlotte, North Carolina, September 11, 1974* (Report NTSB-AAR-75-9). Springfield, VA: National Technical Information Service.

National Transportation Safety Board. (1975). *Aircraft accident report—Trans World Airlines, Inc., Boeing 727-231, N54328, Berryville, Virginia, December 1, 1974* (Report NTSB-AAR-75-16). Springfield, VA: National Technical Information Service.

National Transportation Safety Board. (1976). *Aircraft accident report—Eastern Airlines Boeing 727-225, Kennedy International Airport, June 24, 1975* (Report NTSB-AAR-76-8). Springfield, VA: National Technical Information Service.

National Transportation Safety Board. (1977). *Aircraft accident report—American Airlines Boeing 727-95, N1963, St. Thomas, Virgin Islands, April 27, 1976* (Report NTSB-AAR-77-1). Springfield, VA: National Technical Information Service.

National Transportation Safety Board. (1977). *Aircraft accident report—Pan American World Airways, Inc., Boeing 707-321B, N454PA, Pago Pago, American Samoa, January 30, 1974* (REVISED—October 6, 1977; Report NTSB-AAR-77-7). Springfield, VA: National Technical Information Service.

National Transportation Safety Board. (1977). *Aircraft accident report—Jet Avia, Ltd., Learjet LR24B, N12MK, Palm Springs, California, January 6, 1977* (Report NTSB-AAR-77-8). Springfield, VA: National Technical Information Service.

National Transportation Safety Board. (1978). *Aircraft accident report—National Airlines, Inc., Boeing 727-235, N4744NA, Escambia Bay, Pensacola, Florida, May 8, 1978* (Report NTSB-AAR-78-13). Springfield, VA: National Technical Information Service.

National Transportation Safety Board. (1979). *Aircraft accident report—Japan*

Air Lines Co., Ltd., McDonnell-Douglas DC–8–62F, JA8054, Anchorage, Alaska, January 13, 1977 (Report NTSB–AAR–78–7). Springfield, VA: National Technical Information Service.

National Transportation Safety Board. (1979). *Aircraft accident report—Allegheny Airlines, Inc., BAC 1–11, N1550, Rochester, New York, July 9, 1978* (Report NTSB–AAR–79–2). Springfield, VA: National Technical Information Service.

National Transportation Safety Board. (1979). *Aircraft accident report—United Airlines, Inc., McDonnell-Douglas DC–8–61, N8082U, Portland, Oregon, December 18, 1978* (Report NTSB–AAR–79–7). Springfield, VA: National Technical Information Service.

National Transportation Safety Board. (1980). *Aircraft accident report—Downeast Airlines, Inc., DeHavilland DHC–6–200, N68DE, Rockland, Maine, May 30, 1979* (Report NTSB–AAR–80–5). Springfield, VA: National Technical Information Service.

National Transportation Safety Board. (1981). *Aircraft accident report—Cascade Airways, Inc., Beechcraft 99A, N390CA, Spokane, Washington, January 20, 1981* (Report NTSB–AAR–81–11). Springfield, VA: National Technical Information Service.

National Transportation Safety Board. (1982). *Aircraft accident report—Air Florida, Inc., Boeing 737–222, N62AF, collision with 14th Street Bridge, near Washington National Airport, Washington, DC, January 13, 1982* (Report NTSB–AAR–82–8). Springfield, VA: National Technical Information Service.

National Transportation Safety Board. (1984). *Aircraft accident report—Scandinavian Airlines System Flight 901, McDonnell-Douglas DC–10–30, LN–RKB, at John F. Kennedy International Airport, Jamaica, New York, February 28, 1984* (Report NTSB–AAR–84–15). Springfield, VA: National Technical Information Service.

National Transportation Safety Board. (1984). *Safety study: Statistical review of alcohol-involved aviation accidents* (Report NTSB/SS–84/03). Springfield, VA: National Technical Information Service.

National Transportation Safety Board. (1986). *Aircraft accident report—China Airlines Boeing 747–SP, N4522V, 300 nautical miles northwest of San Francisco, California, February 19, 1985* (Report NTSB/AAR–86/03). Springfield, VA: National Technical Information Service.

National Transportation Safety Board. (1986). *Aircraft accident report—Bar Harbor Airlines Flight 1808, Beech BE–99, N300WP, Auburn-Lewiston Municipal Airport, Auburn, Maine, August 25, 1985* (Report NTSB/AAR–86/06). Springfield, VA: National Technical Information Service.

National Transportation Safety Board. (1986). *Aircraft accident report—Henson Airlines Flight 1517, Beech B99, N339HA, Grottoes, Virginia, September 23, 1985* (Report NTSB/AAR–86/07). Springfield, VA: National Technical Information Service.

National Transportation Safety Board. (1986). *Annual review of aircraft accident data: U.S. air carrier operations calendar year 1982 (Report NTSB/ARC–86–01).* Springfield, VA: National Technical Information Service.

New Zealand Royal Commission. (1981). *Report of the Royal Commission to* inquire into the crash on Mount Erebus, Antarctica, of a DC-10 aircraft operated by Air New Zealand Ltd. Wellington, New Zealand: Government Printer.

Norman, D. A. (1981). Categorization of action slips. *Psychological Review, 88,* 1–15.

Norman J., & Ehrlich, S. (1986). Visual accommodation and virtual image displays: Target detection and recognition. *Human Factors, 28,* 135–151.

North, R. A., & Gopher, D. (1976). Measures of attention as predictors of flight performance. *Human Factors, 18,* 1–13.

NTSB faults commuter safety standards. (1986, October 18). *Flight International,* p. 4.

Oborne, D. J. (Ed.).(1987). *International reviews of ergonomics, 1.* London: Taylor & Francis.

O'Connor, P. J. (1975). Testitis (excessive anxiety about flying checks). *Aviation, Space, and Environmental Medicine, 46,* 1407–1409.

Office of Air Accidents Investigation. (1980). *Aircraft accident—Air New Zealand McDonnell-Douglas DC 10-30 ZK-NZP, Ross Island, Antarctica, 28 November 1979* (Report 79–139). Wellington, New Zealand: Government Printer.

Office of Air Accidents Investigation. (1984). *Aircraft accident brief—Piper PA28R, ZK-EBR, air transport, charter, Kaitaia Aerodrome, 29 June 84* (Reference 84–068). Wellington, New Zealand: Author.

Office of Air Accidents Investigation. (1985). *Aircraft incident—HS748-Mount Cook Airlines/F27-Air New Zealand, air transport, south of Rotorua Aerodrome, 4 Oct 85* (Reference 85-0-429). Wellington, New Zealand: Author.

Office of Air Accidents Investigation. (1986). *Aircraft accident—Cessna 152 ZK-EJX, Rabbit Island, Nelson Province, 1 June 1986* (Report 86–047). Wellington, New Zealand: Government Printer.

178 seconds. (1983, July). *Pilot,* p. 53.

The Optica Tragedy. (1986, November). *Pilot,* pp. 56–57.

Owen, D. H., & Warren, R. (1982). Optical variables as measures of performance during simulated flight. *Proceedings of the 26th Annual Meeting of the Human Factors Society* (pp. 312–315). Santa Monica: Human Factors Society.

Palmer, E. A., Jago, S. J., Baty, D. L., & O'Connor, S. L. (1980). Perception of horizontal aircraft separation on a cockpit display of traffic information. *Human Factors, 22,* 605–620.

Parker, G. B. (1983). Human factors: The next step forward in accident investigation. *ISASI Forum, 16,* 72–77.

Patterson, R. D. (1982). *Guidelines for auditory warning systems in civil aircraft* (Paper 82017). London: Civil Aviation Authority.

Payne, T. A., Dougherty, D. J., Hasler, S. G., Skeen, J. R., Brown, E. L., & Williams, A. C., Jr. (1954). *Improving landing performance using a contact landing trainer* (Contract N6ori-71, Task Order XVI, TR SPECDEVCEN 71-16-11, AD121200). Port Washington, NY: Office of Naval Research, Special Devices Center.

People make poor monitors. (1986, July 26). *Flight International,* p. 1.

Pepler, R. D. (1958). Warmth and performance: An investigation in the tropics. *Ergonomics, 2,* 63–88.

Pepler, R. D. (1960). Warmth, glare, and a background of quiet speech: A comparison of their effects on performance. *Ergonomics, 3,* 68–73.

Perrow, C. (1984). *Normal accidents: Living with high-risk technologies.* New York: Basic Books.

Pfaltz, C. R. (Ed.). (1973). *Advances in oto-rhino-laryngology* (Vol. 19.). Basel, Switzerland: Karger.

Pilotless Cherokee crashes into nudist parlor. (1985, January). *Pilot,* p. 58.

Postlethwaite, A. (1986, May 17). Helicopters in the dock. *Flight International,* pp. 22–25.

Poulton, E. C. (1976). Arousing environmental stresses can improve performance, whatever people say. *Aviation, Space, and Environmental Medicine, 47,* 1193–1204.

Povenmire, H. K., & Roscoe, S. N. (1971). An evaluation of ground-based flight trainers in routine primary flight training. *Human Factors, 13,* 109–116.

Povenmire, H. K., & Roscoe, S. N. (1973). Incremental transfer effectiveness of a ground-based general aviation trainer. *Human Factors, 15,* 534–542.

Prather, D. C. (1973). Prompted mental practice as a flight simulator. *Journal of Applied Psychology, 57,* 353–355.

Preston, F. S. (1973). Further sleep problems in airline pilots on worldwide schedules. *Aerospace Medicine, 44,* 775–782.

Professional Affairs Board, British Psychological Society. (1984). Presenting a case for the economic importance of psychology. *Bulletin of the British Psychological Society, 37,* 253–255.

Randle, R. J., Roscoe, S. N., & Petitt, J. (1980). *Effects of magnification and visual accommodation on aimpoint estimation in simulated landings with real and virtual image displays* (Technical Paper NASA-TP-1635). Washington, DC: National Aeronautics and Space Administration.

Rasmussen, J., & Rouse, W. B. (Eds.). (1981). *Human detection and diagnosis of system failures.* New York: Plenum.

Reason, J. T., & Brand, J. D. (1975). *Motion sickness.* London: Academic Press.

Reason, J. T., & Lucas, D. (1984). Absent-mindedness in shops: Its incidence, correlates, and consequences. *British Journal of Clinical Psychology, 23,* 121–131.

Redding, S. G., & Ogilvie, J. G. (1984). Cultural effects on cockpit communications in civilian aircraft. Paper presented to the Conference on Human Factors in Managing Aviation Safety, Zurich, Switzerland, October 1984.

Rehmann, J. T., Stein, E. S., & Rosenberg, B. L. (1983). Subjective pilot workload assessment. *Human Factors, 25,* 297–307.

Reising, J. M., & Hitchcock, L. (1982). Fitts' principles still applicable: Computer monitoring of fighter aircraft emergencies. *Aviation, Space, and Environmental Medicine, 53,* 1080–1084.

Ricketson, D. S., Brown, W. R., & Graham, K. N. (1980). 3W approach to the investigation, analysis, and prevention of human-error aircraft accidents. *Aviation, Space, and Environmental Medicine, 51,* 1036–1042.

Roscoe, A. H. (1978). Stress and workload in pilots. *Aviation, Space, and Environmental Medicine, 49,* 630–636.

Roscoe, S. N. (1968). Airborne displays for flight and navigation. *Human Factors, 10,* 321–332.

Roscoe, S. N. (1976). Appendix 1: Human factors and crew performance in the St. Thomas accident. In *Accident investigation post-hearing submission to the National Transportation Safety Board: Boeing 727 accident, St. Thomas, Virgin Islands, April 27, 1976.* Arlington, TX: Allied Pilots Association.

Roscoe, S. N. (1979). When day is done and shadows fall, we miss the airport most of all. *Human Factors, 21,* 721-731.

Roscoe, S. N. (1980). *Aviation psychology.* Ames: Iowa State University Press.

Roscoe, S. N. (1982). Cockpit visibility: How window design and scanning habits work against you. *Aviation Accident Investigator, 1*(2), 1-3.

Roscoe, S. N. (1982). Landing airplanes, detecting traffic, and the dark focus. *Aviation, Space, and Environmental Medicine, 53,* 970-976.

Roscoe, S. N. (1983). 747 dives into Arabian Sea. *Aviation Accident Investigator, 2*(9), 1-3.

Roscoe, S. N. (1985). Bigness is in the eye of the beholder. *Human Factors, 27,* 615-636.

Roscoe, S. N. (1986). Designed for disaster. *Human Factors Society Bulletin, 29*(6), 1-2.

Roscoe, S. N. (1989). The zoom-lens hypothesis. In M. Hershenson (Ed.), *The moon illusion.* Hillsdale, NJ: Lawrence Erlbaum Associates.

Roscoe, S. N., & Corl, L. (1987). Wondrous original method for basic airmanship testing. In R. S. Jensen (Ed.), *Proceedings of the Fourth International Symposium on Aviation Psychology* (pp. 493-499). Columbus: Ohio State University, Department of Aviation.

Roscoe, S. N., & Eisele, J. E. (1980). Visual cue requirements in contact flight simulators. In S. N. Roscoe, *Aviation psychology.* Ames: Iowa State University Press.

Roscoe, S. N., & Hull, J. C. (1982). Cockpit visibility and contrail detection. *Human Factors, 24,* 659-672.

Roscoe, S. N., & Jensen, R. S. (1981). Computer-animated predictive displays for microwave landing approaches. *IEEE Transactions on Systems, Man, and Cybernetics, SMC-11,* 760-765.

Roscoe, S. N., Johnson, S. L., & Williges, R. C. (1980). Display motion relationships. In S. N. Roscoe, *Aviation psychology.* Ames: Iowa State University Press.

Roscoe, S. N., & Kraus, E. F. (1973). Pilotage error and residual attention: The evaluation of a performance control system in airborne area navigation. *Navigation, 20,* 267-279.

Roscoe, S. N., & Williges, R. C. (1975). Motion relationships in aircraft attitude and guidance displays: A flight experiment. *Human Factors, 17,* 374-387.

Roscoe, S. N., & Williges, B. H. (1980). Measurement of transfer of training. In S. N. Roscoe, *Aviation psychology.* Ames: Iowa State University Press.

Rouse, S. H., Rouse, W. B., & Hammer, J. M. (1982). Design and evaluation of an onboard computer-based information system for aircraft. *IEEE Transactions on Systems, Man, and Cybernetics, SMC-12,* 451-463.

Rouse, W. B., & Rouse, S. H. (1983). Analysis and classification of human error. *IEEE Transactions on Systems, Man, and Cybernetics, SMC-13,* 539-549.

Ruffell Smith, H. P. (1967). Heart-rate of pilots flying aircraft on scheduled airline routes. *Aerospace Medicine, 38,* 1117-1119.

Ruffell Smith, H. P. (1979). *A simulator study of the interaction of pilot workload with errors, vigilance, and decisions* (Technical Memorandum NASA-TM-78483). Washington, DC: National Aeronautics and Space Administration.

Safety ratings: The best and the worst. (1985, December 1). *Aviation Consumer.*

Saint-Exupéry, A. de. (1931). *Night flight.* San Diego: Harcourt Brace Jovanovich.

Saint-Exupéry, A. de. (1939). *Wind, sand and stars*. San Diego: Harcourt Brace Jovanovich.

Salvendy, G. (Ed.). (1987). *Handbook of human factors*. New York: Wiley.

Sanders, M. S., & McCormick, E. J. (1987). *Human factors in engineering and design*, 6th ed. New York: McGraw-Hill.

Schiff, W. (1980). *Perception: An applied approach*. Boston: Houghton Mifflin.

Schneider, W. (1985). Training high-performance skills: Fallacies and guidelines. *Human Factors, 27*, 285-300.

Schofield, J. E., & Giffin, W. C. (1982). An analysis of aircrew procedural compliance. *Aviation, Space, and Environmental Medicine, 53*, 964-969.

Sharp, G. R. (1978). Vibration. In G. Dhenin (Ed.), *Aviation medicine: Physiology and human factors*. London: Tri-Med Books.

Sharp, G. R., & Ernsting, J. (1978). The effects of long duration acceleration. In G. Dhenin (Ed.), *Aviation medicine: Physiology and human factors*. London: Tri-Med Books.

Shepard, R. J. (1982). *The risks of passive smoking*. London: Croom Helm.

Sheridan, T. B. (1980). Human error in nuclear power plants. *Technology Review, 82*, 23-33.

Sheridan, T. B. (1980). Understanding human error and aiding human diagnosis behavior in nuclear power plants. In J. Rasmussen & W. B. Rouse (Eds.), *Human detection and diagnosis of system failures*. New York: Plenum.

Shiffrin, R. M., & Schneider, W. (1977). Controlled and automatic human information processing: II. Perceptual learning, automatic attending, and general theory. *Psychological Review, 84*, 127-190.

Short cut; misread approach chart. (1986, February). *Pilot*, p. 48.

Shute, N. (1954). *Slide rule*. New York: William Morrow.

Simon, C. W. (1977). *New research paradigm for applied experimental psychology: A system approach* (Technical Report TR-CWS-04-77A). Westlake Village, CA: Canyon Research Group, Inc.

Simon, C. W. (1977). *Design, analysis, and interpretation of screening designs for human factors engineering research* (Technical Report TR-CWS-04-77B). Westlake Village, CA: Canyon Research Group, Inc.

Simon, C. W. (1979). *Applications of advanced experimental methodologies to AWAVS training research* (Technical Report NAVTRAEQUIPCEN 77-C-0065-1, AD A064-332). Orlando: Naval Training Equipment Center.

Simon, C. W. (1981). *Applications of advanced experimental methods to visual technology research simulator studies: Supplemental techniques* (Technical Report NAVTRAEQUIPCEN 78-C-0060-3). Orlando: Naval Training Equipment Center.

Simon, C. W., & Emmons, W. H. (1956). EEG, consciousness, and sleep. *Science, 124*, 1066-1069.

Simon, C. W., & Roscoe, S. N. (1984). Application of a multifactor approach to transfer of training research. *Human Factors, 26*, 591-612.

Simonelli, N. M. (1983). The dark focus of the human eye and its relationship to age and visual defect. *Human Factors, 25*, 85-92.

Simson, L. R. (1971). Investigation of fatal aircraft accidents; "Physiological incidents." *Aerospace Medicine, 42*, 1002-1006.

Smith, J. D., Ellis, S. R., & Lee, E. C. (1984). Perceived threat and avoidance maneuvers in response to cockpit traffic displays. *Human Factors, 26*, 33-48.

Smith, S. L. (1981). Exploring compatibility with words and pictures. *Human Factors, 23*, 305-315.

Sperandio, J. C. (1971). Variation of operator's strategies and regulating effects on workload. *Ergonomics, 14,* 571–577.

Stager. P., Proulx, P., Walsh, B., & Fudakowski, T. (1980). Bilingual air traffic control in Canada. *Human Factors, 22,* 655–670.

Stone, G. C., Cohen, F., & Adler, N. E. (Eds.). (1979) *Health psychology.* San Francisco: Josey-Bass.

Stratton, A. (1974). Safety and air navigation. *The Journal of Navigation, 27,* 407–449.

Student pilot lost at dusk. (1983, June). *Pilot,* p. 53.

Sugarman, R. (1979, November). Nuclear power and the public risk. *IEEE Spectrum,* pp. 59–69.

Taylor, R. M., & Hopkin, V. D. (1975). Ergonomic principles and map design. *Applied Ergonomics, 6,* 196–204.

Taylor, W., Pearson, J., Mair, A., & Burns, W. (1965). Study of noise and hearing in jute weaving. *Journal of the Acoustical Society of America, 38,* 113–120.

Telfer, R. A., & Ashman, A. F. (1986). *Pilot judgment training—An Australian validation study.* Newcastle, NSW, Australia: University of Newcastle, Faculty of Education.

Telfer, R. A., & Biggs, J. (1985). *The psychology of flight training.* Cessnock, NSW, Australia: Civil Air Training Academy (Revised and published in 1988 by Iowa State University Press).

Thorndyke, P. W., & Stasz, C. (1980). Individual differences in procedures for knowledge acquisition from maps. *Cognitive Psychology, 12,* 137–175.

Trammell, A. (1980). *Cause and circumstance.* New York: Ziff-Davis.

Tricky T-tail. (1984, April/May). *New Zealand Flight Safety,* p. 9.

Trollip, S. R. (1979). The evaluation of a complex computer-based flight procedures trainer. *Human Factors, 21,* 47–54.

Troxler, R. G., & Schwertner, H. A. (1985). Cholesterol, stress, lifestyle, and coronary heart disease. *Aviation, Space, and Environmental Medicine, 56,* 660–665.

van Eekhout, J. M., & Rouse, W. B. (1981). Human errors in detection, diagnosis, and compensation for failures in the engine control room of a supertanker. *IEEE Transactions on Systems, Man, and Cybernetics. SMC–12,* 813–816.

Vette, G. (1983). *Impact Erebus.* Auckland, New Zealand: Hodder & Stoughton.

Visual illusions: Runway width and slope. (1975). *FAA Aviation News,* 5(11), 12–13.

Waag, W. L. (1981). *Training effectiveness of visual and motion simulation* (Technical Report AFHRL-TR-79-72). Brooks Air Force Base, TX: Air Force Human Resources Laboratory.

Welch, A. (1980). *The story of gliding* (2nd ed.). London: John Murray.

Welch, A. (1983). *Happy to fly: An autobiography.* London: John Murray.

Welsh, K. W., Vaughan, J. A., & Rasmussen, P. G. (1976). Readability of approach charts as a function of visual acuity, luminance, and printing format. *Aviation, Space, and Environmental Medicine, 47,* 1027–1031.

Weltman, G., Smith, J. E., & Egstrom, G. H. (1971). Perceptual narrowing during simulated pressure-chamber exposure. *Human Factors, 13,* 99–107.

Werblin, F. (1973, January). Control of sensitivity in the retina. *Scientific American, 228*, 70–79.

Weston, R. C., & Hurst, R. (1972). *Zagreb one four—Cleared to collide?* London: Granada.

Westra, D. P. (1982). *Simulator design features for carrier landing: II. In-simulator transfer of training* (Interim Technical Report NAVTRAEQUIPCEN 81–C–0105–1). Orlando: Naval Training Equipment Center.

Westra, D. P. (1983). *Simulator design features for air-to-ground bombing: I. Performance experiment 1* (Interim Technical Report NAVTRAEQUIPCEN 81–C–0105–4). Orlando: Naval Training Equipment Center.

Wheale, J. L. (1984). An analysis of crew co-ordination problems in commercial transport aircraft. *International Journal of Aviation Safety, 2*, 83–89.

Whitfield, D., Ball, R. G., & Ord, G. (1980). Some human factors aspects of computer-aiding concepts for air traffic controllers. *Human Factors, 22*, 569–580.

Wickens, C. D. (1984). *Engineering psychology and human performance.* Columbus, OH: Charles E. Merrill.

Wickens, C. D., & Kessel, C. J. (1981). Failure detection in dynamic systems. In J. Rasmussen & W. B. Rouse (Eds.), (1981). *Human detection and diagnosis of system failures.* New York: Plenum.

Wickens, C. D., Vidulich, M. A., & Sandry-Garza, D. L. (1984). Principles of S-C-R compatability with spatial and verbal tasks: The role of display-control location and voice interactive display-control interfacing. *Human Factors, 26*, 533–543.

Wiener, E. L. (1980). Midair collisions: The accidents, the systems, and the realpolitik. *Human Factors, 22*, 521–533.

Wiener, E. L. (1985). Beyond the sterile cockpit. *Human Factors, 27*, 75–90.

Wiener, E. L., & Curry, R. E. (1980). Flight-deck automation: Promises and problems. *Ergonomics, 23*, 995–1011.

Wierwille, W. W., Rahimi, M., & Casali, J. G. (1985). Evaluation of 16 measures of mental workload using a simulated flight task emphasizing mediational activity. *Human Factors, 27*, 489–502.

Wightman, D. C., & Lintern, G. (1985). Part-task training for tracking and manual control. *Human Factors, 27*, 267–283.

Wightman, D. C., & Sistrunk, F. (1987). Part-task training strategies in simulated carrier landing final approach training. *Human Factors, 29*, 245–254.

Williams, A. C., Jr. (1980). Discrimination and manipulation in flight. In S. N. Roscoe, *Aviation psychology.* Ames: Iowa State University Press.

Williams, A. C., Jr., & Flexman, R. E. (1949). Evaluation of the School Link as an aid in primary flight instruction. *University of Illinois Bulletin, 46*(71).

Williges, R. C. (1984). The tide of computer technology. *Human Factors, 26*, 109–114.

Wolfe, T. (1980). *The right stuff.* New York: Bantam.

Wood, E. C. (1983). Two decades of air carrier jet operation. *Flight Safety Digest, 2*, 1–4.

Woodruff, R. R., Smith, J. F., Fuller, J. H., & Weyer, D. C. (1976). *Full mission simulation in undergraduate pilot training: An exploratory study* (Technical Report AFHRL-TR-76-84, AD-A039 267). Williams Air Force Base, AZ: Air Force Human Resources Laboratory, Flying Training Division.

Index

A4 Skyhawk, 156
Acceleration
  and semicircular canals, 5, 42–45, 52–54, 57
  and sensations of pitch, 47–49, 58
  and sensations of turning, 49–51, 58
  tolerance to *g* forces, 45–47
Accidents. *See also* Controlled-flight-into-terrain; Pilot error; Stall-spin situation
  and alcohol, 171, 221–222
  altimeter misreading, 101
  analysis of causes, ix, 23, 131, 190, 203, 231–233
  and blood glucose, 173
  and carbon monoxide, 172
  classification, 186–189
  control layout, 95
  crew coordination, 214
  design-induced, 113, 212. *See also* Errors
  fuel selector, 95–96
  HUD equipped aircraft, ix, 32–33
  investigation of, vii–ix, 22–23, 62, 188, 230
  and life stress, 174–176
  lives lost in, vii, 181–182
  and loss of texture gradient, 27, 32
  and management deficiencies, 241
  night, 19, 21, 52
  "normal," 239–241
  phases of flight, 184

pressure vertigo, 54–55
rates, 182–184, 186–187
and runway slope, 27
and windshield design, 103
Accommodation. *See* Eye accommodation
Acuity. *See* Visual system
Adrenocorticotropic hormone, 155–156
Age, 134, 166–167, 185
  and auditory sensitivity, 43
  and dark focus, 11, 19–20
  and illness, 148–149
Agnosias, 6
Airbus A320, A330, A340, 212–213
Aircrew team management program, 220–221
Air Florida, 203–204, 211, 233–239
Air India, 106–107
Air Line Pilots Association, 216
Airmanship, vii, 62–64, 71, 76–77, 144, 199
Air New Zealand, 5, 22–23, 30–31, 40, 136, 139, 143–144, 187
Air Traffic Control, 243. *See also* Communication
  clearance, 197, 215
  controller's health, 148–149
  controller's task, 75, 195
  controller's workload, vii, 142, 144, 147–148
  and deregulation, 184
  development of, 15, 181
  errors, 144–145, 189, 231–233
  facilities, 204